The McGraw-Hill
36-Hour Course: Business Presentations

Other Books in The McGraw-Hill 36-Hour Course Series

The McGraw-Hill
36-Hour Course: Business Presentations

Lani Arredondo

McGraw-Hill, Inc.

New York   San Francisco   Washington, D.C.   Auckland   Bogotá
Caracas   Lisbon   London   Madrid   Mexico City   Milan
Montreal   New Delhi   San Juan   Singapore
Sydney   Tokyo   Toronto

Library of Congress Cataloging-in-Publication Data

Arredondo, Lani.
    The McGraw-Hill 36-hour course : business presentations / Lani
Arredondo.
        p.   cm.
    Includes index.
    ISBN 0-07-002840-0 (alk. paper) — ISBN 0-07-002841-9
(pbk. : alk. paper)
    1. Business presentations. I. Title.
HF5718.22.A78   1993
658.4'52—dc20   93-21389
                                             CIP

   2 3 4 5 6 7 8 9 0 DOC/DOC 9 9 8 7 6 5 4

ISBN 0-07-002840-0 (hc)
ISBN 0-07-002841-9 (pbk)

*The sponsoring editor for this book was James H. Bessent, Jr. and the
production supervisor was Donald F. Schmidt. It was set in Baskerville by
North Market Street Graphics.*

Printed and bound by R. R. Donnelley & Sons Company.

This book is printed on recycled, acid-free paper containing a minimum of 50 percent recycled de-inked fiber.

To Bert and Eleanor Voortmeyer,
my parents,
with love and thanks.

Contents

3. Structure: The Framework of a Presentation   75

4. Substance: Developing Convincing Content   113

11. Written Presentations   297

12. Preparing Yourself to Present   317

Introduction

With *The McGraw-Hill 36-Hour Course: Business Presentations,* you gain the benefit of further developing your professional skills coupled with the convenience of independent study. Based on seminars and continuing education classes taught by the author, this course has value for executives, managers, trainers, and a diversity of business professionals. It is presented here in a form that frees you to learn at your own pace and enables you to tailor portions of the material to your individual needs and interests.

Approach

The course incorporates a "building-block" approach to skill development. Successive chapters build upon preceding ones, providing an orderly sequence and continuity to the material. In addition, chapters are structured to progressively step through the principles and techniques that combine to produce winning business presentations.

Chapter Structure—
What You Can Expect

To facilitate learning, chapters are presented according to a common format that recurs consistently throughout the course. Within each chapter, you will find:

- *Objective.*   Each chapter begins with a learning objective. The objective expresses what you will want to have achieved upon completion of the chapter.

- *Key concepts and terms.*   A preview of key concepts clarifies significant points on which you will want to focus as you read. Important terms are listed after the key concepts.

1

■ *Lesson content.* To call attention to the key concepts reiterated in the text, each one is featured within a box. The concept is then explained and discussed in the narrative that follows. Key terms, appearing in bold type, are defined.

■ *Reflection questions.* At various points throughout the lesson, reflection questions appear to prompt you to reflect on the content from your point of view. The questions help to further focus attention on aspects of presenting most pertinent to your situation, and thus facilitate integration of the material.

■ *Summary.* A synopsis recaps the lesson and serves as a concluding reminder of major points addressed in the chapter.

■ *Sample situations.* With an emphasis on applying the course material in practical terms, sample situations describe various aspects of business presentations.

■ *Comprehension checks.* As you progress through the course, you have the opportunity to check your understanding. Questions are presented at the end of each chapter on the material covered in that chapter.

■ *To do.* The subject of presenting lends itself to learning by doing. Therefore, each chapter concludes with a "To Do," a hands-on exercise that directs you to prepare that portion of a presentation covered by the chapter.

How to Proceed—A Schedule for Successful Self-study

There are 12 chapters in *The McGraw-Hill 36-Hour Course: Business Presentations.* Spending an average of three hours on each chapter, you will complete the course in 36 hours. (The optional reflection questions, "To Do" exercises, and final examination at the end of the course are not included in this time estimate.) Bear in mind that chapters vary in length. You may finish one chapter in two and a half hours. Another may take three and a half hours to complete. Remember, too, that people read and digest different types of information at varying rates. You may find you can scan some material rather quickly, but take more time to carefully read and review other parts.

A program of self-study is not intended to be either hurried or delayed. The preferred approach is to stay on track with a skill-building plan you outline for yourself. After completing one or two chapters, you will have a sense of the pace at which you read and absorb the material. Then, you will be better able to schedule your time accordingly.

A "Schedule for Skill-building Study" is included at the end of this introduction. You will find it helpful to map out *your* plan of study by filling in the dates and times you will set aside to complete this course. To avoid conflicts in your schedule, transpose the dates and times to the calendar or daily planner you normally use.

The following suggestions are offered to guide you in developing your schedule of study.

1. (*a*) Determine the amount of time you can allocate to this course each week. (*b*) Consider, realistically, how much material you can cover during that time. Based on (*a*) and (*b*), establish a time frame for course completion. Three possible time frames are shown below.

Per week: 1 chapter (average 3 hours)—12 weeks to complete the course

Per week: 2 chapters (average 6 hours)—6 weeks to complete the course

Per week: 3 chapters (average 9 hours)—4 weeks to complete the course

Completing the course in 12 weeks would correspond to a semester of study. A 4-week program would represent accelerated study.

Resist the temptation to rapidly scan the text and be done with it. While you may pick up a few useful pointers this way, proficiency with presenting will only develop as a result of a thorough consideration of the contents of the course and the practice you will gain by completing the "To Do's."

2. Schedule time to attend to the course each week, preferably on the same two or three days during the week. The consistency that comes from a repeated pattern of study will reinforce your commitment to the program and improve retention of the material you cover during the week.

3. Schedule blocks of time in increments of 1 or 1½ hours when you can fully concentrate on the material. If you choose to pursue an accelerated course of study and schedule study periods in 3-hour blocks of time, it is recommended you take a break every hour to stay refreshed.

4. The following guidelines generally apply to the time you will want to spend on each portion of a chapter.

- 10 minutes: preview the objective, key concepts, and key terms.

- 2 to 2½ hours (depending on the length of the chapter): read the explanatory text, summary, and sample situations. (Take a few minutes more to respond to the reflection questions, if you wish.)

- 20 to 30 minutes: complete the comprehension check at the end of the chapter, check your answers, and review any points about which you are uncertain or have questions.

5. As you read through the material, you will find it helpful to make marginal notes and highlight points that you consider most important, especially as they relate to your situation. It will also be helpful if you keep

a notepad nearby to jot down ideas as they occur to you. (5" x 7" sheets are a convenient size that can be kept inside the covers of your book for ready reference.)

Course Coverage—
What You Will Learn

Chapter 1 serves as an overview to business presentations. It conveys the value of presenting from both an individual and organizational point of view. Communications and creativity are discussed. Types of business presentations are described, foreshadowing the sample situations that appear in later chapters.

Chapters 2, 3, and 4 cover the requisites of planning and preparing the content of a presentation. Chapters 5 and 6 focus on adding impact to the content, with an emphasis on the use of language and audiovisual media.

Beginning with Chapter 7, attention turns to the role of the presenter in relation to the audience. Chapters 8 and 9 continue the discussion of presenter skills, describing "live" presentation techniques and responses to audience reactions.

Chapter 10 focuses on external factors that affect a presenter's effectiveness, including commentary on room arrangements, lighting, noise, colors, and other details. In Chapter 11, selected principles of presenting are applied to written presentations, with guidelines for improving that form of communication as well. Chapter 12 concludes the course of study with insights and suggestions on how to ready yourself to present with confidence.

Before You Start

This introduction to *The McGraw-Hill 36-Hour Course: Business Presentations* would not be complete without encouraging you to incorporate into your course of study the "ABCs" of continuing education.

A = Accountability

Typically, people perform their best when they are accountable for results. Tell one or two people (coworker, manager, associate, friend, or family member) about your plan of study. Consider yourself accountable to them, and ask them to periodically ask how you are progressing.

B = Benefits

The motivational writer and speaker, Zig Ziglar, observed that most people are tuned to the same radio station. The call letters are "WII-FM" (meaning "What's In It For Me"). In other words, people are motivated largely on the basis of the benefits derived from pursuing a particular endeavor. Take a few minutes now to write out what you expect to gain from this course. Keep your "WII-FM" list at hand so you can add to it easily, since additional benefits may occur to you as you read additional chapters. If you find at some point that you are veering off your schedule of study, review the list as a reminder of the benefits you stand to gain by becoming a more accomplished presenter.

C = Commitment

Commit time each week to advance through your course of study. Commit a place where you can study without interruption. Commit to a target date for completing the course.

| Schedule for Skill-building Study | | Start date: _____ | | |
| Business Presentations | | Target date for completion: _____ | | |
Completed	Chapter	Day(s)	Date(s)	Time: from–to
☐	Example	Tues./Thur.	_____	7:00–8:30
☐	1	_____	_____	_____
☐	2	_____	_____	_____
☐	3	_____	_____	_____
☐	4	_____	_____	_____
☐	5	_____	_____	_____
☐	6	_____	_____	_____
☐	7	_____	_____	_____
☐	8	_____	_____	_____
☐	9	_____	_____	_____
☐	10	_____	_____	_____
☐	11	_____	_____	_____
☐	12	_____	_____	_____
☐	Final examination _____		_____	_____

When You Finish—
Final Examination

When you have completed the course, you may wish to take the optional final examination included at the end of this book. Mail it to McGraw-Hill, where it will be graded. With a passing score you will receive an attractive certificate of completion. It is suitable for framing and gives evidence of your commitment to continued professional skill development.

1
Perspectives on Presenting

Visibility is the watchword of success. It is essential for individual career advancement. It can give an organization a leading edge. High-visibility tasks, performed well, serve to establish one's credibility and competence. Few endeavors offer opportunities to attain greater visibility as much as business presentations do. When effective, presentations are a proven means by which you can distinguish yourself from the norm.

This chapter presents an overview of characteristics fundamental to all business presentations. The concepts described form a framework for the aspects of presenting that are detailed in the chapters that follow.

Objective

To understand the value, attributes, and underlying purpose of effective presentations; to be able to explain the processes involved in presenting; and to identify the different types of business presentations.

Key Concepts

1. Presenting serves to help individuals and organizations gain favorable visibility and so achieve their goals, provided the presentation is effective.

2. Five attributes characterize an effective presentation.

3. The purpose of presenting is to persuade.

4. Presenting is a communication process.

7

5. Presenting is a distillation process.

6. Presenting is a creative process.

7. Presentation skills may be applied variously to different types of business presentations.

8. The barriers to presenting effectively can be overcome.

Key Terms

To make full use of the key concepts, you will need to understand the following terms.

Visibility	Cue
Effective	Distill
Balanced	Creative
Persuade	Dynamic
Process	Down-line
Audience	Up-line

Key Concept 1

Presenting serves to help individuals and organizations gain favorable visibility and so achieve their goals, provided the presentation is effective.

In virtually every field, people are engaged in competition. In the context of business and professional endeavors, competition occurs in two forms: (1) externally, in the marketplace and (2) internally, within the workplace. In the marketplace, organizations compete for dollars. Commercial enterprises, for instance, compete for business (sales revenues), government agencies compete for a share of the budget (tax revenues), while charitable organizations compete for contributions (donor revenues). With the second form of competition, in the workplace, individuals compete for positions and advancement.

In both the marketplace and the workplace, people compete to produce desired results. A requisite for competing successfully is improved **visibility**. In occupational settings, visibility refers to being seen, being heard, and getting known. The kind of visibility that engenders greater success relies on capturing people's attention in a favorable manner.

On the matter of capturing attention, business and professional people today face an unprecedented challenge. It is the challenge of finding the means to command attention when the competition for people's time and attention is greater than it has ever been. In the marketplace and in the workplace, prospects, customers, clients, employees, coworkers, managers, executives, and the like are occupied and preoccupied with endless and ever-increasing demands and distractions. To succeed, a person must develop ways to have a highly positive and lasting impact on the people with whom they deal.

Presentations are a proven means for capturing attention. Skillfully done, a business presentation motivates people to respond affirmatively to you and to your message. For individuals and organizations alike, effective presentations are a professional tool that help you create the impact you want and the results that contribute to achieving your goals.

Individual Goals

Goals may be short-term or long-term. An individual's short-term goal may be, for example, to receive recognition for outstanding performance for the month. A longer-term goal may be to reach a particular professional position that signifies career advancement. You can more readily reach your goals, whether short- or long-term, by making skilled business presentations.

With respect to individual goal achievement, presenting has value because well-executed presentations represent opportunities to:

1. Establish yourself as a qualified individual with expertise in and enthusiasm for your subject.

2. Convey that you have mastered the oral communication skills that employers prize.

3. Persuade others to accept and adopt your ideas, recommendations, proposals, or points of view.

4. Highlight your leadership qualities and potential. Managers and leaders who exhibit the ability to convincingly communicate direction, inspiration, motivation, and commitment to others are typically adept presenters as well.

5. Demonstrate initiative, organization, and creativity—attributes of peak performers, promotable personnel, and effective presenters.

Consider the case of an employee who observes that productivity would improve if the methods by which a task is done were changed. In an oral presentation to the supervising manager, the employee clearly describes the recommended change, convincingly relates the advantages to making the change, reinforces the points with visual aids, and volunteers to conduct a training presentation when the proposed method is approved. As this example illustrates, one presentation, done effectively, can serve as a vehicle to convey the five points outlined above. As a result of capitalizing on the opportunities that presentations provide, you increase the probability of achieving your individual goals.

Organizational Goals

An organization is a body of people engaged in a common pursuit. It may be a corporation, a small business enterprise, a professional firm, a governmental, educational, or community-service agency, a political party, an association, or a religious group. For organizations of every type, presentations provide opportunities to:

1. Promote the organization's products, services, interests, programs, and/or points of view.
2. Disseminate information internally, to members of the organization, and externally, to the public.
3. Increase name recognition.
4. Expand consumer acceptance of new products and services.
5. Gain access to and a hearing among those whom the organization seeks to serve (i.e., customers, members, citizens, voters, contributors, and the like).

As with individuals, presentations can augment an organization's efforts to achieve its goals. Business presentations designed to produce results contribute to an organization's goals. Such presentations include product demonstrations, sales presentations, marketing and consumer-awareness seminars, public relations and public service addresses, community outreach programs, and meetings aimed at informing, directing, uniting, or motivating members of a staff or group. In order to fulfill the purpose for which a presentation is done, the presentation must be effective.

Reflection Questions

What are your foremost occupational, professional, or career goals? In the context of your current position, how would giving effective business presentations help you achieve your goals?

Key Concept 2

Five attributes characterize an effective presentation.

To be **effective** is to generate a desired outcome or response. It is to create an intended impression or result. The operative words are "desired" and "intended." All presentations create some kind of impression and produce some kind of outcome. Not all presentations result in the impression or outcome that the presenter intended. All too often the people addressed in a business presentation are left with a negative impression, or an impression so neutral they have no incentive to act in response to the presenter or the presentation. All too often the outcome is disappointing, for the presenter and the audience alike.

Attributes of Effectiveness

Accomplished presenters create positive impressions and produce results that contribute to success. They develop and deliver presentations that are characterized by the following five attributes:

Attention. An effective presentation captures attention at the outset and sustains it throughout the presentation.

Meaningful. An effective presentation is meaningful to the person(s) to whom it is addressed.

Memorable. A presentation is effective when it has a lasting impact and when the audience remembers and reflects on the theme or prominent points after the presentation event.

Activating. A presentation is effective when it moves people to act on the message presented, in the manner in which the presenter intended.

Balanced. To be effective, a presentation must be **balanced**. This means giving equal or similar weight to each of the various elements that must be incorporated in a presentation in order for it to generate positive effects.

On the one hand, for example, a presentation consists of informational content. On the other hand, it is delivered with personal style. If either element—content or style—dominates, to the neglect or exclusion of the other, the presentation will not be effective. Both elements must appear in balance. This principle of balance applies to other components of a presentation as well.

Review the attributes of an effective presentation. Commit them to memory. As various principles, techniques, and skills are discussed throughout this course, they will be related to these attributes.

It is crucial to bear in mind, too, that the standards by which a presentation's effectiveness is measured are based on how the audience is affected. Your aim, for example, is not to make your presentation meaningful from your perspective. That you are presenting the message would suggest that you already find it meaningful. Instead, your aim is to make your message meaningful for the audience. This point will be discussed further in Chapter 2.

Presentations that are attention-getting, meaningful, memorable, activating, and balanced will be effective. In that, they will also fulfill the underlying purpose of presenting.

Key Concept 3

The purpose of presenting is to persuade.

Business and professional people present (or should do so) for a purpose. That purpose is to persuade. To persuade an audience to respond in a given way echoes the fourth attribute of an effective presentation—to move people to act on the message.

The term **persuade** suggests that a change in belief or behavior will occur in and as a result of the person(s) persuaded. It emphasizes the aspect of winning people over to a desired attitude or action, which they are then willing or pleased to adopt. The word *persuade* is derived from a Latin term related to a root word that translates "sweet, agreeable." Thus, to persuade people is to impress a message upon them in an agreeable manner that elicits agreement from them.

Persuasion is not coercion, insistence, instruction, or sales-pitching. It is not a matter of pounding podiums or issuing orders. Such tactics will not win an audience over. On the contrary, a demanding or high-pressure approach to presenting tends to dissuade people.

When a presenter fails to fashion a presentation in keeping with the purpose to persuade, there is a risk that the time, money, and human resource expended may be wasted. What a presenter invests to prepare and deliver a presentation, combined with the time and attention invested by the audience, can be considerable. It is useful to view presenting as an investment. The objective of an astute presenter is to gain the best possible ROI (Return On Investment) from presenting. For that reason, a presenter aims to produce results from presenting, which is more likely to occur when the presentation is persuasive.

Through skillful communication and presentation techniques, effective presenters:

- Persuade people to buy a product or service.
- Persuade people to follow a new procedure.

- Persuade people to learn and apply the information presented.
- Persuade people to approve a project.
- Persuade people to agreeably accept a change.
- Persuade people to lend support to an issue.
- Persuade people to adopt the budget.
- Persuade people to vote for a candidate.
- Persuade people to enact a piece of legislation.
- Persuade people to bring in a certain verdict.
- Persuade people to donate.
- Persuade people to participate.
- Persuade people to respond affirmatively to the presenter's point of view.

As you might surmise (correctly) from the foregoing list, presentation skills apply to an endless and diverse range of subjects and situations. In every case, the purpose of presenting is, ultimately, to persuade.

Key Concept 4

Presenting is a communication process.

The degree to which a presenter is persuasive depends primarily on the presenter's mastery of communication skills. There are those who would argue that persuasion has more to do with selling or negotiation. However, in both selling and negotiating, the person who is a skilled communicator is also more adept at persuading. The ability to communicate effectively is essential to and central to every activity that entails interacting with and influencing people.

The Communication Process

Clearly, presenting is a communication process. A **process**, by definition, is a series of actions. Implicit in the term is the idea of forward movement or progress that leads to an end result. So it is with presenting. A business presentation unfolds through a series of communication actions that are (or should be) aimed at producing a response and yielding an outcome that satisfy the presenter's objective. As Figure 1-1 illustrates, there are numerous factors involved in the process of communicating. A presenter needs to be aware of these factors, and give consideration to their impact on presenting.

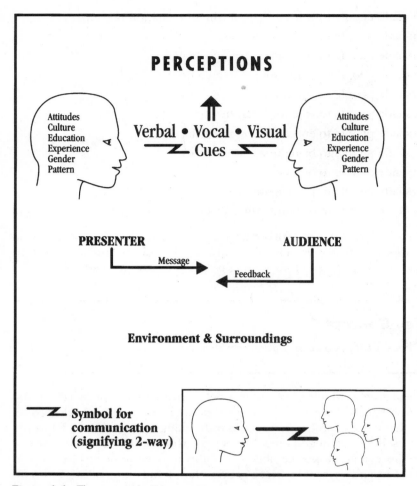

Figure 1-1. The communication process.

The inset in the lower right corner of Figure 1-1 suggests that the demands on a presenter increase as the number of people addressed increases. Presenting to one person entails fewer considerations than presenting to five or fifty or five hundred. At the same time, the potential impact of a business presentation also increases with an increase in the number of people in the audience. A presenter who addresses one person has an opportunity to influence only that one; addressing a greater number of people enlarges the presenter's field of influence.

Communication Factors

In every presentation, whether spoken or written, the following factors influence the nature of the communication and the outcome of the presentation.

Presenter.   The presenter is, of course, the person who delivers the message. In most oral presentations, the presenter is the focal point of attention and bears ultimate responsibility for the outcome of the presentation. It is therefore crucial that the presenter have an acute awareness of the dynamics of communicating and a high degree of proficiency with communication skills.

Message.   The message is the content of a presentation. There are different types of messages that are communicated in different ways. In face-to-face (as opposed to written or electronic) communication, messages may be spoken or unspoken, intentional or unintentional, explicit or implied. Alert communicators, recognizing that messages are conveyed in many different ways, take care to be aware of how and what they are communicating. They also purposefully employ different means to communicate to an audience.

Audience.   In the context of business presentations, **audience** refers to the person or persons to whom messages are presented. The audience is sometimes referred to as the "receiver." However, especially in relation to presenting, the term can be misleading because it implies that those in attendance at a presentation are receiving the message. That is not always the case.

The audience may consist of one person, a small group of a few people, or a large gathering of hundreds or thousands of people. For example, you may make a one-on-one presentation to a manager, and that manager would be your audience. You may present to a group of four or five coworkers or customers, and they would represent your audience. You may deliver a presentation at a community event where a hundred people are present, and they would be your audience. As you proceed through this course, bear in mind that *audience* is a generic term used to describe either the one or the many to whom you present.

Feedback.   Feedback is the audience response to the presenter. As such, it is a reciprocal message. Feedback, like messages, can be expressed in many different ways.

Channels of Communication.   Messages and feedback are expressed in different ways because communication occurs through three different

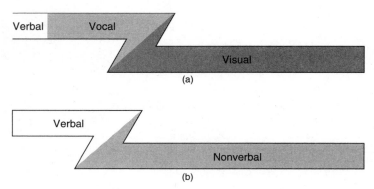

Figure 1-2. Channels of communication.

channels: verbal, vocal, and visual. Verbal communication refers to the words a presenter uses. Vocal pertains to voice characteristics (related to vocal chords). Visual communication entails everything that is seen, including facial expressions, gestures, movements, and numerous other details that will be covered at length in Chapters 5 and 8.

As Figure 1-2 indicates, the three channels vary considerably in terms of their relative impact in face-to-face communication.

Figure 1-2 (*a*) illustrates the findings of Albert Mehrabian, a leading expert on interpersonal communication. According to Dr. Mehrabian's studies, words alone (verbal) account for 7 percent of the impact in face-to-face communication, vocal accounts for 38 percent, and visual 55 percent.

Figure 1-2 (*b*) depicts the findings of John W. Keltner, a specialist in speech communication, who concluded that in interpersonal communication, verbal messages had a relative impact of 35 percent and nonverbal 65 percent.

That different studies produce different findings is not surprising. The process of communication is ever-changing and affected by numerous variables. The significant point to understand and to apply to presenting is this: a presentation does not consist only or even predominantly of words. In fact, as Figures 1-2 (*a*) and (*b*) confirm, the far greater impact of a presentation on an audience occurs through the vocal and visual (nonverbal) channels. An additional consideration for presenters is that frequently the only feedback a presenter receives from an audience is expressed vocally or visually. As subtle as this type of feedback might be, it is crucial for a presenter to perceive the message inherent in it and respond accordingly.

Cues. A presenter and the audience communicate with one another by way of sending and receiving cues. The term **cue** has been adapted from the theater. In a stage production, a cue is an action or line spoken by one player that serves to prompt another player to come on stage or begin speaking. Figuratively, a cue is a signal or hint one person sends to another that indicates what that other person should do next.

The term is appropriate to presenting because when, for example, a presenter speaks a word and gestures in a certain manner, the word and the gesture function as cues. Whether intentional or unintentional, they elicit a response from the audience. Likewise, if members of an audience begin to glance impatiently at their watches (intentionally or unintentionally), that nonverbal feedback acts as a cue that sends the presenter a message. An entire presentation, when delivered, is composed of a complex interchange of cues among the presenter, the audience, and the environment.

Environment and Surroundings. While cues that originate from the environment are generally unintended (although there are exceptions, as Chapter 10 will point out), nonetheless they affect the communication between the presenter and audience. The affects are subtle, but sometimes significant in terms of the degree to which these external conditions can either contribute to or detract from the effectiveness of a presentation.

Environmental factors consist of temperature, noise, lighting, and air quality. Surroundings include those things or conditions that are around the persons communicating, such as the color of the walls, the furniture and fixtures, and other people. Whether the surroundings are familiar or unfamiliar also has an impact on people.

Influencing Factors. The communication process is heavily charged with the influence of factors that reside within the presenter and members of the audience. These factors are attitudes, culture, education, experience, gender, and pattern. They include the thought processes, background, range of interests, intellectual capabilities, and physical, psychological, and emotional conditions that determine how people express themselves, listen, learn, and respond.

Figure 1-1 lists the influencing factors in composite terms. Attitudes, for example, are comprised of a person's biases, perspectives, beliefs, and values. Culture includes not only societal conditions, but also the domestic, political, and corporate cultures within which a person lives and works. For instance, an employee's response to a manager's presentation (or vice versa), will likely be influenced by the corporate culture in which they work. The education factor encompasses both formal and informal types of education, and can be thought of as the body of learned knowledge a person has acquired over the years. Experience is comprised of the personal, social, and occupational experiences to which a person has been exposed. Gender, of course, refers to whether a person is male or female. Although the issue of gender is a sensitive one in many contemporary societies, it is one which studies have found can influence how a person communicates and responds.

Lastly, pattern refers to the predominant thought process that guides the manner in which a person usually thinks, learns, and communicates. In recent years, research has found that the brain exhibits a tendency to favor one hemisphere over another when processing information that is learned or communicated. In lay language, the terms "left-brain" and "right-brain" are commonly used to describe this phenomenon. The terms "concrete" and "conceptual" are used in this text when reference is made to how a pattern of thinking can affect a presentation.

It is critical that a presenter recognize these influencing factors and the part they play in a communication situation. Attitudes, culture, education, experience, gender, and pattern affect virtually every aspect of a presentation. They affect, for example, the words a presenter chooses to express a message, and they influence the nature of the feedback an audience expresses in response.

Perception.   Review Figure 1-1. It points out a significant aspect of the communication process that is especially pertinent to presenting: perception. The action and interaction of the dynamics of communicating have a cumulative effect. They add up to the formation of perceptions. From the beginning of a presentation, throughout, until it is finished, and often even afterwards, the presenter and persons in the audience are forming perceptions. The audience perceives the presenter and the message in certain ways. The presenter perceives the audience, their feedback, and the affect and outcome of the presentation in certain ways.

The audience receives cues from the presenter and the environment: verbal words, vocal sounds, visual sights. These cues are then processed by the person(s) in the audience in the context of the influencing factors that shape how each one thinks and feels. Individuals in the audience then respond with feedback based on how they have processed and perceived the presenter and his or her message. All of this transpires in a matter of nanoseconds. The process can be viewed in terms of this formula:

Reception + Processing = ± Perceptions = ± Feedback = ± Outcome

The formula is deceptively simple. Managing the process is not. A presenter attempts to communicate in such a way as to shape positive perceptions in the minds of members of the audience, in order to generate the affirmative feedback that builds to a successful outcome. Considering the many (and many unseen) variables that affect how both the presenter and people in the audience receive and process information and ideas, a presenter's task is anything but simple.

One of the most important principles to bear in mind throughout this course, and every time you prepare and deliver a presentation, is this: perceptions are more powerful than facts. In other words, people respond

Figure 1-3. Perception.

largely on the basis of what they perceive to be true, rather than on the basis of what, in fact, is true. If you doubt this premise, look around. You will find the power of perception evidenced in virtually every area. It affects what people buy, how people vote, who people date, who they promote—and how people respond to a presenter and a presentation.

The power of perception is such that the very same message will be perceived differently by different people. Figure 1-3, in which the "message" is a simple graphic, illustrates this point.

An office worker might perceive the graphic to represent a file cabinet. A homemaker, chef, or dieter might perceive that it depicts a refrigerator. A driver who spends considerable time behind the wheel of an automobile might see in the figure the back of a truck. A patriot may perceive it as a symbol for Abraham Lincoln's stovepipe hat. An unorthodox reader might turn this book upside down and perceive that the graphic illustrates a kitchen counter or a desk. What do you perceive Figure 1-3 to be?

Perception is more powerful than fact. Accordingly, a skilled communicator takes care to craft and carry out a presentation aimed at fostering perceptions that will be favorable to the presenter and to the message.

Key Concept 5

Presenting is a distillation process.

As early as 1982, social forecaster John Naisbitt, in his book *Megatrends,* called attention to the escalating rates at which information was being generated, processed, and disseminated. He reported that between six and seven thousand scientific articles were written each day; the rate at which scientific and technical data was produced could be expected to increase by as much as 40 percent per year; and the majority of people working in the service sector were employed in the creation, processing, and distribution of information.

Information Overload

The development and increasing use of computer and communication technologies have proliferated the volume of information to which people are exposed every day. An expanding knowledge base, specialization in many fields, and real-time systems (in which message transmission is instantaneous) have added to the complexity of the information with which people have to deal. As a result, an "information glut" exists. In homes, communities, and throughout the workplace, people are inundated with information.

Endless messages are transmitted via the media of radio and television. Still more are communicated through videos, films, audio-cassettes, laser-disk recordings, newspapers, trade publications, books, correspondence, reports, electronic mail, telephone calls, magazine advertisements, direct-mail materials, highway billboards, meetings, training sessions, seminars, and person-to-person conversations. Inarguably, far more information is generated every day than people can absorb or need to know.

It does not take a great deal of skill or discretion to disseminate information. It does, however, require considerable skill and discernment to distill the enormous volume of information that is available. In this, skilled presenters perform an invaluable task for the marketplace and in workplaces that are overloaded with information. They fill the need for professionals who know how to extract that material which is most relevant to a situation and who can communicate with sufficient skill so as to impress the message on people.

In view of the overwhelming mass of information to which most people are exposed, it is not surprising that much of it is not fully received or retained. Listeners and readers (often unconsciously) filter out those messages they perceive to be of little or no importance to them. Therefore, a presentation should not be viewed solely or even primarily as a vehicle for disseminating information. Rather, it should be viewed as a means for conveying and clarifying select information and ideas in such a manner as to prompt the recipients of the information to act on the message.

In view of the overwhelming mass of information to which most people are exposed, it is crucial to avoid overwhelming an audience with a presentation. In the matter of presenting, more is rarely better. Since what people need is not merely more information, a presentation should not be viewed as an occasion to communicate everything the presenter knows about a subject. On the contrary, an effective presentation communicates what the audience needs to see and hear to be persuaded to act on the message.

To effectively combat some of the consequences of information overload referenced in the preceding paragraphs, and to deliver to people material that they will and can better assimilate, necessitates a process of distillation.

Distilling Information

Presenting is a distillation process. To **distill** is to purify, condense, or refine material by extracting the essential elements. Of all the information that may be available on the subject of a presentation, it is the presenter's responsibility to ascertain what material is most needed by and/or most significant to the audience. It is the presenter's role to then deliver only that material which is essential to maintain interest, establish relevance, and convey value to the audience—within the time allotted for the presentation.

There are five stages to the process of distilling information for a presentation, which are introduced here (and explained in greater detail in the chapters that follow).

Research.   In this first stage, background information is gathered, data is collected, and resource material is compiled to gain insights and ideas on the subject. Research includes gathering information on the nature of the audience and the presentation event, as well as collecting evidentiary material on the subject.

Selection.   The reference and resource material obtained from research is reviewed. The main points to be addressed in the presentation are identified and material that will serve to convey the main points is selected. Since the volume of information gathered through research will likely be more than what is needed for the actual presentation, at this stage the presenter is chiefly concerned with determining and choosing the information that will meet the needs of and appeal to the audience and concurrently best serve the presenter's objective. This stage of identification and selection is critical because the overall content of the presentation is determined at this point.

Organization.   The selected material is structured for a well-ordered presentation. The body of information with which the presenter is working is usually further distilled at this stage through the tasks of editing and refining the content in order to tailor it to the nature and time frame of the presentation event.

These first three stages of research, selection, and organization may be done by either the presenter or someone to whom the tasks can be delegated. If the tasks are delegated, at the very least the presenter should be consulted at each stage of the process of distillation. The greater a presenter's involvement, the better prepared the presenter is likely to be before actually delivering the presentation. Moreover, presenters who do their own selection and organization of material tend to gain the advantage of a sense of ownership of the content, which contributes to their conviction and credibility when communicating with an audience.

Presentation/Observation. The distillation process continues during the actual presentation. At this point, it is largely the result of observation on the part of the presenter. A skilled presenter observes and responds to audience reactions and may refine or modify parts of the message "on the spot." A skilled presenter also observes the time in relation to presentation of the topic. If, for example, the first part of the presentation took more time than the presenter had anticipated, subsequent portions of the message will have to be condensed in order to complete the presentation within the allotted time.

In addition, moments before beginning, a presenter may learn that the amount of time allocated for the presentation has been unexpectedly reduced. An earlier speaker or item on the agenda may have taken up more time than scheduled. A client may be late arriving for an appointment, but still wants to finish on time. In such instances, a presenter must distill the content further, immediately before or even during the presentation.

If the subject is one that will be presented again, distilling the content may be a recurring process. After the first presentation on the subject, when the presenter reviews the outcome and assesses what worked and what didn't work as well as intended, she or he may distill the information to make needed adjustments to the material. Subsequent presentations on the same subject would also be distilled to adapt the material to be delivered in different time frames. Content prepared for a one-hour presentation, for example, would need to be condensed when the presenter is given only 30 minutes in which to present the same subject.

Response. In some situations, it is appropriate and advisable to invite questions and comments from members of the audience. When the audience comments or poses questions, there are usually any number of ways in which a presenter may respond. Here again, a presenter exercises discretionary skill to distill, from among the many possibilities, the one most appropriate and concise response.

Presenting is not a matter of reciting a speech from memory. It is not reading from a script or teleprompter. It is not (as one student of mine observed) doing an "information dump" on the audience. Neither is it seeking to impress people with a plethora of facts and figures. An effective presentation is the product of a distillation process that occurs before, throughout, and after the presentation. From out of all of the material available on the subject, considering the time allotted for the presentation, and in relation to the audience addressed, the accomplished presenter distills those select points that encapsulate the essence of the message and best communicate its meaning to the audience.

> ## Key Concept 6
>
> *Presenting is a creative process.*

A **creative** process takes raw material and shapes from it something that is new in form or function. That is exactly what a presenter does during the development and delivery of a business presentation. The raw materials of words and information are fashioned into a novel approach to the subject, fresh insights, or innovative ideas (or updated perspectives on old ideas). The raw materials of overhead transparencies and marking pens, photographic slides, and computer-generated graphics are used to create visual aids. The raw materials of an individual's vocal and visual cues combine to give expression to the subject in ways it has not previously been expressed—because no two presenters are alike in their forms of expression.

Characteristics of Creativity

A dictionary definition of the term *creative* includes the words inventive, productive, imaginative, artistic, literary, constructive, and purposeful. These same words describe characteristics of effective presenters and their presentations. The following points suggest how these words apply to presenters and thus offer a perspective on presenting as a creative process.

Inventive. Devise examples, analogies, or audiovisual aids by which to communicate a timeworn topic in a contemporary way so that the message is perceived to be more timely than worn. Develop techniques to clearly convey a highly complex subject so that the message will be easily understood by laypersons.

Productive. When preparing a presentation, make efficient use of the time and resources available. Present to groups as a means to produce desired results, making creative use of opportunities to influence a greater number of people in less time.

Imaginative. Prior to a presentation, imagine the situation, the audience, and a satisfying and successful experience. Incorporate in the content of the presentation various literary techniques that conjure up mental images in the minds of people in the audience.

Artistic.   Reinforce the message with original and colorful visual aids. Make use of verbal expressions that paint pictures in people's minds.

Literary.   Use techniques derived from literature, such as storytelling, metaphors, alliteration, and verbal illustrations.

Constructive.   Structure a presentation to build a case on the basis of concrete evidence. Present material helpful to the audience.

Purposeful.   Plan, create, and communicate focused presentations, keeping clearly in mind the purpose of presenting.

The Value of Creativity in Presentations

Although every presentation is a product of the creative process, some presentations are obviously more creative than others. Presenters who exhibit a greater degree of creativity enjoy advantages their less creative counterparts do not. Therefore, it behooves business and professional people who are interested in improving their presentation skills to enhance the creativity they bring to presenting.

Creativity enriches a presentation in numerous ways. Creativity is intriguing, and so arouses the curiosity of the audience. A fresh, creative approach to a topic is more memorable than a hackneyed one. The presentation of a creative solution to a problem gains audience attention more so than a routine suggestion that has been heard many times before. Original ideas, or original forms of giving expression to time-honored ideas, often prompt an audience to ponder points that might otherwise be overlooked or considered stale. A unique theme or a new perspective on a subject can be captivating, and may be just what is needed to persuade the audience to act on the message. Creative visual aids can spark interest in statistical and technical data that may otherwise be tedious to listen to for some members of an audience. Many techniques for adding to the effectiveness of a presentation emerge from thinking creatively.

Nurturing Creativity

Many people harbor the popular misconception that creativity is a rare quality reserved for a special few. They perceive that to be creative implies being qualified to join the ranks of the great thinkers, writers, inventors, dramatists, artists, humorists, architects, choreographers, fashion designers, and the like. Creative people, they surmise, have been specially gifted with exceptional artistic, literary, or scientific capabilities. In fact, every person contains the seeds of creativity. Like all seeds, however, creativity must be nurtured in order to bring it to fruition.

Roger von Oech, president of the consulting firm Creative Think, observed, "Knowledge is the stuff from which new ideas are made . . . The real key to being creative lies in what you do with your knowledge."* Every person who presents (or who has an interest in presenting) already possesses a body of knowledge. Creativity is nurtured by applying to that body of knowledge techniques that foster fresh views, spark innovative thinking, and lead to the discovery of ways to present more creatively.

Some techniques that help nurture creative thinking are summarized here. Since the subject of this course is business presentations, the points listed are not intended to represent comprehensive coverage on the subject of creativity. They are an introduction only of approaches that have been found to stimulate creative thinking.

Connect.   The Greek philosopher, Aristotle, suggested the crux of creativity when he advised, "Only connect." A familiar song hints at it, too: "The ankle bone's connected to the calf bone, the calf bone's connected to the knee bone, the knee bone's connected to the thigh bone . . ."—and a whole leg is created as a result.

Connecting is a matter of exploring the possible compatibility or symbiotic relationship that may exist among different elements. To understand its application to business presentations, consider how the concept was just introduced here. Two seemingly unrelated items—a quote from an ancient philosopher and a contemporary ditty—were connected to convey a new point. The point is this: the formation (i.e., creation) of an unexpected connection can produce a surprising effect. The unexpected tends to capture people's attention, which is precisely what a presenter seeks to do.

Connections create more than "special effects." Reflecting on how one point in a presentation might connect with or relate to another can suggest transitions between parts of a presentation. Furthermore, mentally searching for a connection among two or more commonly held ideas can engender new ideas and humorous insights.

Juxtapose.   Positioning information or ideas close together or side by side can enhance a presenter's creativity. This technique can be especially effective when opposites are juxtaposed. The contrast between opposites can add meaning to a message, make it more memorable, or be so startling as to raise audience attention. Try juxtaposing statistical data with an inspiring quotation. Juxtapose a serious story alongside a humorous anecdote. State a fact, then immediately follow with an expression of feeling. The juxtaposition of a con-

---

* Roger von Oech, *A Whack on the Side of the Head* (New York: Warner Books, 1990), p. 6.

servative business suit and a playful approach to a subject would be novel; juxtaposing contrasting colors and shapes could result in more creative visual aids.

Borrow.   Borrowing refers to the practice of taking elements from one context and using them in another. For years, for example, people have borrowed terms from the world of sports and used them in sales, motivational, and political presentations. One technique that can improve both the effectiveness and the creativity of business presentations is that of borrowing literary devices as a means to communicate a message. Literary devices include alliteration, analogies, contrasting structure, metaphors, similes, and visual imagery (all of which will be discussed in detail in Chapter 5).

Record.   It is ironic and unfortunate that one's capacity to think creatively frequently decreases in proportion to an increase in the pressure to be creative. When a presenter faces a deadline on putting together a presentation, the seeds of creativity seem to shrivel. Conversely, a person is often most creative at unexpected times. Therefore, it is useful to keep a notebook or portable recording device on hand for the purpose of recording insights and ideas as they come to mind. Doing so not only makes it easy and convenient to capture creative thoughts, but also serves to reinforce the fact that you are creative. This latter point is significant because, just as success breeds success, so too creativity breeds more creativity.

Question.   Fewer techniques may nurture creativity as much as that of asking questions. Creative thinkers are typically inquisitive. A trait many overtly creative people share in common is a keen interest in exploring possibilities. They probe for clues to the solutions to problems. They muse over unresolved issues. They ask questions.

Creativity is stimulated by asking questions like "What if . . . ?" "Why this . . . ?" "What else . . . ?" "How like . . . ?" "How different . . . ?" Naturally, a presenter would ask the questions in a form that would stir his or her thoughts in relation to the subject or specific considerations of the presentation. For example:

1. What if I approached the subject from this angle? What if I raised this point before that point? What if I expressed the issue in this manner? What if I graphically represented the data in this form?

2. Why this statement? What else would add more meaning to my message? Why this visual aid? What else could have greater impact? Why this seating arrangement? What else might work better?

3. How like Point A is Point B? How are they different? How is this proposed idea like that? How does this differ from that? What can I liken this concept to? What can I contrast it with?

An advantage to asking questions is that they encourage a presenter to consider options, to look beyond the customary way of viewing and doing things. The answers that come to mind are often surprisingly creative and can heighten the effectiveness of a presentation.

Frolic. While connecting, juxtaposing, borrowing, recording, and questioning help to nurture creativity, it is frolicking that frees a person's mind from preoccupations and preconceptions. Mental pressures and fixed ideas can stifle creativity. When they are relieved, that whole body of knowledge from which creativity springs becomes more open to exploration. Fresh ideas and new possibilities formulate more readily.

Frolicking calls to mind images of carefree children at play, romping about, their laughter unrestrained. Like their younger counterparts, adults who take time off to have fun tend to be more inventive. Presenters who develop the ability to adopt a playful attitude—toward themselves, the audience, and the subject of the presentation—discover their inherent creativity. They discover another quality essential to effective presenting, too: humor.

Business presentations can be serious business. The subject may be serious. The occasion for which the presentation was called may be serious. People in the audience may be wearing serious expressions on their faces. The demands on a presenter, to get the job done and achieve goals through the avenue of presenting, may be serious. However, treating any (or worse, all) of these factors with too much gravity will squelch creativity—and the effectiveness of the presentation.

An accomplished presenter takes seriously the skills and disciplines of structuring presentations that will be effective. You may recall that one of the attributes of an effective presentation is balance. Even a serious subject needs the balancing affect of humor, just as a serious presenter needs the counterbalance of frolicking good fun. Fun fosters spontaneity which in turn stimulates creative thinking.

As you proceed through this course, consider creative ways to apply the skills described in the chapters to the business presentations you develop and deliver. At various points, you may find it helpful to return to this section to review the techniques for nurturing creativity. Connect, juxtapose, borrow, record, question, and have fun.

Dynamic Processes

The foregoing pages have offered perspectives on presenting as a function that encompasses communication, distillation, and creative processes. These processes are **dynamic**: active, energetic, and continuously changing. The term **dynamic** is derived from a Greek word, "dynamikos," which translates "power." The best business presentations (i.e., those that are dynamically effective) are powerful means for reaching people and having an impact on them.

Key Concept 7

Presentation skills may be applied variously to different types of business presentations.

All business presentations have in common:

- The ultimate purpose to persuade
- The communication, distillation, and creative processes through which a message is developed and delivered

Obviously, not all business presentations are the same. They differ with respect to:

- The occasion, motivation, or need that prompted the presentation
- The presenter
- The message
- The audience
- The environment and surroundings
- The time frame
- The degree of effectiveness
- The outcome

Types of Business Presentations

Despite the preceding differences, a presentation can be categorized on the basis of the types of business presentations that commonly occur. By identifying a presentation as to its "type," a presenter is better able to ascertain:

1. What background information should be researched and to what degree
2. Which presentation methods, skills, or techniques it would be most appropriate to incorporate in the presentation and the manner in which to apply them
3. How to tailor the content and style of the presentation

One form of categorizing presentations is in terms of the relationship of the audience to the presenter. In this respect, a presentation is one of two types:

1. External
2. Internal

An external presentation is one given to an audience from outside the organization that the presenter represents. A presentation by a sales representative to customers would be an example of an external presentation. Internal refers to those situations in which the presenter and the audience come from within the same organization, such as when a manager addresses staff members.

A presentation may be further categorized in terms of the predominant characteristic(s) of the presentation, as follows:

1. Promotional

2. Informational

3. Down-line

4. Up-line

Promotional.   A promotional presentation concentrates on promoting a product, service, idea, solution, or recommendation. Promotional presentations may also aim at promoting a person or platform, as in the case of political presentations that promote a certain candidate or party line.

Informational.   In this type of presentation, the emphasis is on conveying information. The information may be in the form of technical material, scientific data, survey or statistical findings, policies, procedures, methods, or techniques.

Down-line and Up-line.   Both are internal presentations. The terms **down-line** and **up-line** are derived from a traditional organizational hierarchy in which positions are structured in vertical relationship to one another. A presentation by an executive to managers, from a manager to supervisors, or from a supervisor to employees would be down-line (i.e., the communication flows down the organizational line). Conversely, a presentation by an employee to a supervisor, from a supervisor to managers, or from a manager to executives would be termed up-line.

Two or three of the types just described may be evident in one presentation. Consider, for example, a presentation by an employee to a manager on the subject of recommendations for automating the workplace. Is this a promotional, informational, or up-line presentation? Two questions help determine the answer. First, what is the predominant characteristic of the presentation? (In this case, it is up-line.) Second, what is the presenter's primary intent? If it is to promote one recommendation over others, then the presentation would be considered up-line/promotional. If it is to inform the manager of the options, then the presentation would be an up-line/informational type.

Reflection Questions

What types of presentations do you currently do? What other type(s) would it be beneficial for you to do as a means of achieving your goals?

A Common Purpose

With all types of presentations, bear in mind that the ultimate purpose of presenting is to persuade. In the foregoing example, the presenter's ultimate purpose would be to either (a) persuade the manager to adopt the recommendation promoted by the presenter, or (b) persuade the manager to review the information presented. It is easy to recognize the "purpose to persuade" in the former case. However, even in the latter, the end objective is the same. Business and professional people typically have more to do than time in which to do it all; and (as previously discussed) there are increasing volumes of information with which to deal on a daily basis. Consequently, in this example, there is no guarantee that the manager will take the time to review the information presented—unless the presentation is persuasive.

Adaptability

Adept presenters have at their disposal a full complement of skills and techniques with which to accomplish the purpose of presenting. They are more likely to achieve their purpose when they have mastered the ability to adapt—to discern, select, and accentuate the material, methods, and techniques which would be most appropriate in a given situation. The quality of adaptability is one which distinguishes an outstanding presenter from the norm.

A presenter cannot adapt to different situations without first recognizing the different types of business presentations. Throughout this course, reference will be made to the different types previously outlined, notably in the sample situations that appear at the end of each chapter, beginning with Chapter 2.

Key Concept 8

The barriers to presenting effectively can be overcome.

A feature in the October 22, 1990 issue of *Fortune* magazine reported that more than 25 million business presentations occur every day. Studies of workplace activity and productivity have found that business and professional people spend, on average, from one-third to one-half of their time in meetings—a setting in which presentations are common. Clearly, presentations represent a substantial investment of time, energy, money, and human resource. To justify and capitalize on such an investment, it is imperative that business presentations be effective.

From the standpoint of the individual, a business presentation represents a potential opportunity. When a presentation is effective, the opportunity is gained. When ineffective, it is an opportunity lost.

Ineffective Presentations

All too often, presentations are needlessly ineffective. The presenter does not achieve his or her objective. The presentation lacks the attributes that are hallmarks of effectiveness. The audience is not persuaded to accept or act on the message. The outcome for everyone involved is sadly disappointing. Such a situation can be traced to one or a combination of the following barriers.

Anxiety about Speaking before a Group. Surveys of the general public, college students, employees in the workplace, and CEOs of Fortune 500 companies have found that what Americans fear most is public speaking. Anxiety about speaking before a group can paralyze a presenter.

Inadequate Planning and Preparation. Whether a presenter knows of an upcoming presentation one month or one week in advance, an all too common tendency is to put off preparing until a day or two before the presentation. The presenter is ill-prepared and the audience perceives it. A lack of planning and preparation not only results in an ineffective presentation, but also triggers and further fuels anxiety about presenting.

Disorganized Content. When the material in a message is disorganized, it may be because the presenter put off preparing until the last minute. At other times, however, it is a matter of not knowing how to go about organizing information. In either case, a message that is not well-ordered is more difficult for an audience to assimilate. This increases the probability that the audience won't respond affirmatively, in keeping with the presenter's objective.

Failure to Relate to and with the Audience. A common misconception is that presenting is synonymous with orating. It is not. An oration is typified by a speaker who talks at the audience, frequently from the speaker's point of view. In an effective business presentation, the presenter seeks to understand the point of view of the person or persons in the audience, relates the message to them, and builds a relationship with them. Presenters neglect doing so if they (*a*) are fixated on their own point of view, (*b*) are unaware of the importance of this aspect of presenting, or (*c*) have not yet discovered or developed the relational techniques that are essential to an effective presentation.

Inattention to Details and Arrangements. In addition to the many factors involved in preparing and delivering the content of a presentation, there are numerous details and arrangements to be considered: meeting-room reservations, seating, audiovisual equipment, and supplies and handouts, to name a few. Attending to these details and arrangements is the ultimate responsibility of the presenter. Overlooking even the smallest detail or failing to confirm and check arrangements can undermine the effectiveness of a presentation.

Environmental Factors. Within the environment in which a presentation occurs, factors such as room temperature, lighting, noise, odors, and the proximity of people in the audience (to one another and to the presenter) can have a favorable or unfavorable effect on a presentation.

Breaking the Barriers

With the exception of some environmental factors over which a presenter may not have control, the barriers that are listed above are self-imposed. Therefore, they can be overcome. People choose to set themselves up for failure or to set themselves up for success. People who present can choose to set themselves up for success, through learning, skill development, preparation, and practice.

Reflection Questions

What barriers currently hinder you from presenting as effectively as you would like? What aspects of presenting do you most want or need to improve?

Summary

Business presentations are a means by which individuals and organizations can enhance their visibility and advance toward achieving their goals. The degree to which a presentation serves these aims is related to how effective the presentation is. Effective presentations are attention-getting, meaningful, memorable, activating, and balanced. Furthermore, a business presentation is most effective when it satisfies the purpose of presenting, which is to persuade.

A business presentation is a complex and dynamic function, encompassing the communication process, the distillation process, and the creative process. These processes and their related skills apply to all types of business presentations: internal and external, promotional, informational, up-line, and down-line. By gaining an understanding of the processes involved in presenting and developing proficiency with presentation skills, a person can overcome the barriers to presenting effectively.

Comprehension Check

The answers to the following appear on page 333.

1. During the communication process, both the presenter and the audience form _____.
   a. attitudes
   b. visual cues
   c. perceptions
   d. creative ideas
   e. thought patterns

2. Creativity can be nurtured by _____.
   a. taking a presentation seriously
   b. asking questions
   c. organizing the message
   d. understanding influencing factors
   e. overcoming the barriers to presenting effectively

3. The purpose of presenting is to _____.
   a. distill information
   b. persuade the audience
   c. achieve goals
   d. recommend solutions
   e. inform the audience

4. Of the three channels through which a presenter and audience communicate, _____ have the greatest impact.
   a. nonverbal cues
   b. verbal cues
   c. perceptions
   d. vocal cues
   e. attitudes

5. To complete the sentence that follows, select the five attributes that are characteristics of an effective presentation. An effective presentation _____, _____, _____, _____, and _____.
   a. is humorous
   b. gets and keeps attention
   c. activates the audience

d. is researched
e. creates perceptions
f. is memorable
g. entertains the audience
h. is balanced
i. is meaningful
j. maximizes visibility

To Do

The chapters that follow will be more meaningful and memorable for you if you apply the information to a presentation that has practical value for you. It will be most useful if you select a presentation on a subject related to your occupation or profession. It may be a presentation you currently do and want to improve, or it may be a presentation you will have to or want to make in the future.

Write the subject of the presentation you will develop as you proceed through this course.

Is the presentation:

1. Internal?

2. External?

What type of presentation is it?

1. Promotional

2. Informational

3. Up-line

4. Down-line

2
Planning Your Presentation

In the preceding chapter, an effective presentation was defined as one which produces the desired result. The same definition could be applied to virtually every endeavor. An effective military campaign is one which achieves victory. An effective sports team wins the game. Effective managers provide leadership to increase productivity. Effective salespeople attain quota. In every case, the effort to produce the intended result begins prior to the actual event. It begins with planning. Military strategists, coaches, organizational leaders, and salespeople know that their efforts are more likely to succeed when they are guided by a plan. Effective presenters know it, too.

In this chapter, you will become acquainted with the planning process as it relates to business presentations. You will gain a view of the value of planning as a precursor to producing a successful presentation. Each concept will step you through the considerations and questions that planning entails.

Objective

To recognize the variables involved in planning for different types of presentations; to name the factors that govern the outcome of a presentation and, for each one, describe aspects to be considered when planning; to apply the use of a checklist when planning for a presentation; and to understand ways to overcome the common obstacles to presenting.

Key Concepts

9. Planning is the essential first step in the process of presenting.

10. The extent to which planning occurs depends on a number of variables.

11. Planning focuses on the primary factors that govern the outcome of a presentation.

12. Through planning, the role and responsibilities of the presenter are determined.

13. Planning concentrates on the nature and needs of the audience.

14. Planning takes into account the setting in which a presentation will occur.

15. Planning clarifies scheduling and time-frame considerations.

16. Effective presenters use a planning checklist to speed and simplify the planning process, and to confirm arrangements for the presentation.

17. Devising means to assess results is an integral part of planning.

18. The obstacles to planning for an effective presentation can be overcome.

Key Terms

Understanding the following terms is essential to understanding and applying the key concepts.

Proactive	Payoff
Systematic	Resource
Plan	High-stakes, low-stakes
Presentation event	Sources
Variables	Action plan
Setting	Demographics

Key Concept 9

Planning is the essential first step in the process of presenting.

Respected author and management scholar, Lester R. Bittel, affirmed that, "It has been demonstrated time and again that organizations and individuals that engage in systematic planning have better success records than those that do not."* The findings apply to presenters as well as to managers. When given the opportunity to deliver a business presentation, the presenter functions as the "manager" of that presentation (whether the person literally occupies a management position or not). An effective presenter, like an effective manager, plans.

Managers perform four basic tasks: planning, organizing, leading, and monitoring results. Effective presenters perform those same tasks. They plan for the presentation, organize the material, lead the audience through the message, and monitor the outcome. The best managers are proactive rather than reactive. So, too, are the best presenters. **Proactive** presenters, through planning, act in advance. They anticipate conditions and work toward developing a presentation that will act on the audience—and prompt the audience to act. Failing to plan proactively, a presenter runs the risk of having to react on the spot to unexpected conditions that can plague an unplanned presentation. To anticipate conditions and therefore avoid, or at least minimize surprises, plan.

Planning, whether by managers or by presenters, is **systematic** in nature. It is an orderly method by which the variables in a given situation are considered and then arranged into a plan. The **plan** is a framework for action, a blueprint that delineates factors on and around which the presentation will be built. Figure 2-1 depicts presenting as a cycle that begins with a plan and ends when the plan is completed.

Planning is done for the **presentation event**, that is, for the entire context within which the message occurs. A staff meeting, a sales call, a seminar or

* Lester R. Bittel, *The McGraw-Hill 36-Hour Management Course* (New York: McGraw-Hill Publishing Company, 1989), p. 81.

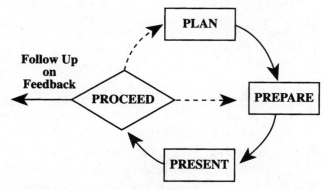

Figure 2-1. Business presentations process.

training session, a political speech, a conference keynote address—each is an example of a presentation event. By planning for the presentation event, a presenter is better prepared to know what to expect and how to capitalize on the opportunity the occasion represents.

The single most important benefit to be derived from planning is that it serves to set a presenter up for success. Through planning, a presenter gains information and insights that contribute to and are necessary for both preparing and presenting an effective presentation (as Figure 2-1 indicates). It is the point at which the distillation of information begins, the point at which a presenter identifies factors that will affect the communication process, and it often triggers the onset of the creative process. Furthermore, out of planning comes an understanding of conditions— favorable and potentially unfavorable—of which a presenter must be aware in order to tailor the message to satisfy the purpose of the presentation and avoid oversights that can undermine it.

Advantages of Planning

Planning offers additional advantages as well. It serves to enhance a presenter's probability of success for the following reasons:

1. Planning clarifies and confirms details of the presentation event that can be crucial to an effective outcome.

2. Planning crystallizes a presenter's thinking in terms of those aspects of the presentation the presenter controls, compared with those the presenter does not control, but can manage. For example, a presenter can control the content of the message, but may not be the person who establishes or controls the time frame. However, a presenter can manage the time in terms of how it is used during the presentation. There are also aspects of a presentation which a presenter may not be able to foresee, and therefore cannot plan how to best control or manage them. However, by planning, a presenter is better prepared to respond (as opposed to react) should the unpredictable arise—such as a heckler in the audience, a medical emergency, or a power failure.

3. Planning demonstrates a presenter's planning skill, commitment to the presentation event, and conscientious attention to detail. In a manner of speaking, planning is one way a presenter conveys, "I mean business."

4. Planning minimizes crises. As "systematic" is the antonym of "chaotic," so systematic planning avoids a chaotic presentation situation. It is damaging to both the presenter and the presentation when chaos reigns, when at the eleventh hour the presenter is scrambling to come up with a message and frantically attend to last-minute details.

5. Planning makes more efficient use of the presenter's time. Although planning takes time, it is time well invested. If one has 30 minutes in which to present, the planning that was done prior to the presentation could result in new customers, more voters, new donors, better motivated employees, better educated students—more people who act in an affirmative response to the presenter's message. If a presenter neglects to plan, the desired result may not be achieved and the time spent presenting is time lost.

6. Planning provides direction. The value of having a direction is clearly stated in the familiar story of Alice in Wonderland. At one point in the story, Alice is wandering around Wonderland when she comes to a fork in the road. There she meets the Cheshire Cat. "Pardon me, sir," Alice says, "I wonder if you could help me. Which road would you suggest I take?" "That depends," answers the Cheshire Cat. "What is your destination?" "Nowhere in particular," Alice answers. "Then," replies the Cheshire Cat (grinning broadly), "any road will do."

One of the first questions that arises when planning a presentation is akin to "What is my destination?" In other words, what is the end result the presenter wants to reach? To what point of view does the presenter want to bring the audience via the message? There is usually more than one way to bring an audience to the desired result. By analogy, planning provides a roadmap that clarifies the direction a presenter should take.

7. Planning encourages follow-up to the presentation event. In some situations, the purpose of the presentation is not fulfilled until after the fact, when the presenter follows up on the action proposed by the presentation. There is often a temptation to consider the job done once the presentation is over. However, a presentation plan is not complete (as Figure 2-1 suggests) until the presenter follows up on the feedback from the presentation.

8. Planning boosts a presenter's confidence for the actual presenting. The authors of *The One-Minute Manager* contend (and many behavioral psychologists agree), "People who feel good about themselves produce good results."* Conversely, people who produce good results feel good about themselves. Doing a good job of planning fuels enthusiasm for the presentation event. The very act of acting on a presentation in a positive, productive way can alleviate the anxiety some people feel about presenting.

For the numerous reasons just listed, planning is the first and an essential step in the entire cycle of a business presentation. There is a danger in viewing the act of presenting itself as an isolated event that begins when the presenter starts to speak and ends when the presenter sits down. The danger

---

* Kenneth Blanchard and Spencer Johnson, *The One-Minute Manager* (New York: Berkley Books, 1983), p. 19.

lies in the fact that, without initial planning and subsequent preparation, there is a greater probability that the presenter will appear and the message will sound isolated from the audience and from the context in which the presentation occurs. There is a further danger that the presentation will be considered the terminal point of the process when, in fact, it might well be only a beginning.

Presenters sometimes neglect this essential first step of planning. The reasons are explored later in this chapter. Suffice it to say at this point that, as with any other task, the more regularly you plan, the easier it becomes. With practice, you will find you can quickly complete a plan for a business presentation. Familiarity facilitates.

Reflection Question

How will planning for the presentations you do (or expect to do in the future) be of benefit to you?

Key Concept 10

The extent to which planning occurs depends on a number of variables.

Some presentations require very little planning. Others lend themselves to an extensive planning effort. A plan for one business presentation may be completed in a matter of minutes, while another may take hours or even days to plan. In some cases, planning may occur far in advance of the presentation event. More often, planning will start closer to the date of the actual presentation. The differences are occasioned by a number of **variables** (factors that change or vary from one situation to the next).

Presenting is, by its very nature, variable. There is no more uniformity to business presentations than there is among the people who do them, and therefore little a presenter can count on as predictable. For that reason, it behooves the professional to consider in advance, and confirm prior to a presentation, every detail that can influence the outcome.

Variables That Affect Planning

The variables that affect planning are considered in relation to the factors that govern the outcome of a presentation (examined under Key Concepts 11 through 15). These include the presenter, audience, subject, time frame, and **setting**. Setting is an inclusive term that refers to the environment and surroundings within which a presentation occurs. The setting of a presentation may be an office, conference room, meeting facility, convention center auditorium, outdoor platform, or arena, together with conditions in and around the site.

The following variables determine both the extent to which planning needs to be done for a given presentation and how far in advance of the presentation the planning should start.

1. *Frequency.* A quick assessment of what planning might entail for a particular presentation can be made by asking, "How often has the presenter done a presentation on this subject to this type of audience in this time frame in this setting?" If the answer is "frequently," then planning *may* be a routine task that can be accomplished quickly. The word *may* is emphasized because a second question follows. On most occasions, has the presenter succeeded in producing the desired result? If the answer is "yes," it is probable that less planning would be required than if the answer were "no." One reason a presenter may not have experienced success, even with frequent presentation of the same subject in similar circumstances, is that the presenter neglected to plan adequately.

In the matter of business presentations, some people are novices. They are new to presenting, or to the type of audience, or the subject, or the setting. In that case, comprehensive planning is not only essential to prepare for a successful outcome, but also useful for learning and skill development. Other presenters are polished veterans, skilled at presenting, quick to adapt to different audience situations, conversant in numerous subjects, and at ease in any setting. Veteran presenters recognize the value of planning and always do it, although it usually takes them less time. One of the advantages to presenting often is that with repeated experience, a presenter gains the ability to plan more quickly and proficiently.

2. *Familiarity.* Although related to frequency, familiarity is considered separately because it cannot be assumed. It is determined by asking, "How familiar is the presenter with the audience and the subject? Very familiar, moderately familiar, or barely familiar?" A presenter may have done a presentation on the same subject frequently, but may not be familiar with the audience for a particular presentation. Then, planning would concentrate on points pertaining to the audience.

Obviously, the need for planning occurs in inverse proportion to the presenter's level of familiarity. A presenter who is very familiar with the audience and the subject will need to do far less planning than a presenter for whom either the audience or the subject, or both, are new.

3. *Origin.* The extent to which planning is done is also affected by who originated the request for a presentation: an outside party, the presenter's

organization, or the presenter. Another way to view this variable is in terms of whether the presentation is "theirs," "ours," or "mine." If an outside party (such as a client, association, or community organization) requested the presentation, it is "theirs." If the idea of doing the presentation originated with the presenter's organization or employer, then it is "ours." If the presenter asked to do the presentation, it is self-originated or "mine."

Typically, a presentation requested by an outside party takes more planning than one originating from within the presenter's organization. With an in-house presentation, the presenter is usually already familiar with certain conditions. Presentations that are self-originated usually take even less time to plan, because presumably (although not always) the presenter knows about the subject and how to apply it to various audiences and settings.

4. *Representation.* This variable identifies whether the presentation is delivered by someone perceived to be speaking on their own behalf or as a representative of an organization. A salesperson who presents to a customer does so as a representative of a company. A political candidate represents a party or platform. A training professional who conducts an in-house seminar is perceived to represent the organizational point of view. In such cases, when the presenter is in the role of "representative," care needs to be taken to plan the presentation accordingly. In contrast, citizens who present their own views at a public hearing, for example, or self-employed persons who present on their own behalf, have more latitude to speak as individuals.

5. *Type.* Various types of presentations were identified in Chapter 1: external or internal (i.e., in terms of the relationship of the audience to the presenter), promotional, informational, down-line, and up-line. The nature of the presentation as to its type affects the planning task. Given the importance of knowing the audience (a point emphasized later in this chapter), a presentation addressed to an audience that comes from outside of the presenter's organization typically takes more planning than an internal presentation does. As to the other types of presentations, the degree of planning varies according to the other variables listed here.

6. *Content.* In Chapter 3, organizing material for the content of a presentation is discussed in detail. What must be considered during the planning stage, however, is the nature of the content of the message. Is the information on which the content will be based complex or relatively simple? Is material readily available or will it need to be extensively researched? Can sources of information be accessed quickly and easily? When the information is complex, requires extensive research, and/or is time-consuming or difficult to access, planning and preparation must begin far enough in advance to ensure that the presenter will have a fully prepared message and sufficient time to prepare for presenting it.

7. *Nature of the presentation event.* Some presentation events are relatively simple in nature, such as an internal presentation from one person to another conducted in an office. Others are more complex. When a person has been asked to present a keynote address to hundreds of people at a convention, there are more details to be considered and the planning of the presentation would be more extensive.

8. *Potential payoff.* The **payoff** is what a presenter and/or organization stands to gain should a presentation prove successful. Although the potential for gain or the risk of loss are inherent in every presentation, the value of the expected payoff should be considered to determine how much resource to invest in planning. The term **resource** refers to both material and human resources: time, money, skills, talent, energy, and effort.

When there is a great deal at stake in terms of the potential payoff, a presentation is termed **high-stakes**. Conversely, a presentation is **low-stakes** when the potential is relatively nominal. What and how much are at stake vary with each situation. In one situation, a presentation may be done to persuade a customer to buy a product that generates substantial profit for the presenter and the organization represented. Obviously, this would be a high-stakes presentation. In another situation, a presentation may be done to persuade employees to adopt a new procedure. If the recommended change does not have a significant impact on the overall operations or profitability of the organization, the presentation would be considered low-stakes.

Naturally, a high-stakes presentation warrants a greater investment of resources than does a low-stakes presentation. When assessing what is at stake, bear in mind that payoffs are not always measured exclusively in terms of immediate monetary gain. Payoffs of presenting successfully include:

- Credibility

- Good will

- Cost reduction (short-term or long-term)

- Profit (short-term or long-term)

- Visibility

- Value to the audience

These are, of course, interrelated. A presenter who gains credibility through a skillful presentation is more likely to build good will with the audience, which is then more likely to respond affirmatively to the message. A positive response can lead an audience to buy or approve a presenter's recommendations, which may mean value to the audience and enhanced visibility for the presenter. Conversely, a presenter who loses credibility as a result of a poorly planned and ill-prepared presentation risks losing the good will of the audience, and subsequently the prospect of gain.

The relative importance of what is at stake varies from presentation to presentation. The examples that follow suggest the potential payoff that would likely be most important when weighing how much resource to expend on the planning of a presentation.

- When a community leader or political candidate presents to citizens and voters: credibility and good will.

- When a staff analyst for a government agency presents report findings: potential cost reduction.

- When a company (such as an advertising, architectural, construction, design, or engineering firm) presents a proposal for a multimillion dollar project: profit potential.

On the matter of planning relative to what is at stake, professionals apply this rule of thumb: decide on the basis of what serves the best interests of the business over time. Ego considerations can cloud a person's judgment. A presenter may overplan in an attempt to achieve the impossible—perfection. To avoid any risk of losing credibility, a presenter may invest too much resource in a low-stakes presentation. An astute presenter weighs the planning effort and required resources against the payoff expected from a successful presentation.

Reflection Question

What are the potential payoffs to your presenting more effectively?

Key Concept 11

Planning focuses on the primary factors that govern the outcome of a presentation.

As depicted in Figure 1-1, a presentation entails a presenter who delivers a message to an audience in a specified time frame within a given environment and surroundings (setting). Which is the most important factor? They all are. Each one can detract from or contribute to the effectiveness of a presentation. Taken together, they govern the outcome of a presentation.

The message is the content of the presentation. Since an effective message reflects careful consideration of the other factors, it is prepared after the planning stage. Preparing the message is covered in depth in Chapters 3 through 6. From the standpoint of planning, this chapter concentrates on the following primary governing factors:

- Presenter
- Audience
- Setting
- Time frame

Questions Guide
the Planning Process

One helpful approach to planning—systematically, thoroughly, and creatively—is to ask questions. Questions seek answers that reveal information, contingencies, and possible concerns of which a presenter should be aware before presenting. The questions that do that best are open questions which begin with the words:

- Who
- What
- When
- Where
- How
- Which
- and sometimes, Why

For example:

- Who will I be addressing when I present?
- What is the desired outcome?
- When am I expected to start and finish?
- Where can I find material for the message?
- How soon should I start preparing?
- Why is this presentation worth doing?

The answers to the questions asked during the planning stage provide invaluable information and insights. They equip a presenter to develop and deliver a more effective presentation.

Key Concept 12

Through planning, the role and responsibilities of the presenter are determined.

---

c.1

The person who fills the role of presenter is determined by the origin of the presentation. As you may recall from the previous discussion of variables that affect planning, the request for a presentation may be initiated by an outside party, the organization the presenter represents, or the individual presenter.

Selection by the Organization

There are occasions when an outside party solicits a presentation from an organization, or when an organization seeks, and has been granted by an outside party, the opportunity to present. In situations such as these, the organization selects the person who will be the presenter. For example:

- A government agency selects a staff member to make a presentation at a public hearing, council or board meeting, or community event.
- A professional services firm selects a staff member to present to a selection committee in response to an RFP (Request For Proposal).
- A company selects an employee to present to a customer, at a trade association meeting, or at a public relations event.

Unless the outside party specifies who they want to make the presentation, it is up to the organization to decide who will present. In some cases, the decision is a foregone conclusion. There may be only one person on staff who is available and sufficiently qualified on the subject. Then the organization selects the presenter by default. In other words, "This is the only person we've got." Choosing a presenter on that basis may not be the decision that is in the best interests of the business.

In other instances, organizations blindly follow a tradition of selecting the presenter on the basis of a person's position. They automatically opt to have the presentation delivered by the CEO, the department chair, the senior partner, or the upper-level manager. Again, unless the outside party specifically asked for someone by position, choosing a presenter on that basis may not be the decision that is in the best interests of the business either.

What choice of presenter would be in the best interests of the business? Clearly, the best choice would be a person who is well-versed in the subject and a skilled presenter as well. In some cases, presentation skills are an even more important consideration than the person's knowledge of the subject. Unless the presentation event calls for a highly technical topic or in-depth treatment of an esoteric subject, it is preferable to choose the person who is the best communicator and presenter to represent the organization. Then, the presentation plan would include some provision for having the selected presenter study up on the subject in advance of the presentation.

Individual Choice

On other occasions, the presenter is the individual who initiates the presentation event or who regularly presents as a function of her or his job. This is the case with most presentations. Common examples include the following:

- An employee asks to make an in-house presentation at a staff meeting.
- A self-employed person initiates opportunities to present to prospective customers, community or service organizations, or association meetings.
- Sales representatives, training professionals, and often supervisors and managers present as a routine part of their professions.

When a presentation is done because of individual choice or occupation, there is an even greater expectation that the person presenting is prepared to do so. A person prepares to present by giving attention to the development of presentation skills, organization of the message, and planning.

Planning Responsibilities

A presenter's first responsibility is to plan for the presentation. A professional who wants to be effective when presenting needs to do an effective job of planning as well. The discussion that follows refers to the presenter as the person who attends to planning. However, the tasks of planning may be delegated. If some tasks are delegated, the presenter should at least be involved to the extent that he or she gains a full understanding of the audience, the time frame, and the setting. Bear in mind that the tasks and details related to planning do not apply to every presentation. As mentioned previously, some presentation situations require relatively little planning. Others are more complex and require careful, comprehensive planning.

Identify Contacts. Depending on the relative simplicity or complexity of the presentation event, a presenter may identify one person as the primary point of contact or several people who will need to be contacted. The primary contact is usually the person who has requested or approved the presentation, or who is coordinating the presentation event. A primary contact provides details regarding time, location, setting, and the size and nature of the audience. Either the primary contact or others may assist the presenter in arranging travel and accommodations, equipment and supplies, handout materials, or other details that may apply.

In situations when a presenter will be appearing as a guest speaker, an additional detail to clarify is who will introduce the presenter. The presenter is expected to provide a brief *curriculum vitae* (an autobiographical sketch) to the person who will be making the introduction.

Record Details of the Forthcoming Presentation. When a presentation is scheduled, the presenter should keep a written record of:

1. The date and time of the presentation.

2. The type of presentation, as to whether it is external or internal, promotional or informational, and up-line or down-line.

3. The nature of the presentation event. The presenter would indicate if the presentation is, for example, a one-on-one situation; a small-group meeting, a seminar or training session; a sales, customer service, public, or community relations event; an agency hearing, council, or board meeting; or a large-group conference or convention. Understanding the nature of the event helps a presenter better prepare a message (and supporting materials like handouts) that will be most appropriate to the event. For example, it is appropriate to refer to prepared notes when addressing a large group from behind a podium in a more formalized setting. It would not be appropriate to do so when making a presentation one-on-one, to a small group meeting, or in a sales situation.

4. The theme of the event (if applicable). The theme of the event is a consideration when the presenter will be appearing as part of a conference or convention program. Typically, conferences and conventions (and sometimes meetings of service organizations and associations) have a theme. It adds to the presenter's effectiveness when the theme of the event is incorporated into the message. It is one of those subtle touches that pleases people and often gets the presenter invited back.

5. The subject of the presentation. Making note of the subject is especially important in the case of presenters who speak frequently and on more than one subject. The presenter may also find it helpful to note the origin of the subject as "theirs," "ours," or "mine" (discussed under Key Concept 10, item 3). This detail is an indicator of the latitude a presenter has when preparing the message for presentation. When the subject is assigned, the presenter needs to prepare content according to the assignment. When the subject is selected by the presenter, one can be far more flexible in modifying the content to suit one's own objectives.

The specific title of the presentation is also noted. The title may, however, be decided at a later time, especially if the presenter is going to prepare a new message. Frequently, a title doesn't come to mind until the presenter is in the process of drafting the message. There is no urgency to decide on a title, unless the presentation is being done at someone's request and they ask for the title in advance in order to publicize the presentation.

6. The potential payoff. Indicating the payoff alerts the presenter to consider, "How much in the way of resources can be justified for this presentation?" In the case of high-stakes presentations, it is an item that can also be useful to negotiate for more resources, if needed.

Locate Sources.   **Sources** provide a presenter with information and services. They may be internal (within the presenter's organization) or external (outside sources). If, for example, a presenter needs to research local-area statistics, a local Chamber of Commerce, a branch office of the U.S. Small Business Administration, economic development agencies, and area colleges and universities represent sources of information. Businesses that do travel planning, media preparation, printing, photocopying, and graphic design are sources of services a presenter may need.

Identifying sources of information and services during the planning stage can save a presenter time, effort, and aggravation later on when one's energies are better spent preparing for the presentation. It also helps a presenter estimate in advance the time and expense that may be associated with gathering information and using services. The presenter can then evaluate the expense in relation to what is at stake and determine if the expense is justified by the potential payoff.

Establish an Action-Plan Schedule.   To avoid the pressures of preparing a presentation at the last minute, and risk an unfavorable outcome as a result, a presenter who plans effectively develops an action-plan schedule. An **action plan** projects what actions or tasks need to be done in order to bring the presentation process to a successful conclusion. The schedule assigns dates to each task and, if applicable, indicates the person responsible for performing the task. An action-plan schedule is especially useful when:

- There is a considerable lapse of time between the inception of the presentation process and its completion.

- Readying the presentation will entail extensive research, development of materials, and/or personal preparation on the part of the presenter.

- Some tasks will be delegated to others.

When you prepare an action-plan schedule, be sure to transpose dates on which tasks are to be done to the calendar or planner you normally use.

Confirm All Arrangements.   Once you have identified and scheduled all arrangements for your presentation, don't assume that nothing will change. Confirm the details at least one week prior to the date of the presentation, or earlier if the presentation will entail extensive preparation. Neglecting to confirm can result in a needless waste of time and can place a presenter in an awkward situation, as the following examples illustrate.

- Marlene had scheduled a presentation of a proposal to a management committee. When she arrived at the customer's office, it was vacant. In the three weeks that had transpired since she initially set up the appointment, the company had declared bankruptcy and was out of business.

■ In March, Stan was invited to appear as a guest speaker at the May luncheon meeting of a trade association. When he showed up to give his presentation, he was told there had been a change in personnel at the association. Due to a scheduling conflict, Stan was not expected to speak at the luncheon as originally planned.

■ Lee was asked by his manager to deliver a 30-minute presentation at a staff meeting. The night before the meeting, Lee worked late in order to finish preparing his message. The next morning, he learned that the meeting had been cancelled three days before because the manager was called out of town.

Don't expect that the person or organization for whom the presentation is being done will advise you of any changes. People become preoccupied with their own priorities and concerns; your schedule is not likely to be foremost in their minds. When it is your presentation, it is your responsibility to confirm it.

Key Concept 13

Planning concentrates on the nature and needs of the audience.

Among the factors a presenter considers when planning, none has more effect on the outcome of a presentation than the audience. Although it would seem the point is self-evident, apparently it is not. Many presenters deliver a message in a manner that would suggest they are either unaware of or unconcerned with what matters to the people they address. As a consequence, their presentations prove ineffective.

One highly successful presenter observed, "The most important secret of salesmanship is to find out what the other fellow wants, then help him find the best way to get it."* Presenting is a form of selling, and the audience is the presenter's customer. In every situation, what a presenter ultimately hopes to do is prompt the audience to "buy": to accept and approve the ideas, information, proposal, or point of view presented. To do so requires getting to know what the audience (the customer) wants, which requires getting to know the audience. Then, and only then, can a presenter prepare a message that will best serve the needs and interests of the audience.

---

* Frank Bettger, *How I Raised Myself from Failure to Success in Selling* (New York: Simon & Schuster, 1949), p. 44.

The value of understanding the nature and needs of the audience will become increasingly apparent as you progress through this course. An effective presenter persuades. To persuade, you must appeal to people. You must know about the people with whom you will be communicating, then apply what you know by tailoring your message to them. Virtually every aspect of an effective presentation—the content, language, audiovisuals, platform behavior, responses to audience feedback—is considered in relation to the audience being addressed. These areas are examined in later chapters. For the purpose of this chapter on planning, the key characteristics you want to discover about the audience are summarized here.

Two techniques help a presenter better understand an audience, and how to appeal to them to generate an affirmative response. One technique is to analyze the audience in terms of demographics. The other is to ask questions. With both techniques, it is important to remember that an audience is a composite of individuals (with the exception of situations in which a person presents one-on-one to another person). While a presenter may not be able to fully ascertain the traits of each individual, one can gain invaluable insights by viewing a group in terms of its predominant characteristics.

That people in the audience are present for the same occasion suggests they share some characteristics in common. Employees attending an in-house training program, as different as they may be from one another, all share in common the fact that they work for the same organization. That would be a predominant characteristic of the audience. The same is true of citizens attending a public hearing, voters attending a rally, men and women sitting on a jury, members attending a service club meeting, or people in attendance at a convention. In every case, the audience (as a whole) can be viewed in terms of predominant characteristics.

Demographic Profile

The term demographic is derived from the Greek word *demos* (meaning *people*) and the English *graphy* (meaning *pictorial*); **demographics** provide a presenter with a "picture of people." To form a demographic profile of an audience, analysis can be performed scientifically and extensively, especially given the variety and volume of data currently available. However, for the majority of presentations, it is sufficient to identify a few key demographic characteristics of the audience, information that can usually be obtained relatively quickly and easily. These are:

1. Age group
2. Education
3. Gender

4. Geographic location

5. Occupation

6. Social and economic status

7. Special interests (such as professional, political, ethnic, cultural, or religious affiliations)

Identifying the predominant characteristics of an audience provides a presenter with insight into people's needs, interests, concerns, and factors that are likely to influence their response. Studies by sociologists, behavioral psychologists, and market researchers have found that different types of people respond differently to the same item or issue. Differences in response are frequently attributable to these demographic variables.

To appreciate the value of developing a demographic profile of an audience, imagine that you have been asked to speak on the subject of "The High Cost of Substance Abuse." Over time, you will present to various audiences, which will include:

- A high school assembly attended by teenagers who live in an economically deprived area of Los Angeles.

- A conference of MBA graduates recently hired into management positions with Fortune 500 companies.

- A community meeting of parents, 30 to 45 years of age, who reside in affluent suburban neighborhoods.

- A national policy meeting of owners and coaches of professional sports teams.

As the foregoing examples suggest, that a message is presented on the same subject does not imply that it will be the same presentation in every situation. On the contrary, to generate the greatest impact and persuasive appeal, an accomplished presenter modifies the message and the way it is delivered based in part on the demographic profile of the audience to be addressed.

Although a demographic profile of an audience serves to guide a presenter as to how to modify the message, it is only a partial indicator. An astute presenter will:

- Refrain from making assumptions based on personal experience or biases. Credible presenters sharpen their objectivity, keep abreast of trends and events, and evaluate the demographic profile of an audience in relation to current news, opinion polls, information gathered from applicable trade or industry sources, and insights gained from asking questions.

- Recognize that a demographic profile is an "average." It does not fully reflect the pluralistic nature of most audiences. Workplaces and communities today are increasingly diverse, making it increasingly important for a presenter to be alert and sensitive to individual differences.

■ Remember that demographics do not take into account all of the factors to be considered when analyzing an audience. Other considerations will likely surface when you ask questions.

Ask Questions

Earlier, reference was made to the value of asking questions. The answers bring to light information that may be crucial to the success of your presentation. From all of the possible questions that might be asked, select those that are appropriate to the situation and that focus on what you need to know to be effective. Identify:

1. Questions you need to ask the contact person. Some questions can only be answered by the person who is your primary contact, or someone to whom they may refer you. There are times when, even if your questions could be answered elsewhere, it is preferable to talk with the contact person directly (in a meeting or telephone conversation). Doing so can be an opportunity to build rapport and demonstrate your interest in the presentation event.

2. Questions you can research yourself. Some answers can be obtained by reviewing printed material. When a presentation is for an organization, it is useful to obtain the latest annual report, copies of company newsletters, the organization's mission statement, strategic or marketing plan documents, company or product brochures, and the like. When a presentation is aimed at one (or a few) individuals, it is helpful to find out and become familiar with the publications to which the person subscribes and books he or she counts among his or her favorites. You can learn a great deal about people from the material they read.

3. Questions you can answer yourself. Develop a demographic profile of the audience, consider the answers you've gained from the preceding two points, and reflect on these in relation to your observations and experience. Doing so, you will discover you can answer some questions yourself.

Following are questions to consider for the purpose of discerning the nature of the audience. As you look them over, you will notice many are worded in terms of *this* audience. The adjective *this* is intended to emphasize the importance of thinking in terms of not just any audience, but the specific audience at which a given presentation is aimed. An effective presenter does not ask, "How do I present to an audience?" Rather, an effective presenter asks, "How do I present *this* message to *this* audience on *this* occasion?"

- How many people are expected to attend this presentation? (For presentations to smaller groups, find out specifically who will attend and their respective job titles or occupational positions.)

- What are the organization's goals?

- Who has decision-making responsibility and authority? Which people act in advisory capacities, or in some way influence decisions?

- On what criteria will they base their decision? How would this audience rank each criterion in order of priority or relative importance?

- What do members of this audience have at stake? What is the potential payoff for them if they are persuaded to accept my message?

- From what kind of "corporate culture" does this audience come? What are the predominant characteristics of that culture?

- What are the objectives of the people in this audience? Are they attending to acquire information, to make a buying decision, to evaluate a proposal, to improve their professional skills, to be motivated, to spend a day away from their workplace routine?

- What does this audience want? What do they need?

- What does this audience value?

- What does this audience know about this subject? What do they need to know in order to be persuaded? What will help this audience understand and accept my message?

- What does the audience know about me? What do they need to know to be more receptive to me and to my message?

- How do people in this audience think? How do they feel about this subject? What preconceptions or misconceptions might they have that would be important to correct?

- What information and techniques would gain attention? What will promote a favorable response? What could generate a negative reaction? What would motivate this audience? What would demotivate them?

- What "language" (i.e., specialized terminology or jargon) do the people in this audience speak?

- How homogeneous is this audience? How diverse? What diversities should I be aware of and sensitive to?

- What other presentations will this audience hear on this same subject that may compete with mine?

- What other presentation(s) will they hear immediately before and after my presentation?

■ Are there any other details or considerations I should know about? This last question should always be asked. If you establish rapport with the contact person, he or she will often volunteer useful information. In one instance, for example, a presenter was advised that the chief decision maker had difficulty hearing in one ear. Knowing that, the presenter reinforced the verbal message by using more visual aids and spoke from a position on the side of the decision-maker's good ear.

The Advantage of Knowing the Audience

You may recall from the discussion of the communication process in Chapter 1 that an audience forms perceptions on the basis of influencing factors. These include attitudes, culture, education, experience, gender, and pattern (a person's predominant thought process). A demographic profile and answers to questions help you identify and understand the variables that influence audience response to you and to your presentations. It has been suggested that "knowledge is power." The more you know about your audience (and apply what you know to your presentation), the more powerful your impact on the audience will be.

Reflection Question

What do you most need to learn about the audiences to whom you will present? (One approach to answering this question is to consider, "If I could ask only three questions about the audience, which three questions would I most want to ask?")

Key Concept 14

Planning takes into account the setting in which a presentation will occur.

The setting in which a presentation will occur affects both an audience and a presenter. Some sites and surroundings are more conducive to presenting than others. Details of the physical environment—and what can be done to make it more conducive to an effective presentation—are discussed in Chapter 10.

In addition to the physical setting, a presentation takes place in a psychological environment. Each person in an audience brings to a presentation a frame of mind, a point of view, a set of "psychological luggage" in which is packed feelings and thoughts. Some aspects of the psychological environment can be brought out during the planning stage by the questions a presenter asks. In addition to those listed under Key Concept 13 (regarding the audience), ask the following questions as well.

- Will people in this audience be present by choice or under orders to attend? Are they likely to be receptive, indifferent, resistant, or hostile toward me and my message?

- What events have occurred recently that may have an impact on the receptivity of this audience? Has there been "good news" it would be beneficial to reference? Has there been "bad news" I should avoid mentioning?

- What will be the prevailing mood of this audience? The nature of a presentation event understandably affects the way a majority of people in the audience are likely to feel about it and react to it. The mood at an upbeat recognition luncheon will probably be positive. On the other hand, the prevailing mood at a meeting to announce a reduction in personnel is likely to be somber.

- Will alcohol be served? If so, when? If alcohol is served immediately before or during a presentation, the presenter should expect the unexpected. In some situations, the mood of the audience will be more favorable; in others, the effect is negative if people become noisy and disruptive.

Other factors that influence the psychological environment cannot be anticipated, no matter how extensively a presenter plans. The familiar adage, "You can't please all of the people all of the time," applies to presenting. Even the best of presenters is not in a position to manage the many variables that affect the setting in which a presentation occurs. However, planning and asking questions help a presenter prepare for probabilities, and give a presenter an opportunity to modify the message when applicable. Moreover, by being attuned to the psychological environment, an observant presenter will more readily perceive and adjust to nonverbal cues that signal audience response.

An additional question is essential to planning for a presentation, and encompasses both physical and psychological factors. At the very least, a presenter should ask, "What is the nature of the setting: formal, businesslike, or casual?"

The setting suggests certain norms regarding expected behavior and attire, not only on the part of the audience, but also on the part of the presenter. A presenter who appears in casual attire in a businesslike setting runs the risk of being perceived as less than professional. A presenter who behaves with formality in a casual setting runs the risk of being perceived as detached from the audience. Again, the nature of the presentation event offers clues into the nature of the setting. A legislative hearing governed by strict protocol tends to be a formal setting, whereas an off-site, weekend retreat is usually more casual. Notice the qualifying terms "tends" and "usually." Effective presenters are careful not to make assumptions, and then discover too late that they were wrong. Instead, ask questions that give you answers that enable you to be well prepared.

Key Concept 15

Planning clarifies scheduling and time-frame considerations.

A cardinal rule of business presentations is *deliver the message in the allotted time*. Doing so is imperative when one's presentation is not the only item on a meeting or program agenda, or on someone's calendar of appointments for the day. Presenters who don't respect people's time risk losing the respect of the audience. The thoughtful presenter heeds the following five points.

During the Planning Stage

1. Clarify the time the presentation is scheduled to start, and how much time is allocated for the presentation. Reconfirm the schedule prior to the date of the presentation.

2. Consider the nature of the presentation in relation to the time frame. Will the presenter be the sole speaker, or will the presentation include participation by members of the audience? If the latter, how much time will audience participation consume? Will time be reserved for a question-and-answer period at the end? Is the time frame sufficiently long to allow for a break or two? All of these factors affect the net time remaining for delivery of the message.

3. Having estimated the net time available for the message, determine how much material will comprise the content of the spoken presentation. It is a needless waste of time to prepare a message that would take an hour to present when the time frame allocated for the presentation is 20 minutes. On the other hand, it is needlessly embarrassing to prepare only 20 minutes worth of material when one hour has been allotted for the presentation.

On average, 40 pages of typewritten text (typed double-spaced in 10-pitch pica type) equate to one hour of speaking. In other words, each 15 minutes of speaking is, on average, the equivalent of 10 pages of typewritten material. The phrase "on average" is reiterated for emphasis. Obviously, some presenters speak rapidly and others more slowly. Some presenters ad lib more than others. The formula is a "ballpark" estimation only. With experience, a presenter knows how to adjust the foregoing formula to reflect her or his own rate and style of speaking.

After the Content Is Prepared

4. Give thought to how the presentation could be expanded or condensed in case the need arises to speak for a longer or shorter period of time. Even though a presenter prepares a message that conforms to the planned time frame, it is not uncommon to find that others do not conform to the plan. If a previous item on a meeting agenda is concluded ahead of schedule, a presenter may be asked to speak longer. More often, less time than planned is available. Other speakers on the program run over their allotted time. A meeting agenda is packed with more items than there is time available to cover. The client shows up late for the appointment. The professional presenter is prepared for such contingencies, and demonstrates flexibility in dealing with them.

The Day of the Presentation

5. Arrive early. Professionals operate on "Lombardi Time." The term is named after Vince Lombardi, the championship football coach of the Green Bay Packers during the 1960s. The story is told of a rookie player who showed up for the first practice session of the new season right at the scheduled time. When he arrived, he was surprised to find the other players already on the field and the practice well under way. Reportedly, coach Lombardi explained that if it's important enough to show up for, it's important enough to show up early.

Experienced presenters have learned not to take anything for granted, because circumstances do not always conform to plan. By arriving early, a presenter has time to ensure that everything is readied for the presentation. The extra time also provides an opportunity to calmly collect one's thoughts and be better mentally prepared to address the audience.

The Best Time to Present

In some situations, an organization, a customer, or an upper-level manager establishes the schedule for a presentation. On other occasions, scheduling is at the presenter's discretion. When you have the option of selecting the day and time for your presentation, bear in mind that some days and times are better than others.

Refrain from scheduling a presentation on Mondays and Fridays. People are often preoccupied on the days before and after a weekend. The same holds true for holidays. Refrain from scheduling a presentation on the days before and after a holiday, and during the periods surrounding major holidays like Thanksgiving and Christmas. In view of the ethnic diversity in the workplace, be cognizant of holidays that may be observed by people whose backgrounds are different from your own.

As to the time of day, it is preferable to present during "prime time," when your energy level is at its peak and when the audience is likely to be most alert. For many people, prime time is during morning hours. If you are presenting to an audience from one organization, find out what time their workday begins. Refrain from scheduling a presentation any earlier than a half-hour afterwards, in order to give people time to arrive and settle in at work. Avoid scheduling too close to noon, since an audience tends to grow restless as lunchtime approaches. In general, early afternoon should also be avoided, since people are more sluggish during the hour or so immediately after lunch. Taking these factors into consideration, the preferred times to schedule a presentation are on a Tuesday, Wednesday, or Thursday between 9:00 a.m. and 11:45 a.m.

Positioning a Presentation

If you present in business situations in which you compete with others, know enough about the competition (and your relative strengths and limitations) to know how to position your presentation with respect to the order in which the presentations are scheduled. The order in which an audience views presentations can influence their perceptions, and consequently their ultimate decision. To feature your presentation most favorably:

■ Against strong competition, try to position your presentation as the first one on the agenda. You gain the opportunity to establish the buying criteria and set the standard for a quality presentation. Doing so, the presentations that follow may be perceived as disappointing by comparison.

■ Ask to appear last when presenting against lesser competitors. If the previous presenters have failed to persuade the decision maker(s), the strength of your presentation will have a greater impact coming at the end. It can be perceived as what the audience has been waiting to hear.

First and foremost: deliver a well-planned, prepared, and polished presentation that will be the most meaningful and memorable to members of the audience, regardless of the position of your presentation in relation to competitors.

Key Concept 16

Effective presenters use a planning checklist to speed and simplify the planning process, and to confirm arrangements for the presentation.

A planning checklist is a helpful tool. It helps step you through the details you want to be sure to cover when planning for a presentation. It provides a written record of information that is useful, not only for the one presentation, but also as a reference for future presentations. For example, statements of objectives and lists of sources may apply to more than one presentation you do. The checklist also serves as a reminder of this important principle of planning: when in doubt, find out.

The planning checklist that follows is a three-part form. Part I is a cover sheet that outlines the arrangements, objectives, and action-plan schedule for a presentation. Part II focuses on the audience, summarizing characteristics of a demographic analysis and some of the key questions to ask about the nature and needs of the audience. Part III covers the setting and facilities considerations. You may find you can use this checklist as is, or you may prefer to amend it to suit your situation.

Addendum to the Planning Checklist: High-stakes Action Plan

A notation appears as the last line on the cover sheet of the Presenter's Planning Checklist. It reads: "For high-stakes presentations: detail action on project planner/calendar." A high-stakes presentation is one in which the payoff is substantial—if the presentation is successful. The prospect of achieving substantial gain warrants a substantial investment of time and resources in the planning and preparation of a high-stakes presentation. It also warrants a more detailed action plan than the summary form that appears on the cover sheet of the planning checklist.

The planning of a high-stakes presentation is similar to the planning of any significant project, and should be treated accordingly. On many occasions, highly qualified (sometimes the most qualified) organizations and individuals fail to achieve their objectives because they fail to adequately plan and prepare a winning presentation. Such disappointments may be avoided by developing a comprehensive action-plan schedule.

Presenter's Planning Checklist   Part I: Cover Sheet

Date prepared: _____ Date confirmed: _____

Presenter _____   Date of presentation _____
Subject _____   Title _____
Event _____   Type ___Internal ___External
Theme _____   ___Promotional ___Informational
Requested by _____   ___Down-line   ___Up-line
Contact _____   Telephone no. _____
Organization _____
Address _____

Time   Start at ___ End by ___ = Time frame: ___Hours ___Min.
            Less time for Q & A, breaks,
            and/or audience participation: ___Hours ___Min.
        Net time for presentation of message: ___Hours ___Min.

Contacts: Name   Organization   Telephone no.

      _____   _____   _____
      _____   _____   _____

Sources: _____   _____   _____
          _____   _____   _____
          _____   _____   _____

Schedule: Action   Start date   Completion date
      Research (collect info.)   _____   _____
      Prepare content   _____   _____
      Practice delivery   _____   _____

Estimate of time to research, prepare, and practice: _____ Days/Hours
Estimate of what is at stake (i.e., potential payoff): _____

For high-stakes presentations: detail action on project planner/calendar

Planning Checklist   Part II: The Audience

Date prepared: _____

Presenter _____   Date of presentation _____
Event   _____   Title _____
Persons _____   (If small group, list names and positions)

Demographic analysis

Age   _Teens   _Young adults _Mature adults _Seniors
Education   _H.S.   _College   _Technical   _Advanced
Gender   _Female _Male   _Mixed group
Occupation/Profession _____
Socio-economic status _____
Special interests/affiliations _____

Key questions

This organization's chief goals? _____
The nature of the corporate culture? _____
Who makes or influences decisions? _____
Key decision-making criteria? _____
What are the wants/needs of this audience? _____
_____
What does this audience value? _____
What do they know about this subject? _____
What do they need to know? _____
How does this audience think? _____
How does this audience feel? _____
What type of terminology or references are appropriate to this audience?
_____
What other factors should I be aware of? _____
To gain further insights, obtain and review the following material.
Internal publications: _Annual report _Newsletters _Brochures
External publications: this audience reads _____
_____

Planning Checklist   Part III: The Setting

Date prepared: _____

Presenter _____   Date of presentation _____
Event   _____   Title _____
Nature of event: ___Formal   ___Business/Professional   ___Casual
What immediately precedes my presentation? _____
What immediately follows my presentation? _____

Site   ___Office   ___Conference room   ___Meeting room
            ___Auditorium   ___Other _____

Seating   ___Classroom: ___Conventional rows or __T __U __V
            ___Theater   ___Other _____

Fixtures   ___Podium   ___Draped head table   ___Equipment stand
                        ___Other _____

Equipment ___Flip chart   ___Computer (PC/Desktop)
          ___Overhead projector ___Video player & monitor
          ___Slide projector   ___Visual board
          ___Screen   ___Other _____
          ___Sound system
             ___Microphone: ___Hands-free   ___Hand-held

Supplies   ___Bio. for intro.   ___Marking pens
            ___Brochures   ___Name tags; ___Tent cards
            ___Business cards   ___Samples
            ___Hand-outs   ___Other _____
            ___Props _____

Lighting requirements _____
Color considerations _____

Food/Beverage service _____ at _____
(specify type and time) _____ at _____
            Alcohol served? ___No. If yes, when? _____

A detailed action-plan schedule identifies:

- Tasks to be performed to ready a quality presentation.
- Dates and times the tasks will be performed.
- Members of the presentation team (if more than the presenter are involved in the project) and their respective responsibilities.

Activities, dates, times, and the names or initials of members of the presentation team should be tracked on a form of planner that suits the needs of the project. Wall planners, visual date organizers, and manual or computerized task-tracking systems are readily available from office supply stores and catalogs. The date of the presentation to the audience is posted first. Working backward from that date, the following action-plan steps are then scheduled and posted on the calendar/planner.

1. Planning meeting(s): identify governing factors, objectives, responsibilities of team members, time lines, resources, and budget
2. Research
3. Develop structure (draft the framework of the presentation)
4. Develop substance (draft narrative)
5. Review meeting(s)
6. Develop supporting material (draft audiovisuals, handouts)
7. Practice presentation
8. Revise and refine: content, delivery, and supporting materials
9. Produce supporting materials
10. Arrange facilities, equipment, supplies (travel and shipping, if applicable)
11. Confirm all arrangements and audience attendance
12. Final simulation: a "dress rehearsal" of the presentation in its entirety, preferably presented with a "mock" audience that role-plays the parts of those who will be attending the presentation

The order in which the tasks are listed is not necessarily the order in which they always occur. If extensive lead time is required to arrange facilities or to produce visual aids, these would be scheduled early on in the sequence of activities. Some of the activities listed above may occur concurrently. For example, research may continue while the structure of the presentation is being developed. Other activities may occur repeatedly, such as review meetings and practice sessions.

If planning or tasks essential to producing a quality presentation are delayed, oversights and stress can accumulate. The result can be a less than effective presentation. Allow sufficient lead time before the date of the presentation to the audience to ensure that all tasks can be accomplished in an excellent manner.

When a presentation is being prepared by a team, it is also important to consider who is best suited to lead the presentation-project team. The team leader need not be the person or persons who will do the actual presenting. The most skilled presenter may not be the most adept at the planning, administration, delegation, and follow-up skills required of a project team leader. When a great deal depends on the outcome of a presentation, select as team leader that person best suited to the role.

Key Concept 17

Devising means to assess results is an integral part of planning.

Figure 2-1 depicts presenting as a cyclical process that begins with planning. The cycle comes full circle when, once the actual presenting is done, the presenter proceeds to the next step. One next step (represented by dashed lines) may be to take the same message and replan and reprepare it for presentation again—to another audience, for a different setting, or in a different time frame. Another next step is to follow up on feedback from the audience. This step is represented by a solid line to indicate that follow-up is an essential conclusion to the process of presenting.

To be effective has been defined as producing an intended outcome. Without feedback, a presenter cannot be sure that the presentation achieved the desired outcome. Too often, people who present are pleased by the outcome if members of an audience nod and smile in an agreeable manner. Such a response may occur more out of courtesy than a conviction to act. Too often, presenters are gratified if an audience applauds. Applause may be a conditioned response more than an indication of agreement with the message. The only way to ascertain if the purpose of a presentation has been satisfied is to devise a method for eliciting feedback that measures audience response to the message. In some cases, follow-up after the presentation is also necessary. When it is, follow-up should be done on a timely basis so as to "strike while the iron is hot."

Forms of Feedback and Follow-up

The manner in which a presenter invites feedback depends on the nature and objectives of the presentation. In general, one or a combination of the following methods may be used to gain audience feedback.

1. *Person-to-person.*   At the conclusion of the presentation, the presenter asks a direct question of the audience. The answer will provide the feedback that enables the presenter to assess the effectiveness of the presentation. For example, after a sales presentation, one might ask a question like, "Based on what you've seen and heard, how many widgets do you want to order for your company today?" After a training presentation, the presenter might ask something like, "How will you use these techniques to do your job better?" The audience response to a direct question gives the presenter immediate feedback that indicates the degree to which the objectives have been achieved.

2. *Telephone calls.*   A day or two after the presentation, the presenter follows up by telephone with the contact person or decision maker. The presenter conveys his or her interest in the outcome of the presentation and asks questions to measure its effectiveness. Although the wording would be modified to reflect the subject and the situation, the questions asked would focus on the following points:

- How satisfied were you with the presentation?

- What was the group's response to the message?

- To what degree did my proposal meet your expectations and objectives?

- When would it be convenient for you to meet with me to discuss this matter further? In some situations (notably after promotional presentations), a presenter will want to set up an in-person appointment when such follow-up is required in order to bring about the desired result.

3. *Meetings.*   In addition to follow-up appointments with external audiences (e.g., customers and prospective clients), a presenter may meet with members of an internal audience to determine the outcome of a presentation. If a manager, for example, used a business presentation to introduce a new policy or to encourage employees to work together better as a team, the effectiveness of the presentation could be determined in part through follow-up meetings with workgroup supervisors, department heads, or the employees themselves.

4. *Feedback forms.*   Whenever appropriate, the use of feedback forms is recommended. Written evaluations often offer the most candid feedback, and provide records that can be reviewed immediately after a presentation and over time. If a person presents frequently, an ongoing record of feedback can be useful to identify trends, such as whether audience feedback is improving or declining and in what areas.

A sample of a feedback form, set up in two parts, follows. Part I asks the audience to rate various factors on a scale of 1 to 4. Feedback based on 4- or 6-point scales are preferable to 3 or 5. An even-numbered scale forces a deci-

Feedback Form   Date _____

Subject _____   Presenter _____

We welcome your evaluation of this presentation. Please give us your candid response.

Part I. Rate the following factors by checking the appropriate box.

	(4) Excellent	(3) Good	(2) Fair	(1) Poor
Overall presentation	☐	☐	☐	☐
Content	☐	☐	☐	☐
Presenter	☐	☐	☐	☐
Materials	☐	☐	☐	☐
Facility	☐	☐	☐	☐
Relevance to you	☐	☐	☐	☐
Value for you	☐	☐	☐	☐

Part II. Comments or suggestions

_____

_____

_____

How will you make use of the information presented?

_____

_____

_____

(Optional) Name   Telephone number

_____

sion toward a "more" or "less" favorable response. With an odd-numbered scale, the indecisive person tends to mark the midpoint, and feedback frequently comes back as "average." A numbered scale provides feedback that is more objectively measurable. Boxes to be checked encourage an audience to respond by making it easier and faster to complete the feedback form.

Part II asks the audience for comments and suggestions. It is the open-ended, subjective section of the feedback form. As an optional entry, space is added at the bottom of the form for the respondent's name and telephone number. This is considered an optional item since some people will give more candid feedback if they can submit an evaluation anonymously. Others have no reservations about identifying themselves. With a name and telephone number on the form, a presenter can follow up on feedback that is especially "excellent" or "poor."

How to elicit feedback to measure the effectiveness of a presentation, and how and when to follow up, should be decided when planning. Doing so reinforces the purpose of presenting. It causes a presenter to consider in advance what techniques may need to be incorporated in the content of the message (such as asking direct questions during a sales presentation). Moreover, a method for assessing results is a natural conclusion to the planning process.

Reflection Questions

Of presentation you have done in the past, have there been aspects for which you neglected to plan? As you reflect on the material covered thus far in this chapter, what points do you think you will find most helpful in planning for future presentations?

Key Concept 18

The obstacles to planning for an effective presentation can be overcome.

Whether a presentation is high-stakes, low-stakes, or somewhere in between, some degree of planning is essential if the presentation is going to be effective. Yet many presenters neglect this crucial first stage. Following are the reasons most often cited as to why people don't plan.

Obstacles to Planning

1. Planning takes time.
2. Planning is interrupted by daily tasks.
3. Don't know how to plan.
4. Attempts at planning are side-tracked by routine tasks with which a person is more familiar.
5. Procrastination.

Each of these obstacles to planning can be overcome by putting into practice the guidelines that follow.

Overcoming the Obstacles to Planning

1. Recognize that the time you invest in planning for a presentation will reap rewards. You can work harder, or you can choose to work smarter. Planning is a first step toward working smarter. The improved outcome you will experience more than compensates for the time spent planning for a presentation.

2. Minimize interruptions from daily tasks by making planning a priority. Delegate or temporarily set aside the routine tasks that threaten to derail your planning efforts. When applied to professional endeavors, a principle commonly referred to as the 80/20 Rule suggests this: 80 percent of the time in the workplace typically spent on routine tasks yields only 20 percent of results achieved. Conversely, 20 percent of a person's time devoted to goal-related priorities will yield 80 percent of the results. When a presentation represents an opportunity to advance toward your goals, planning is a priority that warrants time and attention.

3. With respect to concerns about not knowing how to plan, this chapter has provided guidelines to overcome that obstacle. The next time you have a presentation to do, review this chapter and use the planning checklist. Use it again for the next presentation, and the next. With practice, you will find you have learned how to make use of tools and techniques that simplify and speed your planning efforts.

4. With repeated use of a planning checklist and the questions that guide the planning process, you will gain skill, confidence, and a comfort level planning for presentations. The fourth obstacle—being side-tracked by more familiar tasks—is overcome by becoming familiar with planning.

5. Procrastination is one of the most common barriers to planning and to effective presenting. Presenters who put off preparing until the day or two before a presentation do not allow sufficient time to order their thoughts or the message, or to practice skilled delivery. As a consequence, they feel more stressed. Stress accentuates anxiety about presenting, which results in an unsettling experience presenting, which fosters further procrastination on the next occasion.

Procrastinating produces a vicious cycle of repeated procrastination and the risk of poor performance. Factors that contribute to procrastination include frustration with the task, uncertainty, anxiety, conflicting demands, fatigue, distractions, and the habit of procrastinating. To overcome these obstacles to success:

- Learn and apply the principles and practices of effective time management.
- Develop a business presentation one "SIP" at a time. "SIP" is an acronym for Short-Interval Planning and Short-Interval Preparation. It suggests planning and preparing a presentation over several shorter increments of time. Refrain from waiting until a block of time is available to complete all planning and preparation in one sitting. Schedule sufficient lead time to develop a presentation in stages over time. It makes the process more manageable and more pleasant. You also gain the advantages of having more time to mentally process ideas, to think more creatively, and to function without the pressure that produces counterproductive stress.
- Master presentation skills. Doing so builds confidence, which releases energy and enthusiasm.
- With every presentation you do, identify aspects that represent value to you. A common trait of human nature is to pursue with greater eagerness those activities that are aligned with one's interests, values, or purpose. Review your personal and professional goals, and remind yourself that business presentations are a means to achieving your goals.

Reflection Questions

What obstacles to planning have you experienced? What will help you overcome them?

Summary

Planning is an essential precursor to presenting. The numerous benefits to be derived are summed up in this principle: planning prevents poor performance. Through planning, the role and tasks of the presenter are established; the characteristics of the audience are identified; the nature of the setting is determined; and the time frame for the presentation is confirmed. As a final consideration in planning for a presentation, a presenter decides on methods to elicit evaluative feedback and for follow-up. Although obstacles to planning can inhibit the process, every obstacle can be overcome, especially when weighed against the value of planning.

Sample Situations

Situation 1: External/Promotional Presentation

Jack Sprack is president of the Pro-Fits Company, makers of quality footwear and accessories for athletes. Harvey Hightops, program chairman of the Association of Collegiate Coaches and Sports Trainers, has invited Jack to speak at the Association's annual convention on the subject of the latest advancements in sport-shoe design. Jack is somewhat apprehensive about the speech. Although he has gained prominence as the CEO of a very successful company because of his business acumen, he never played sports in college, or at any other time for that matter. He has presented to entrepreneurs and corporate executives in business settings, but never to a convention audience of people in the field of athletics.

Completing the planning checklist alleviates Jack's concerns. He discovers that it triggers useful ideas. He finds the following aspects of the checklist particularly helpful.

Type of presentation. In view of the subject on which Jack was asked to speak, initially it seemed this would be an informational presentation. However, Jack realizes the event offers a golden promotional opportunity (provided he does not deliver a blatant sales pitch). By presenting a message that will appeal to coaches and trainers, he can establish his credibility and that of the Pro-Fits Company.

Contact. Considering the contact person prompts Jack to make a telephone call to Harvey. Jack asks key questions that appear on Part II of the checklist. He is then able to form a mental picture of the audience, and better discern what will interest them. Jack discovers similarities to audiences he has addressed in the past (which bolsters his confidence), as well as characteristics unique to this group (which he is now better prepared to address). At the same time, Jack develops greater rapport with Harvey, who is in a position of influence with the Association's members.

Sources and publications. Reflecting on what he now knows about the audience, it occurs to Jack that there are many books and video tapes readily available which are authored by or feature renowned coaches and athletes. Jack asks his secretary to obtain and screen a selection of these and to make note of terminology, stories, and quotations he might be able to use in his message. He also asks her to call Harvey Hightops and request that he send to Jack a sampling of Association newsletters and program brochures from past conventions and for the upcoming one. These will further familiarize Jack with the nature of the event.

Equipment and supplies. Jack reviews Part III of the planning checklist with his secretary. Discussing the section on supplies, they come up with a couple of creative ideas. Jack will wear a business suit, since that portion of the agenda during which he will present will be professional in nature. However, as a humorous attention-getter, Jack will wear a pair of Pro-Fits bright neon-green sneakers. They will also distribute to each member of the audience an advertising specialty: shoelaces with the Pro-Fits name and logo imprinted on them.

Now, Jack is excited and confident about his forthcoming presentation. He has gained insights and information that will make it easier to prepare the content of his speech. Also important, planning has started him thinking about how to shape his presentation to both serve the audience and promote his business.

Situation 2: Internal/Informational Presentation

Susan Antell is a training associate who was recently hired to work for a large organization. With a Ph.D. in Behavioral Sciences, she was selected to present a program in management skills for new supervisors. Susan conscientiously set about doing extensive research, compiled material for the course, prepared visual aids, and produced workbooks for the participants. After the first session, Susan was surprised and disappointed to learn from her manager that the two days of training were not evaluated favorably. Although participants indicated they liked her as a presenter, overall the course was rated only "fair."

Susan's manager gave her copies of the feedback forms collected at the end of the training. The manager suggested she review the forms and this chapter on planning. The feedback forms showed that the aspects of content, relevance, and value were rated fair to good. Participants had added comments like, "Too much material," "Strategies and paradigms not useful," "Content confusing," and "Session too short."

The feedback and this chapter helped Susan identify factors that contributed to the unsatisfactory evaluations. An after-the-fact analysis of the audience revealed that most new supervisors had a high school education, had started with the organization in entry-level positions, and had been promoted up through the ranks over time. Since she had not considered these characteristics before presenting, Susan used terminology, models, and examples which did not aim at the level of understanding or interests of those who had attended the training. In addition, she realized she had based the content on the total hours available for the session. Having neglected to deduct time for breaks, interaction, and questions from the group, some trainees had been overwhelmed by the amount of material covered in a limited time frame. Now, Susan knew what to do to improve the program before presenting it again to the next group.

Situation 3: External/Promotional Presentation

Joe, Barbara, and Jan are partners in a design consulting firm. They are among the most qualified, talented, creative professionals in their field in the geographic area they serve. For that reason, they are especially frustrated by their lack of success when they respond to competitive RFPs (Requests for Proposal). After one particularly disappointing year, they assessed the results of the oral presentations they had made to selection committees. They calculated they had won a contract on only two occasions out of every ten. Whenever they failed to make a winning presentation, they lost the money invested in producing models and packaging proposals (not to mention the time it took).

Barbara called a meeting of the partners. Jan complained that it was always a last-minute rush trying to get everything ready to present. Joe complained that you never knew what to expect. He reminded them of that recent presentation when they had no idea who two people on the selection committee were. Barbara raised the point that being surprised by the competition was just as bad. They were often unaware of other firms that had also been invited to present proposals.

After a lengthy and candid discussion, the partners agreed that they needed to take the same care planning their presentations as they took planning the projects they designed. In the future, as soon as an RFP was received, they would establish a project plan to track the process of preparing the proposal and presentation.

Comprehension Check

The answers to the following appear on page 333.

1. The planning process is guided by _____.
   a. demographics
   b. questions
   c. delegation
   d. assumptions
   e. settings

2. Planning is an essential precursor to presenting because, by planning, a presenter _____.
   a. reduces the amount of research that needs to be done
   b. demonstrates analytical abilities
   c. predicts the variables that affect evaluations
   d. fosters teamwork among those involved in a presentation project
   e. considers the factors that govern the outcome of a presentation

3. The frequency with which a person presents is _____.
   a. a common obstacle to planning
   b. a benefit of planning
   c. a variable that affects how much planning may need to be done
   d. a primary factor that governs the outcome of a presentation
   e. an objective of an effective presentation

4. One way to gain insight into the nature of an audience is to _____.
   a. review company literature or publications the audience reads
   b. listen to the contact person's terminology
   c. form assumptions based on past personal experience
   d. clarify the potential payoff from the presentation
   e. become familiar with the facilities

5. To overcome a common obstacle to planning, a presenter should _____.
    a. present frequently
    b. become familiar with the use of a planning checklist
    c. assign a team leader for a presentation project
    d. write objectives for every presentation
    e. confirm the arrangements for the event

To Do

At the end of Chapter 1, you were asked to identify a presentation you will develop during this course. To conclude this chapter, complete a planning checklist for that presentation. (For your convenience, the form of checklist introduced in this chapter is duplicated on the following pages.)

If the presentation you have selected for this course is a hypothetical situation, use your imagination and draw from your experience to envision a likely situation for which to plan.

3

Structure: The Framework of a Presentation

How many business presentations have you attended during the past six months? Consider every situation in which you have heard and viewed a speaker: meetings, seminars, sales calls, workshops, conferences, conventions. Of the total number of presentations in which you have been a member of the audience, how many would you describe as "effective"? If your experience is like that of most people, the answer is "too few!"

Among the most common complaints expressed by people who attend presentations are that:

- The speaker failed to address our interests or concerns.
- The presentation was too long, too detailed, too technical.
- The presentation was disorganized.
- The presenter was unprepared.
- The speaker rambled.

Such complaints indicate that people in an audience want a relevant, focused, well-organized message delivered by a presenter who is well-prepared. This chapter concentrates on the first stage in preparing the kind of message that an audience (a speaker's "customer") wants to hear.

Objective

To understand the stages of preparing a presentation; to formulate objectives and a core concept; and to make use of techniques for outlining a message that will be well-organized and effective.

Key Concepts

19. Structuring the message is the first stage in preparing a presentation.
20. Both audience and presenter benefit from a well-organized presentation.
21. Before structuring the message, a presenter should first determine the most effective approach to the subject for a given audience.
22. Objectives and a core concept are the foundation of the structure of an effective presentation.
23. An effective presentation consists of five components.
24. Memorable messages conform to the Rule-of-3.
25. A few simple techniques help to generate ideas for a message.
26. An outline lends structure to a presentation by arranging ideas and information in an orderly manner.

Key Terms

To make full use of these concepts, you will need to understand the following terms:

Structure	Clicker culture
Approach	Key points
Buying motives	Transition
Objective	Rule-of-3
Focus	Retention stress
Core concept	Mnemonic
Opener	

Key Concept 19

Structuring the message is the first stage in preparing a presentation.

Table 3-1. Aspects of Presenting

	Prepare	to	Present
Action	Develop content		Deliver content
Nature	Informational		Relational
Deals with	The "what"		The "how"
Who	You, the presenter		Them, the audience

As Figure 2-1 indicated, planning for a presentation is followed by two aspects: prepare and present. These aspects of making a business presentation are summarized in Table 3-1.

Preparing a presentation consists of four stages, illustrated in Figure 3-1.

Each of these four stages, through which a presentation is fully developed, are covered in separate chapters in this course. Preparing the substance of a presentation (discussed in Chapter 4) entails composing the content that will comprise the "meat" of the message. Style (Chapter 5) refers to the language and forms of expression through which the message will be communicated. Support (Chapter 6) involves the preparation of materials that augment the message, such as audiovisuals. However, before these three stages are prepared, the message must first be structured.

The term **structure** applies to anything composed of parts arranged together, or to the function of building or constructing. Implicit in the term is the idea that parts are put together in such a manner that the item constructed will hold up. Speakers who want their presentations to "hold up"—under audience scrutiny, objections, or indifference—invest the time to prepare a well-structured presentation.

A well-structured presentation is, first, built according to audience specifications. In other words, as a skilled architect designs a building to satisfy the needs and appeal to the tastes of the client, so a skilled speaker designs a presentation to suit the needs and interests of the audience. In a structured presentation, the various parts of the message are interrelated, as are the parts of a building. Some parts lead naturally to others. Some parts support others. Every part of a well-structured message serves the purpose of the presentation.

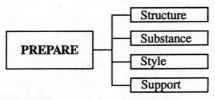

Figure 3-1. Preparing a presentation.

Amount of Preparation

The variables that affect planning for a presentation (discussed in Chapter 2) are the same factors that determine the time and effort required to structure and prepare a message. For example, a high-stakes presentation (i.e., one with a substantial potential payoff) would warrant a greater investment in preparation than a low-stakes presentation.

When the planning for a presentation has been thorough, the time and effort to prepare are usually reduced because the presenter is guided by the insights and information gained from planning. Decisions about how to structure the message and what to include can be reached more quickly. Understandably, experience also reduces preparation time, especially when a presenter is well-acquainted with the subject and the nature of the audience. Familiar with what is required to prepare an effective presentation, proficient presenters typically work through the process with relative ease.

Key Concept 20

Both audience and presenter benefit from a well-organized presentation.

A chief characteristic of a well-structured presentation is that the message is organized. It proceeds from point to point in a logical, orderly manner. That it does so is advantageous for both the audience and the presenter.

From the standpoint of the audience, it is much easier to digest and retain an organized presentation than it is to try listening through a disorganized, muddled message. Organization enables listeners to more readily follow the speaker's train of thought. Provided the speaker expresses points that are of interest to the audience, people are more likely to feel that their time and attention are justified. The presentation will be for them a more useful and gratifying experience.

For presenters, there are also benefits to structuring a presentation in an organized manner. A message that unfolds as an orderly sequence of points is easier to remember, and therefore takes less time to rehearse. As a result, it is easier to present. Organization helps minimize or eliminate rambling—a flaw that is potentially fatal to a presenter's effectiveness. Typically, a presenter who delivers a well-organized message is perceived more favorably than one whom the audience perceives to be disorganized. In sum, organization boosts a presenter's credibility and serves to build a better case, both factors in persuading the audience to respond affirmatively to the message.

The best argument for structuring (and then presenting) a well-organized message is that doing so alleviates the common complaints cited at the beginning of this chapter. The discipline of organizing information and ideas tends to keep a presenter focused on the aim of the presentation. Moreover, while performing the task of structuring a message, a person is concurrently (sometimes unconsciously) becoming better prepared to present it.

Key Concept 21

Before structuring the message, a presenter should first determine the most effective approach to the subject for a given audience.

The saying, "There's more than one way to skin a cat," connotes that a situation can be handled in various ways. The principle applies to presentations. With respect to presenting, the familiar adage translates, "There's more than one way to approach a subject."

An **approach** is a way by which a person can be reached or a method by which an activity can be carried out. When communicating a message to people, numerous approaches to any subject are possible. Some approaches are preferable to others. What is the most effective approach to a subject? The question is answered by considering the following factors:

- Perspective
- Persuasion
- Perception

Perspective

A common trap into which many presenters fall is that of approaching a subject from a single point of view: theirs. Doing so can produce an indifferent or negative response from an audience. It can trigger the most frequent complaint about presentations, "The speaker failed to address *our* interests or concerns."

Since the purpose of presenting is to persuade, the perspective with which a presenter should approach a subject is that of the person(s) to be persuaded. Therefore, the preferred approach is one which takes into account the point of view—the interests, needs, concerns, background, expectations, and hopes—of the audience.

To gain understanding of the perspective of an audience is a primary reason for planning. Armed with a profile of the audience (developed from a planning checklist and the considerations discussed in Chapter 2), a presenter is better equipped to ascertain how to best approach an audience. Where a divergence of perspectives exists—between those of the audience and that of the speaker, or among different members of the audience—a solution lies in finding commonalities. In other words, at what points do the differing perspectives converge? "What," the astute presenter will ask, "do we (or they) have in common?"

Consider the case of a business consultant preparing to present a proposal to a company recommending a Total Quality Management (TQM) program. The consultant's view is that TQM is inarguably the superior strategy for making enterprises more competitive in the global marketplace. From planning the consultant learned something of the perspectives of the four people who will be attending the presentation.

The owner of the company, which currently concentrates on a regional market, is concerned about the cost of implementing a TQM program. The product and distribution managers are feeling somewhat threatened that the TQM concept of self-directed work teams will undermine the authority of their positions. An executive secretary is favorable to the idea of improving quality, but is uncertain about what disruptions will be caused by a change in the way the company currently operates.

Before structuring the presentation, it would be helpful for the consultant in this case to ask, "What do all of us—presenter and audience alike—have in common?" Shared views might include the following issues.

- *Regard for the business.* An interest in seeing the organization not only survive, but also thrive.

- *Concern for security.* Securing the company's future and individual job security.

- *Financial considerations.* Improving business revenues and individual earnings.

- *Personal satisfaction.* Gained from the contributions each person can make to the success of the program.

By identifying different perspectives as well as commonalities, a presenter can determine how to tailor the message for greater appeal to the audience. By reflecting on different perspectives, a presenter often discovers new meanings in a message and an innovative approach that will have more impact than a hackneyed one.

Earlier, the term **approach** was defined as *a way by which a person can be reached.* It is a definition that conveys the essence of presenting, which is an activity aimed at reaching people. A salesperson who presents solely from his or her perspective typically spotlights the features of the product or service. On the other hand, a salesperson who presents from the prospect's perspective will, more effectively, communicate what the product or service will do for the customer. Training professionals experience greater success reaching people when they tailor presentations to incorporate the perspectives of participants and students. Executives and managers who deliver down-line presentations will more effectively reach employees when they present a message in terms of the interests and concerns of employees, not management. Conversely, employees who present up-line are more likely to reach managers and executives when they approach a subject from the perspective of management.

When a presentation fails to achieve its objectives, all too often the reason is the use of an approach that was inappropriate to the audience. Neglecting the perspective of the audience has accounted for salespeople losing business to competitors, managers losing credibility and staff support, employees losing out on promotions, and politicians losing votes. To structure a winning presentation, begin by asking the following questions (which echo the attributes and purpose of an effective presentation outlined in Chapter 1):

- What will get and keep the attention of the members of *this audience?*
- What will make the message meaningful to *them?*
- What will make it memorable for *them?*
- What will move *this audience* to act on the message as I intend?
- What will provide balance among possible differing points of view?
- What will serve to persuade *this audience,* consistent with my objectives?

Persuasion

An **approach** is also understood as a method by which an activity is carried out. An effective method for carrying out a presentation is to address the primary buying motives of the person(s) in the audience. In the context of business presentations, the term **buying motives** is used in a broad sense to mean the principal reason(s) people accept, approve, or adopt what is presented to them.

Inherent in every business presentation is a proposal. Clearly, a sales presentation proposes that a customer buy the salesperson's product or service. Less evident, perhaps, but nonetheless part of every other type of presentation is an underlying proposal. A presentation of an instructional nature proposes that students learn information and adopt it into their manner of thinking or doing things. An up-line presentation by a manager may propose, for example, that a chief executive approve funding for a new program. In a down-line presentation, a supervisor may propose that entry-level employees accept the benefits to be derived from job-skills training. Although presentations vary with respect to the nature of what is proposed, all do propose something that the presenter recommends the audience *buy*.

Before structuring a presentation, a presenter should consider: "What will prompt this audience to buy my message?"

Persuasive presenters modify their approach on the basis of one or a combination of several buying motives (listed here in alphabetical order):

- Pleasure
- Power
- Practicality
- Prestige
- Profit
- Purpose

By way of example, effective presentations by an architectural firm would appeal to the respective buying motives of clients. A proposal presented to an executive committee for new corporate offices may highlight the motives of power and/or prestige; to a family building a custom home—pleasure and/or practicality; to real estate developers—profit and/or prestige; to a nonprofit community action agency—practicality and/or purpose. These examples suggest possible buying motives. From one audience to the next, however, what motivates listeners may vary. (Again, the planning checklist is a tool that helps presenters identify the buying motives of a given audience).

Every buying motive represents a form of personal satisfaction. People are moved to approve, accept, or adopt (i.e., *buy*) that which they perceive will satisfy what they need, want, or value. As noted in the introduction to this course, it is common for people to consider "What's In It For Me." A presenter who, through planning, understands the nature of the audience can then present a message that unmistakably conveys what's in it for them. Speakers who consistently produce successful outcomes recognize the imperative of communicating in terms of what motivates the listener, *not* what motivates the speaker.

Perception

As the foregoing discussion points out, an effective approach reaches people in an audience by addressing their perspective and carries out the presentation persuasively. How successful a presenter is at reaching and persuading people depends in large part on how the presenter is perceived. Thus, an additional question for a speaker to consider when structuring a presentation is: "How do I want to be perceived by this audience?"

Typically, people who deliver winning presentations are perceived to be:

- *Credible.* The audience finds the speaker believable. They perceive that the presenter's ideas, information, or recommendations are well thought out, reliable, and trustworthy.

- *Competent.* The audience considers the presenter knowledgeable, capable, and qualified on the subject. A corollary to competence is being prepared. A speaker who is perceived to be ill-prepared (no matter how well qualified in fact) risks being perceived as incompetent.

- *Confident.* The speaker is viewed by the audience as a person who is self-assured, a person of conviction who does not waffle on issues. People are not inclined to put their confidence in a speaker who is perceived to be lacking in confidence.

- *Caring.* People perceive the presenter cares about the subject, the event, the opportunity to present, and, most important, the audience. People are not inclined to be persuaded by a presenter who displays an attitude of indifference.

- *Convincing.* People in the audience feel sure about the veracity or feasibility of the speaker's message. This last characteristic is an outcome of the first four. Convincing presenters demonstrate a high degree of credibility, competence, confidence, and care.

The characteristics outlined above are hallmarks of those leaders, managers, salespeople, training professionals, and workers in every field who experience success. They are hallmarks of the most effective presenters.

These characteristics are also interrelated. Credibility and competence occur as a result of education and training, experience, and preparation. Confidence is an outcome of increasing credibility and competence, and frees a person to express that they care.

On the matter of confidence, it is helpful to remember a principle set forth in the first chapter of this course (under Key Concept 4: Communication Factors). *Perception is more powerful than fact.* If you feel confident, let your confidence show. If your confidence wavers, practice the principle, "Feel it or fake it." As you fake being confident, you will begin to feel more confident. The key to a successful experience in a presentation situation is not that you are, in fact, confident. It is that the audience perceives you to be so.

According to Lou Holtz, championship football coach and acknowl-
edged leader and motivator, "The answers to three questions will determine
your success or failure. (1) Can people trust me to do my best? (2) Am I
committed to the task at hand? (3) Do I care about other people and show
it? If the answers to these questions are yes, there is no way you can fail."*
The premise applies to presenting. It expresses qualities the most effective
presenters demonstrate. It suggests that a person consider the following
question when preparing to present:

> "By this approach, will people in the audience perceive that I am trust-
> worthy and committed and that I care?"

Other Factors That Affect Approach

The preceding points have emphasized the audience as the primary factor
in determining how to approach a presentation. Although not as important
as audience considerations, other factors influence the approach. They
include the subject, setting, and time frame of a presentation.

Subject.   Some subjects lend themselves to serious treatment. Other subjects can be treated humorously. Most subjects are best approached in a manner that blends both the "comic" and the "tragic," so to speak. During the
presentation of a grave or pressing matter, comic relief can be effective (provided it is tasteful). Conversely, weaving into a lighthearted or humorous subject some points for more serious reflection can add impact to the message.

Setting.   A speaker's approach should be consistent with the setting of the
presentation event. For example, in a professional organization where it is
generally understood people are there for the purpose of getting down to
business, the effective presenter will adopt a professional, no-nonsense
approach.

Time Frame.   Presenters frequently feel that their subjects warrant in-
depth coverage. However (as noted previously), it is crucial to respect the
time frame allocated for a presentation. Depending on the time available, a
speaker may use a condensed approach that presents a broader overview of
the subject, or a comprehensive approach that explores the subject in
detail.

Presenters are rarely in a position to say or do everything they want to in
a manner they might prefer, without concern or regard for who they are

---

* Howard E. Ferguson, *The Edge* (Cleveland, Ohio: Getting the Edge Company, 1991),
pp. 1–4.

addressing and in what situation. Instead, like a tailor, the accomplished presenter alters the message to fit the nature of the audience, subject, setting, and time frame. The approach is to a speaker what a pattern is to a tailor. Before cutting cloth, a tailor takes certain measurements to determine the best fit. Before structuring a presentation, a speaker measures the factors that determine the best approach.

Reflection Questions

For the presentations you do (or expect to do), how will you tailor the approach in order to be more effective? Which factors would it be most beneficial for you to incorporate in the approaches to your presentations?

Key Concept 22

Objectives and a core concept are the foundation of the structure of an effective presentation.

The structure of a presentation provides a framework for the message. It is a skeleton of points the speaker will make. It indicates the overall shape the message will take when the presentation is fully prepared. In that, the structure of a presentation is like the framework of a building. The framework delineates the various components. Although incomplete when only the framework is in place, something of what it will be like when the project is finished is apparent. An additional similarity is that the framework is based on a foundation. The foundation of an effective presentation consists of objectives and a core concept.

Objectives

Objectives are critical to the preparation of a presentation. In terms of the earlier reference to Alice in Wonderland, an **objective** represents the presenter's "destination." It is the aim of the presentation, the object of the endeavor, a statement of what will be achieved as a result of presenting. An objective may be thought of as "the guiding light" of the entire presentation. The surest guidance is provided by objectives that are attainable, measurable, and time-targeted.

An objective that is attainable states what the presenter can reasonably expect to achieve within the parameters (such as time frame) of the presentation event. An objective is stated in measurable terms so the presenter can determine that the objective has been attained. The time target identifies the time frame within which the presenter intends to achieve the objective.

A presenter formulates two objectives: a primary objective and a supporting objective. Both should take into account the type of presentation, the nature of the event, the audience, the setting, and the time frame.

Primary Objective. The primary objective reflects the purpose of presenting, which is to persuade. It also reflects one of the attributes characteristic of an effective presentation, namely, that the audience is moved to act affirmatively in response to the message. A clear time-targeted statement of a primary objective would read, "By the conclusion of this presentation, the audience will be persuaded to . . ."

The statement would be completed by answering the question, "What do I want to persuade the audience to do?" For most business presentations, the primary objective is to move people to do one of the following:

- Buy
- Fund
- Invest
- Use
- Choose
- Change
- Approve
- Accept
- Adopt
- Award

The following examples suggest how these terms translate specifically into statements of a primary objective. Although the wording may be modified depending on the situation, the intent remains essentially the same.

"By the conclusion of this presentation, the audience will be persuaded to . . ."

. . . buy (or purchase) widgets from Miscellany, Inc.

. . . fund a community care program.

. . . invest in a retirement plan.

. . . use (or follow) the new procedure for processing client files.

. . . choose (select, or vote for) the party's candidate at the election.

. . . change (adjust, amend, or modify) their attitude in the workplace.

. . . approve my qualifications for promotion.

. . . accept budget reductions.

. . . adopt the proposed amendment to the General Plan.

. . . award the contract for the Hi-Rise Project to the XYZ Company.

A presenter may determine that the desired objective is not realistically attainable "by the conclusion of the presentation." Then, the time target on the end objective would be extended to a later date, and the presenter would schedule a further action as a follow-up to the presentation. The objective for the presentation itself would then read as an interim objective. For example, "By the conclusion of this presentation, the audience will be persuaded to . . ."

. . . recognize the value of purchasing widgets.

. . . recommend the new procedure.

. . . reflect on the benefits of a more positive attitude.

. . . give me opportunities to demonstrate my qualifications for promotion.

. . . evaluate the proposed amendment.

. . . consider the advantages of awarding the contract.

Whether the objective is stated in terms of the desired "end" result or an "interim" action will depend on what the presenter ascertains can be accomplished with the audience being addressed, in the setting in which the presentation will occur, and in the time that is available. When preparing the framework of a message, the imperative is to state explicitly the reason for doing the presentation.

Supporting Objective. The supporting objective is so named because it supports the primary objective. It describes the audience attitude and/or ability the presenter will strive to develop during the course of the presentation. The function of the supporting objective is to lead to the achievement of the primary one. There are four graduated levels at which a supporting objective may aim: (1) understanding, (2) acceptance, (3) ability to, or (4) application. The fourth level, application, parallels the primary objective in that it means the audience is persuaded to do it.

Using the subject of this chapter as an example, assume the primary objective is, "By the conclusion of this presentation, the audience will be persuaded to use the techniques recommended for structuring an effective presentation." The supporting objective might be stated like this, "By the conclusion of this presentation the audience will . . ."

. . . understand the stages of preparing a presentation.

. . . accept the value of structuring a presentation.

. . . be able to use a model outline.

. . . do it (i.e., apply the techniques to an actual situation).

Depending on the subject of the presentation and the time available, a supporting objective may be singular or composite. If singular, it would be stated: (1) understand, or (2) accept, or (3) be able to, or (4) do it. If composite, the supporting objective would be stated: (1) understand and accept, (2) accept and be able to, (3) understand and be able to, or (4) all four levels combined.

Notice how both types of objectives, primary and supporting, are formulated in terms of the audience. Doing so underscores the fact that the overriding consideration in a presentation is not the presenter. It is the audience. It also tends to clarify the role of the presenter. A presenter's role, for example, is not to sell; it is to persuade the audience to buy. It is not to teach, but to prompt the audience to learn. It is not to dictate; it is to motivate people to follow. No one (including the best of presenters) can compel people to vote a certain way, bring in a certain verdict, approve a proposed project, adopt a procedure, work together as a team, or accept change.

What the skillful presenter can and does do is gain sufficient understanding of the audience to identify what will appeal to its members. Then, the presenter builds a framework for the presentation, beginning with the formulation of specific objectives. Specifically stated objectives provide the direction that guides a presenter through the process of preparing and presenting a winning message. Direction alone, however, is not enough. Equally important is focus provided by a core concept.

Core Concept

Outlined at the begining of this chapter are five of the most common complaints about presentations. All are related to a lack of preparation.

Three are a direct result of a lack of focus on the part of the presenter. A presenter who fails to establish and maintain the focus of a presentation cannot expect the audience to stay focused on the subject.

Focus refers to a condition of clarity. It is also defined as a central point at which attention is directed. The effective presenter clarifies the central point of the message during this first stage of structuring a presentation. This central or focal point is stated as a **core concept**. The core concept is the heart of a message. It is the prominent theme, the chief idea, the main thesis that the presentation will be designed to convey. Every part of a presentation—the statistics, the stories, the visual aids—should grow out of the core concept. If all of the verbiage of a presentation were stripped away, the core would remain. Communications consultant, Brent Filson, observed, "Keeping your speech grounded in one idea [the core concept] can make the difference between the audience guessing about what you're saying and knowing exactly what you're saying."*

Writing the Core Concept of a Presentation

A core concept expresses what a presenter would want the audience to say if they were asked at the end of a presentation, "What did you hear in this message?" Since it is intended to provide focus and to clarify the essence of the message, a core concept is written in one sentence. Reducing the core concept to a single sentence crystallizes a person's thinking.

A core concept is formulated by first rough drafting a paragraph that describes the main meaning to be communicated to the audience. The paragraph is reviewed, then condensed. Unnecessary words are eliminated; others are revised until the paragraph is pared down to one precise and succinct statement. A core concept for this chapter, for example, might read, "Every effective presentation is built around a framework of well-organized material that elaborates on the core concept to achieve the presenter's objectives."

Applying the Objectives and Core Concept

Once written, the core concept and the objectives are reviewed from time to time throughout the process of preparing a presentation. Doing so helps to ensure the use of material that contributes to the message, and that will ultimately lead to achieving the primary objective. When compiling and selecting material, the "litmus test" for inclusion is, "Does it support the objectives or the core concept?" Material that does not should not be used. When this principle is applied, and the core concept is kept clearly in mind, a presentation will more likely exhibit the following qualities.

---

* Brent Filson, *Executive Speeches* (Williamstown, Mass.: Williamstown Publishing Company, 1991), p. 53.

■ *Concentration.* The focus gained by clarifying the core concept of a message can improve a speaker's concentration during both the development and the delivery of a message. A speaker whose attention is concentrated is less inclined to slip into the rambling that an audience finds distracting and disconcerting.

■ *Consistency.* Most presentations use material that has been compiled from various sources. Many communicate a variety of points. As a result, a presentation can appear disjointed. However, by checking content against the objectives and core concept, a more unified and harmonious message is produced because an underlying theme is expressed consistently from start to finish.

■ *Cohesiveness.* The core concept and objectives act as "glue" that holds together the various elements of a message. The diversity of information, ideas, terminology, examples, audiovisuals, and the like are interrelated. The presentation is strengthened by the mutual reinforcement that occurs when all elements reflect common objectives and one core concept.

Writing out objectives and a core concept offers an additional advantage, especially to novice presenters. Knowing where and how to begin to prepare a message is baffling to some people. A person staring at a blank writing tablet grows increasingly frustrated when words for the message are slow in coming to mind. Formulating objectives and describing the core concept can give a presenter a "jump-start." The very act of working them out and writing them out activates a person's thinking and accelerates the process of preparing.

Key Concept 23

An effective presentation consists of five components.

Once the foundation for a presentation is in place (that is, the objectives and core concept are written), you are ready to prepare the framework of the message. An effective presentation will contain the following components, listed below in the order in which they are presented.

1. Opener
2. Preview
3. Body
4. Review
5. Close

The function of each component is described next. Guidelines for drafting a preliminary outline to structure a message are discussed in the key concepts that follow. Techniques and examples for developing the content (substance) of a message are covered in Chapter 4.

Opener

The **opener** functions as an invitation to the audience to give attention to the message. It is sometimes referred to as the *hook,* which depicts the intent to catch hold of the audience. The opener may be thought of as the appetizer to the main course of a meal. The term **opener** connotes that which will "open up" the audience to be receptive to the speaker and eager to hear the message.

As the first words voiced by a presenter, the opener is crucial. In just a few moments at the outset of a presentation a speaker establishes a tone, a mood, and expectations in the minds of people in the audience. For that reason, clarity and conviction are essential to a favorable start. So, too, is brevity.

In the case of the opener, less is generally better. Typically, a presenter has as little as 60 to 90 seconds in which to capture people's attention. A compelling, crisp, and quick opener is therefore important. In a "clicker culture," it is imperative. The term **clicker culture** is derived from findings that television viewers in the United States switch channels (click the remote control) as often as every minute and a half. More patient viewers may stay tuned to the same program for up to as long as four minutes. In either case, attention spans are short. In 1992, during the political campaigns that preceded elections in the United States, the average "sound bite" (a broadcast excerpt from a speech or commentary) clocked at 20 to 30 seconds.

What do these findings have to do with presenting? For presenters who hope to have an impact on people, they suggest that a traditional speech-making approach to an audience is no longer appropriate. Television has a powerful influence on people's listening and viewing behaviors. With its constantly changing visual images and variations in sounds, television has created a new norm regarding what people have come to expect they will see and hear. If people are not captivated, they will "tune out." Mentally, they will switch to a channel of thought other than that which is being presented. That people are attending a presentation does not guarantee that they are attentive. A presenter must seize and sustain attention. The primary function of the opener is to command audience attention from the very outset of a presentation.

The opener may serve a secondary function as well: to introduce the speaker and/or the subject. When the presenter is not known to the audience and has not been introduced by someone else, a brief introduction to establish the presenter's authority to speak on the subject would be added at the end of the opener.

When the subject is one with which the audience is not familiar, the opener may conclude with a brief statement or two to orient the audience to the topic. This orientation may convey the significance of the subject, provide background information, define the use of a unique term or a term used in a unique way, or establish a point of common ground between the audience and the presenter.

It is advisable to keep introductory and orientation comments to a minimum or they will detract from the impact of the opener. Once a presenter has captured the attention of the audience, the purpose of the opener is defeated if it is followed by lengthy explanations, background dissertations, or a self-serving introduction. It is preferable (when the topic lends itself to doing so) to incorporate introductory remarks early on in the presentation within the first point in the body of the message. The *first* thing an audience wants to hear is an answer to the question, "Why am I here?" (in other words, "What's in it for me?"). An effective opener hints at the answer and thus entices the audience to "stay tuned" for the rest of the message.

Preview

The preview anticipates the main message. It is a concise statement that prepares the audience for what they are about to hear. It is not unusual for people to come into a presentation preoccupied. In the workplace, people often have on their minds concerns other than those relating to the subject of a presentation. After the opener has gained audience attention, the preview directs it to the issues to be addressed. It also functions as a bridge to the body of the presentation.

Body

The body *is* the message. The other components of a presentation are accessories to the body of information and ideas. The opener and preview set up the audience for the body. The review and closing cap it off. The body itself is the reason for the presentation event. As the opener must gain people's attention, the content of the message (and the way it is delivered) must sustain it.

The body is composed of three elements:

- Key points
- Substantiating material
- Transitions

Key points are the main ideas communicated in the body of a presentation. They are called *key* because they open the way to the audience understanding and accepting the message.

Substantiating material consists of information and ideas that explain and support (substantiate) the key points. It is the substance of a presentation (covered in Chapter 4).

Transitions, although relatively minute, are an essential part of a presentation. A **transition** is a bridge that leads the audience from one key point to the next. It acts as a summary-preview internal to the body of a message. A transition summarizes one key point and introduces the next, as indicated by the following statements.

- "Having considered *x*, let's go on and look at *y*."
- "In addition to these results in Department A, the organization has experienced success in Department B."
- "We've focused attention on widgets. Equally important are gadgets."

Transitions alert people in the audience that the message is advancing. Speakers know when they are leaving one point and beginning the next. The audience does not. Without transitions, a presenter can be part way into a new point before the audience perceives a change from the previous point. When this occurs, the message can appear incomplete or confusing to an audience. Transitions help keep the audience on track with the message. They can also serve to bring people back. If someone has tuned out mentally during the course of a presentation, a transition may regain their attention because it signals a change.

Review

The review restates the key points of the message. This reiteration of key points—prefaced in the preview, addressed in the body, and summarized in the review—is purposeful. It capitalizes on a principle of persuasion known as "frequency and recency." The principle contends that people are persuaded, in part, by what they have heard frequently and recently. Few, if any, people in an audience are attentive every moment throughout a presentation. Even if they were, they are bombarded (sometimes during the course of one presentation) with volumes of information and ideas that compete for their consideration. Spotlighting the key points one last time in a review offers the added reinforcement that can imbed the points in the thoughts of the audience.

To gain the benefit of reinforcement and at the same time avoid sounding redundant, variety is added to the manner in which key points are expressed in the preview, the body, and the review. Synonyms may be used. The points may be stated in contrasting terms (provided they are stated in such a manner that the audience will clearly understand the contrast). For example, if a key point were "enjoy gains," it might be stated in those terms and later restated as "avoid loss." The points may be presented from a different angle or expressed using literary devices such as metaphors or analogies.

In addition to summarizing the key points, the review signals that the presentation is nearing completion. This represents a change from the rhythm of the body of the message, and any change in pace or direction can heighten attention. A strong review can alert the audience to sit up and take notice of the "grand finale."

Close

In an effective presentation, the close functions as more than a ceremonious conclusion that does little more than thank the members of the audience for their time. An effective close calls the audience to act on the message. It appeals to, encourages, or directly asks the audience to do something. The "something" is that which will equate to achievement of the primary objective.

A presentation was previously described as a means to an end. The close communicates the end to which the presenter has guided the audience. As the culmination of a message, the close should be a strong, succinct statement or question that concludes the presentation on a definitive note. A definitive close leaves no doubt that the presentation is over. Presentations that lack structure (that neglect the orderly arrangement of the five essential components) typically trail off ambiguously at the end. They leave people in an audience dangling, wondering whether the presentation is finished yet and uncertain about what to do with the message they received.

A quality close brings a presentation to an end on a high note. A high note expresses a positive, upbeat point. Even in the most negative or dreadful subjects, some positive feature can be found. A negative topic, if it is considered from the opposite standpoint, reveals a positive aspect. The audience that leaves feeling good is more likely to remember the presentation as a pleasant, productive experience and so think favorably of the presenter.

Staying on Track

An analogy may be drawn between a presentation and taking an audience on a journey aboard a train. Figure 3-2 illustrates the components of a presentation from the viewpoint of this analogy.

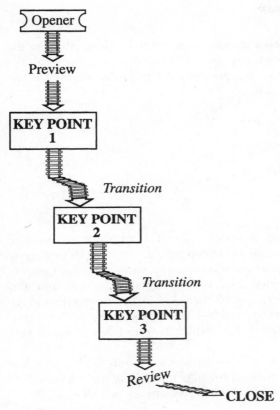

Figure 3-2. Staying on track.

The *opener* can be likened to a "ticket to ride." It is the invitation to the audience to come on board. The *preview* is an abbreviated itinerary. Each *key point* is a "tourist attraction"—a significant stop as the journey proceeds toward the intended destination. Information and ideas (represented by the tracks) substantiate the key points. Transitions act as "switches" that, leaving one key point, redirect to the next. The *review* is a retrospective of the journey and announces arrival at the *close,* which expresses the primary objective of the journey.

Throughout, the presenter serves as the engineer, conductor, and tour guide who is responsible for staying on track and for keeping the audience on track, too. Before the journey (i.e., the actual presenting) begins, the presenter is the travel planner who decides the destination and develops the surest, most enticing way to get the audience there.

Preparing the Components
of a Presentation

As Figure 3-2 illustrates, when a message is presented it proceeds from the opener to the preview, through the body, to the review, and ends with the close. However, when structuring a presentation, the components are prepared in the order shown below.

1. Body

2. Preview

3. Review

4. Opener

5. Close

1. The body of the message is structured first. It naturally follows that, having formulated objectives and a core concept, the next step is to identify the key points that will support them. Initial and early attention to structuring the body is recommended because the body takes the most time and thought to prepare. Moreover, points included in the body affect every other component. If changes are made—in the objectives, the core concept, or the body—other components (which haven't been prepared yet) won't have to be reworked.

At this first stage of structuring, it is sufficient to identify the key points of the message. Depending on the length and complexity of the presentation, the substance may be prepared in a number of sittings over time.

2. and 3. The preview and review are easily prepared after the key points of the body have been identified. The preview is simply a sentence that announces the key points contained in the body. The review recaps the same points.

4. The opener not only serves to capture audience attention. It also heralds the theme of the message. Therefore, it is prepared after the body. Doing so allows time to consider and compose different types of openers, which a skilled presenter will do in order to have various options from which to choose the most appropriate and attention-getting opener.

5. The close is prepared last since it is that point at which a speaker asks the audience to act on the message. Before preparing the close, the presenter should review the components that precede it to confirm that they lead naturally and contribute to the intended conclusion. If they do not, some aspect of the presentation should be changed: either the objectives or the key points in the body of the message.

Key Concept 24

Memorable messages conform to the Rule-of-3.

As previously stated, the key points in the body of a message are identified first. An effective presentation follows the Rule-of-3. The **Rule-of-3** contends that every great message communicates at least one, sometimes two, but rarely more than three key points. The Rule-of-3 should be applied to every presentation for the following reasons.

■ It produces a better-organized message. Isolating key points establishes categories into which substantiating material can be grouped.

■ It lends clarity to a presentation. Presenters who follow the Rule-of-3 are less likely to ramble.

■ It adds focus to a presentation. Rather than an open-ended assortment of endless facts and figures and ideas and information, the message is crystallized into the most significant points a speaker wants to impress upon the audience.

■ Improved organization and added focus make the message easier for a person to present and easier for an audience to assimilate.

■ The Rule-of-3 reflects the natural way in which people mentally store information. When asked about a telephone number or address, people often respond by reciting the numbers in pairs of two or sets of three. A number like 5133, for example, is usually grouped in pairs and pronounced "fifty-one thirty-three." This tendency represents the brain's effort to organize data in a form that can be more easily and quickly recalled.

The benefits to following the Rule-of-3 can be summed up in one most important advantage: it makes a message easier for the audience to remember. Among the attributes of an effective presentation is that it is memorable. There is little reason to present if the audience won't remember enough of a message to act on it.

Factors in the contemporary workplace and in society inhibit how much an audience is likely to retain. Information overload (a problem discussed in Chapter 1) is one such factor. The volumes of communications to which people are increasingly exposed contribute to **retention stress**: a mental tension that results from being inundated with information. When physically overstressed, the body eventually "shuts down" (a condition described as "burn out"). A similar condition occurs when the mind is overstressed. After being bombarded with messages throughout the day, every day, the mind will limit how much new information will be absorbed.

It is not surprising that studies have found people remember as little as 10 percent of what they hear. The remaining 90 percent is filtered out for any number of reasons. It may be because the message does not have sufficient impact to hold a person's attention. It is not considered meaningful or relevant. It is too garbled or confusing. It is not perceived to be significant. This course presents techniques for increasing the amount of material an audience receives and retains. The Rule-of-3 is one such technique.

The Rule-of-3 is based on the premise "the more they hear, the less they will remember; the less they hear, the more they will remember." It facilitates retention because it simplifies and concentrates the message into *the* most significant points. The one, two, or three key points to select for presentation are determined by considering the following questions.

- What points will best support my objectives?
- What points will best express the core concept?
- What points will alert this audience to pay attention?
- What points will be most meaningful to this audience?
- What points do I want this audience to most remember?

When identified, the key points form the framework for the body of a presentation. As such, they guide research efforts and the subsequent preparation of substantiating material.

Reflection Questions

If you have not previously applied this principle, how will the presentations you do change by following the Rule-of-3? How might they improve?

Key Concept 25

A *few simple techniques help generate ideas for a message.*

Assume that you are in the process of structuring a presentation. You have written objectives and a core concept. You've made note of some possible points, but you are not completely satisfied with them. You may have identified one or two key points, but you aren't sure how to develop them further. Like many people, you feel pressured when it comes to preparing a message. You find yourself staring at a writing tablet with very little written on it. Your pen is poised, ready for action, but no thoughts related to your presentation come to mind. What you need is a jump-start, a way to get you moving on the message. Four techniques for generating ideas are described in this section: free-form sketch, index cards, stick-on notes, and walk and talk.

Free-form Sketch

Sometimes referred to as mind-mapping, the technique of freely sketching one's thoughts is a productive adaptation of doodling. When deep in thought, many people doodle. The drawing of forms and squiggles on paper acts as a kind of substitute for writing out ideas before they have fully formulated. Free-form sketching one's thoughts offers the freedom of doodling while capturing ideas on paper as they come to mind. It frees a person to think more creatively. It removes the concern with details (like spelling, wording, sentence structure, organization, and outlining) that constrain the thought process. It can foster fresh ideas and depict relationships between them.

The only supplies needed to do a free-form sketch are a blank piece of paper and a pencil. The subject of the presentation or a key point is written in the center of the paper and circled.

When a thought comes to mind, it is added to the paper, circled, and connected by a line to the idea that triggered it. When no new ideas seem to be forthcoming, a person's thinking may be prompted by posing open questions: who, what, when, where, how, which, and why?

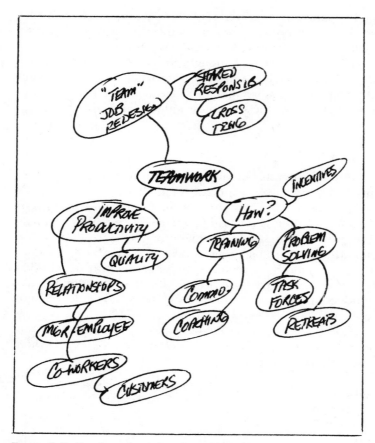

Figure 3-3. Free-form sketch (mind-mapping).

Figure 3-3 is a sample of a free-form sketch of ideas. Not every idea that is sketched will necessarily be used. Extraneous ideas are erased or crossed out. Ideas the presenter chooses to develop further can be highlighted with a marking pen. Ideas that logically belong together are marked with alphanumeric notations to indicate groupings: A1, A2, A3; B1, B2, B3. The free-form sketch then provides a basis for outlining the message.

Index Cards

Using this technique, each separate idea or item of information is written on an index card. The cards are then spread out on a desk, counter, or table top. Viewing ideas together and in relation to one another facilitates the task of sifting through and sorting material. Index cards are used because they can easily be removed, rearranged, or replaced with different cards on which new items have been written.

It is also helpful to keep a supply of cards or note paper close at hand to record ideas or items of information when they come to mind (which is often at times other than when a person is working on a presentation). It is easier to capture ideas in writing as they occur than it is to try to recall them later.

Stick-on Notes

This technique combines aspects of the free-form sketch and index card methods. A key point (or preliminary thought for a possible key point) is written across the top of an 8½ × 11″ or 8½ × 14″ sheet of paper. Initially, a presenter may start with three, four, or a half a dozen such pages. Ideas are individually written on small (1½ × 2″) stick-on notes and attached to the appropriate larger sheet of paper that represents a key point. Ideas that are not clearly related to one of the key-point pages are posted to a blank sheet(s) of paper so the idea is captured until a decision is made about what to do with it.

Stick-on notes offer the creative freedom that helps to generate ideas, together with the flexibility of easily rearranging, revising, or removing items. They can also be posted at various positions on the key-point pages in a manner that simulates a rough outline.

Walk and Talk

People tend to think faster when they stand. They also tend to communicate more naturally when they talk. Recognizing these tendencies, this technique suggests standing and walking around while recording ideas into a hand-held portable dictation or audio-recording unit. The recordings are then transcribed to capture the ideas on paper.

The preceding idea-generation techniques are useful for the following reasons.

■ They are easy to do. For people for whom the process of preparing a presentation is tedious, any of these techniques should make it more enjoyable. The more enjoyable a task, the less inclined a person is to procrastinate.

■ They can generate ideas in record time. Ideas are jotted down (or recorded) as quickly as they come to mind, without taking the time to compose complete and accurate sentences.

■ They remove the pressure of having to produce prematurely a logical, organized, correctly prepared outline. Early on in the process of structuring a presentation, the best ideas may still be in the formative stage. At this point, attempting to force-fit embryonic thoughts into a system of organization can be counterproductive.

■ They nurture creative thinking. The facility with which thoughts are captured is freeing. So, too, is the fact that there is no "right" or "wrong" way to do any one of these techniques.

■ With the first three techniques, ideas are written out in a manner that speeds and simplifies the subsequent preparation of an outline.

Reflection Question

Of the four techniques described for generating ideas, which one(s) do you think you will find most helpful?

Key Concept 26

An outline lends structure to a presentation by arranging ideas and information in an orderly manner.

How does it all get put together: the many ideas, the facts and figures, the researched information, the material that has been collected? A presentation takes shape when the various items and points are arranged in an outline. An outline is most easily prepared when three preliminary steps are completed first: selection, sequencing, and labeling.

Select Material

Often, potential material has been gathered from various sources, or more material is available than there is time in which to present it all. Presenters who generate many ideas may find upon further consideration that not all of the ideas apply. Before outlining ideas and information from a random assortment of items, an effective presenter sifts through (distills) all material and selects only those items that are appropriate to use. Each item (idea or piece of information) is selected or eliminated on the basis of the following criteria.

■ It is essential to satisfy the objectives.

■ It is useful to shape audience perceptions.

- It is consistent with the approach to this audience.
- It substantiates a key point.
- It adds value (i.e., contributes to the attributes of an effective presentation).
- It is unnecessary. (Eliminate it.)

An item of information or idea should not be selected simply because it appeals to the presenter. Every item should be viewed in terms of its potential appeal and/or probable impact on the audience.

Determine the Sequence

Key points for the body of the message have been identified. Information and ideas to be included in the presentation have been selected. The next step is to determine the sequence in which they will be outlined, that is, the order in which the material will be presented.

An effective presentation guides listeners through a logical "sequence of events" (so to speak) to make it easy for people in the audience to follow along. When an audience finds a speaker's train of thought confusing or difficult to follow, people are inclined to be critical of the presentation. If a presentation is so lacking in order that it makes no sense to the audience at all, people will likely "tune out."

There are several ways in which material can be arranged. Provided the arrangement produces a logical sequence, with continuity from one point to the next, any one of the following methods may be used.

Chronological Order. Arranges points in the order in which events have happened or will occur in time. Depending on the subject, the message would address (1) past, (2) present, and (3) future; or (1) the initial phase, (2) an intermediate phase, and (3) the final phase.

Spatial Arrangement. Presents points in terms of space or geographic area. A presentation on an organization's results across the country, for example, would proceed from results in (1) the East, to (2) Central regions, to (3) the West. (If an organization had four regions—East, North, South, and West—an exception to the Rule-of-3 would allow four key points.)

Topical Method. Identifies main topics within the message. For example, a presentation may address (1) sales, (2) service, and (3) support; or (1) product development, (2) manufacturing, and (3) distribution. As these examples indicate, a topical approach also relates the topics in sequence. Logically, product development precedes manufacturing, which is followed by distribution.

Crescendo.   Presents points from the least important to the point of greatest importance. The term "crescendo," borrowed from music, refers to a gradual increase in force. This arrangement builds to a high-impact finish. It presents last the point that the speaker wants the audience to most remember.

General-to-Specific.   Begins with a broad issue and works down to the more detailed point. This method is effective when presenting a positive message. For example, a presentation to employees announcing year-end bonuses might convey that (1) organizational results were outstanding, (2) departmental performance was excellent, so (3) individual employees will receive bonuses.

As the example indicates, arranging points in a descending manner, from generalities to the individual situation, can produce a heightened effect. It is therefore often the preferred sequence for sales presentations. A salesperson may relate (1) overall findings, (2) findings as they apply to an industry or profession, and then (3) implications for this prospect in particular. For instance, (1) on average, computerized billing increases productivity by so much; (2) using computerized billing, the legal profession has improved productivity by this much; (3) think what it could do for your firm. The general-to-specific arrangement starts with an overall result and progressively translates it into personalized reasons—to buy, to benefit, to act on the message.

Specific-to-General.   Begins with detail and builds to broader statements. This approach is useful when the message is unpleasant. For example, in a presentation to employees announcing corporate reductions in personnel, the points might proceed from (1) specific percentage of decrease in the sales of widgets, to (2) decline in the industry as a whole, to (3) overall, resulting in reductions in staffing around the country (ergo, our organization will also be laying off personnel). The specific-to-general approach can reduce a potentially negative impact by gradually relating points before presenting the ultimate result.

Comparison Method.   Considers two key points in comparison with one another. Common examples include presentations that feature problems compared to solutions, revenues compared to costs, gains compared to losses, and the like. The point presented last would be that one which the presenter wants to emphasize. The effect of comparing gains to losses, for example, differs from the effect of comparing losses to gains.

Label Key Points

Key Concept 23 described the five components that comprise a presentation and the order in which they are prepared. The body of a message—

made up of key points and related material—is outlined first. Not only are key points outlined in sequence. They are also labelled to designate the idea or information to which each point refers.

It is easier for people in an audience to remember the key points of a message if the points are labeled using a mnemonic device. A **mnemonic** (pronounced *ni mon ik*) is an aid to memory. To demonstrate how mnemonics help to make key points more memorable, the following mnemonic devices each include an example. The examples are based on a presentation on the subject of "Work."

Acronym. An acronym is a word that is formed from the first letters of other words. Example: The LAW of Working Successfully. LAW is a label for the following key points: (1) L = Learn job skills; (2) A = Accept responsibility; (3) W = Willingness to go the extra mile.

Alliteration. Repetition of the same first sound in a group of words is alliteration. Alliteration is most effective with consonants that have a crisp, bold, or poetic sound. Example: the letter "s" repeated with the key points (1) satisfaction, (2) self-esteem, (3) success.

Reiteration. With this technique, a repeated word or theme is used to label each key point. Example: the word "work" is reiterated with the key points (1) work to benefit self, (2) work to benefit others, (3) work to benefit the community.

Familiar Fundamentals. The 3-Rs and ABCs commonly refer to the fundamentals of a subject, and they are generic references with which most people are familiar. Examples: the ABCs of work might cover the key points (1) attitudes, (2) behaviors, (3) career advancement. The 3 Rs might address (1) reasons to work, (2) responsibility to work, (3) rewards of work.

Abbreviations. Some organizations are best known by their abbreviated names: AT&T, IBM, the IRS, the FBI, PPG, to name a few. When it is appropriate to the subject and can be applied honestly without appearing to be a gimmick, labeling key points using the letters of an abbreviated name can be effective. A presentation by an AT&T representative, for example, could address the key points of (1) Access, (2) Timeliness, and (3) Team support. A motivational presentation by an IBM manager to employees could emphasize (1) Innovation and (2) Boldness to gain (3) Momentum for the future.

People in an audience typically remember as little as 10 percent of a presentation. Under the best of circumstances, using all of the right techniques, even the most effective presenters can increase audience retention to little more than about 50 percent of a message. Recognizing that people will not remember all of a presentation raises the question, "What do you *most* want people to remember from your message?" The answer is the 1, 2, or 3 key points.

How can a presenter make it easier for an audience to remember the key points? As the foregoing examples suggest, mnemonic labels serve to impress the key points on people's minds. The example of key points used to create the acronym "LAW" could have been labeled (1) develop job skills, (2) accept responsibility, (3) perform above and beyond the call of duty. However, the use of an acronym (LAW: Learn, Accept, Willingness) makes the points more memorable. The key points of satisfaction, self-esteem, and success could have been labeled (1) job satisfaction, (2) confidence, (3) success. However, the points are more memorable when mnemonic labels are used—in this case, alliteration.

To devise mnemonic labels:

1. For each key point, write any label that initially comes to mind.

2. Look over the words used to describe the key points. Find substitute words, as in the case of using "learn" for the acronym LAW instead of the word "develop." (A thesaurus or dictionary of synonyms is a helpful reference for this purpose.) Consider rearranging or revising words: as with the use of "satisfaction" instead of "job satisfaction."

3. Confirm that the labeling of key points is relevant to the subject and will not be perceived as contrived. Irrelevant or gimmicky labels should not be used.

Prepare an Outline

When the preliminary tasks of selection, sequencing, and labeling key points are completed, a presenter then prepares an outline of the message. An outline represents the general plan of a presentation. For each component, an outline delineates the ideas and items of information that will be communicated. The key points of the message represent "categories" under which related subpoints of substantiating material will be grouped.

Types of Outlines. An outline may be abbreviated or comprehensive. An abbreviated outline uses only key words or phrases to convey what will be addressed at each point. Experienced presenters conversant with the subject of a presentation usually find abbreviated outlines adequate. A comprehensive outline is more detailed. With a comprehensive outline, complete sentences are written out to more closely approximate the narrative of the presentation. A full-sentence outline is often preferred when a person is new to presenting, dealing with a new subject, or delivering a message that has been prepared by someone else.

With respect to full-sentence outlines, one caution should be observed. A presenter who hopes to be effective will not rely on them. It can be tempting to treat pages of a prepared narrative like a script. Doing so is not presenting. It is reading aloud. Before the actual presentation, a comprehensive outline should be converted into an abbreviated one. An abbreviated outline is sufficient to prompt a prepared presenter from one point to the next and encourages a person to speak more naturally.

Either type of outline is intended to serve two purposes: (1) to organize the content of a message and (2) to help a speaker stay on track. A third purpose is served by developing an outline; it helps a presenter get prepared. It is one thing to organize ideas on paper; it is another matter to organize one's thoughts. If for no other reason, presenters should prepare an outline as a means to putting their thoughts in order.

Guidelines for Outlining. An outline should clearly (1) distinguish key points from subordinate points and (2) depict the relationships among all points in a presentation. The following guidelines should be observed when preparing an outline.

1. Express only one idea or item of information within each unit of the outline.
2. Refrain from overlapping points, which can lead to confusion.
3. The relative importance of each item is signified by symbols: Roman and Arabic numerals, and alphabetic characters. The Roman numeral "I" usually designates the first key point, followed by an uppercase "A" as the symbol for the first subordinate point, and so on. Apply symbols consistently throughout an outline to clearly distinguish the relationships among points.

For a presentation on the subject of geography, for example, a conventional key-word outline might look like this:

I. Continents
   A. Countries
      1. Provinces
      2. States
        a. Cities
II. Oceans
   A. Rivers
      1. Lakes
        a. Streams

As this example illustrates, an outline is hierarchical. It shows points in terms of their relative importance—from the greatest to the least.

A Model Outline Worksheet

Presenters are sometimes reluctant to prepare an outline because they are uncertain about how to begin. The model outline worksheet that follows provides an easy-to-use blueprint that identifies the components of a well-structured message.

A model outline is especially useful for occasions when a presenter is asked to speak on short notice or extemporaneously. Ideally, every opportunity to present would be preceded by sufficient lead time to do a thorough job of planning and preparation. Realistically, that is not always the case. When a presenter has little time in which to prepare, it is helpful to be able to recall a mental image of the model outline and structure a message "on the spot," if need be.

Summary

To structure an effective presentation, a presenter determines the best approach, formulates primary and secondary objectives and the core concept of the message, and then outlines components in a logical sequence that leads to achieving the objectives. In order to be most effective, a presenter will adhere to the Rule-of-3, practice techniques for generating ideas, and label key points in a manner that will make the message more memorable.

Sample Situations

Situation 1: Competitive Sales Presentation

Matt McGee is a distributor for an office furnishings manufacturer. Along with three other vendors, Matt was invited to present a proposal for furnishing the offices of a company that had relocated to larger facilities. Matt was surprised when he learned that the company selected another vendor. He had given his standard sales presentation, the one with which he had been successful many times before. He had explained the features of each item in detail, stressed the economy of his recommendations compared to his competitors', and emphasized the fact that his product line was backed by a national corporation. Although he had spoken 20 minutes longer than the time allotted for each vendor's presentation, Matt had felt the many points he wanted to make warranted an extended time frame.

Since the proposal had represented a substantial amount of business, Matt investigated the situation further. After talking with the company's executive secretary and the vendor who was awarded the contract, Matt realized he had used the wrong approach. He discovered (too late) that

Model Outline Worksheet   For subject: _____

1. Write objectives and the core concept of the message.
2. Prepare in this order: 1-Body (select, sequence, and label key points; add substantiating material; note transitions between key points. Follow the Rule-of-3). 2-Preview. 3-Review. 4-Opener. 5-Close.

Opener

Preview (introduce key points)

Body

    I. Key point _____ (substantiate)

                                                                                    (transition)

    II. Key point _____ (substantiate)

                                                                                    (transition)

    III. Key point _____ (substantiate)

Review (summarize key points)

Close

the president of the company was a leader in the business community and a vocal proponent of local entrepreneurial enterprise. With increased profits from her company's growth in recent years, the president had precipitated the move to a more prestigious, upscale, comfortable location. It occurred to Matt (albeit after the fact), that he had not identified the buying motives of the president (prestige, power, and pleasure). The oversight resulted in a failure to present key points that were meaningful to the prospect. Furthermore, to complete his presentation in the allotted time frame, Matt realized he should have used a condensed rather than a detailed approach.

Situation 2: Telephone Presentation

Terry Towne is a sales representative for New Century TechnoProducts. Terry had been trying to obtain an appointment with the general manager of a company to present a proposal for a system to replace a competitor's equipment. Having recently completed training in presentation skills (in which she learned about the Rule-of-3), Terry had identified the three key points she would emphasize once she gained the opportunity to make her presentation.

When Terry telephoned the company again, she was put through to the general manager. "I'm taking your call," he said, "because of your persistence. If you can give me three good reasons why I should meet with you, you've got your appointment." With the confidence that comes from being well prepared, Terry related the key points of her proposal. Not only did she get the appointment, she secured the order as well. (Although the names have been changed, this situation actually occurred as it is described. It confirms the value of focusing a message on two or three key points, and the benefits of being well-prepared.)

Situation 3: Job Interview

A job interview is a form of presentation. It may be either external or internal. If it is for a promotion to a position within the organization for which one already works, it would be an internal/up-line presentation. All job interviews are (or should be) promotional in nature.

Imagine that you are preparing to interview for a job that represents the next career move to which you aspire. With respect to this sample situation, identify a person or position (generally or specifically) with whom you would likely interview. For example, it may be a personnel agent or director, the head of a department, a business owner, an upper-level manager, or an executive.

What would be the best approach to the interviewer you've identified? What three key points would best communicate your abilities and qualifications? How would you state these key points in a manner that would make them more memorable? What information (from your experience and education) will serve to substantiate each key point?

Comprehension Check

The answers to the following appear on page 333.

1. According the the Rule-of-3 _____.
   a. a presenter has three minutes to capture the attention of the audience
   b. an effective presentation contains at least one but not more than three key points
   c. there are three factors to consider when determining the best approach
   d. the three most common buying motives are power, pleasure, and profit
   e. a presenter should write three objectives: a primary, a secondary, and an audience objective

2. The factors that most determine the best approach to a subject in relation to a given audience are _____.
   a. time frame and setting
   b. opener, preview, and close
   c. objectives and core concept
   d. perspective, persuasion, and perceptions
   e. factors identified on the planning checklist

3. Alliteration is _____.
   a. formulation of a new meaning for a company name
   b. repetition of the same first sound in a group of words
   c. a system of outlining a presentation
   d. repetition of the same first word in a title
   e. a method for persuading an audience

4. One technique for generating ideas is _____.
   a. develop a structured outline of the message
   b. review the planning checklist for ideas
   c. free-form sketch thoughts as they come to mind
   d. analyze the buying motives of the audience
   e. listen to an audio-recording of the core concept

5. List the five components of an effective presentation, first in the order in which they are prepared, then in the order in which they are presented.

   Prepare in This Order   *Present in This Order*

   _____   _____
   _____   _____
   _____   _____
   _____   _____
   _____   _____

To Do

At the end of Chapter 1, you were asked to identify a presentation you will develop during this course. The "To Do" for Chapter 2 suggested completing a planning checklist for that presentation. To apply the principles and techniques described in this chapter:

1. Write a primary and a supporting objective for your presentation.

2. Write the core concept of the message you want to communicate.

3. Try doing a free-form sketch to generate ideas for the message.

4. From the free-form sketch you have drawn, select two or three ideas for the Key Points that will comprise the body of your message.

   Key Point 1:

   Key Point 2:

   Key Point 3:

5. Look over the Key Points you have selected. Are they listed in a logical sequence? (If not, rearrange the order in which they are listed.) Have you used mnemonic labels for the Key Points? If not, consider how the labels might be revised to make use of an acronym, alliteration, reiteration, familiar fundamentals, or an abbreviated name.

4

Substance: Developing Convincing Content

When pleading a case, a trial lawyer seeks to persuade the jury to reach a certain conclusion. In doing so, the lawyer presents evidence that substantiates his or her case. Not only for lawyers, but also for anyone who makes business presentations, providing evidence is an essential factor in the process of persuading people. Substantive evidence comprises the content of an effective presentation. Together with the manner in which it is delivered, it is what convinces people to respond affirmatively to the message.

The previous chapter dealt with structure, ending with the creation of an outline that represents a "skeleton" of a presentation. This chapter concentrates on how to "flesh out" a presentation with substance: content that both validates and adds meaning to the message.

Objective

To identify the various types of material used to develop the substance of a presentation; to describe resources for locating information; and to apply guidelines for selecting material that will be most appropriate and effective.

Key Concepts

27. To be effective, a presentation must be believable.

28. The body of a presentation is developed from various types of material (evidence) selected to substantiate the presenter's message.

113

29. The opener is prepared from one or a combination of different forms of expression that best capture audience attention.

30. An effective close asks the audience to do that which will satisfy the speaker's objectives.

31. Countless resources are readily available for finding material from which to prepare the substance of a presentation.

32. Selection guidelines help a presenter determine which material to choose and how much to use for a given presentation.

Key Terms

To make full use of the key concepts, you will need to understand the following terms:

Believable	Anecdote
Substantive	Scenario
Evidence	Application close
Balance	Database
Verbal illustration	Litmus test
Analogy	

Key Concept 27

To be effective, a presentation must be believable.

If audience members do not believe the presenter, it is highly unlikely they will accept or act affirmatively on the message. Three factors determine the believability of a business presentation: who is presenting, how the message is presented (in terms of style, presence, and platform behavior), and what is presented (the content). With respect to who presents, some people—by virtue of position, affiliation, or reputation—are assumed to be credible. The messages they present are therefore readily accepted. However, most speakers do not enjoy such an advantage, and so must rely on building believability through the other two factors. How a message is presented is addressed in subsequent chapters. As to what is presented, the content will be believable (or not) depending in large part on how substantive it is.

Two terms in the preceding paragraph warrant definition: **believable** and **substantive**. Information and ideas that are **believable** are deemed to be true, trustworthy, and reliable. The audience perceives that the points the speaker makes are valid and therefore worthy of consideration. **Substantive** refers to that which is actual (i.e., true), and will hold up because it is strong and solid. In the context of presenting, substantive content holds up—against questions, scrutiny, debate, skepticism, or doubt—because it is composed of material that verifies the reliability or truth of the message.

Evidence Is Essential

What lends believable substance to a message? Evidence does. **Evidence** includes material that demonstrates or clarifies what is true or what is not true. By providing proof that validates and clarification that illuminates the message, evidence serves to convince people in an audience.

As discussed under the next Key Concept 28, different forms of evidence can be used to substantiate a message. When considering what material to use, it is crucial to bear in mind the attributes of an effective presentation (see Chapter 1). Among these is balance. **Balance** gives equal or proportionate attention to different types of evidence, as Figure 4-1 illustrates.

Some forms of evidence are concrete in nature; that is, they are factual, objective, and quantitative. Other types are conceptual—more feeling, subjective, and qualitative. For example, statistics are concrete; stories are conceptual. One type of evidence is not necessarily better than the other. The most convincing presentations blend both types, in balance.

Marketing studies have found that most consumers, on hearing or seeing a commercial message, respond first in terms of how they feel about it. They then seek facts to support their initial feelings. People subconsciously check facts against feelings (and vice versa) in every situation in which they communicate: in the workplace, at home, in social situations, and in presentations. People begin to form impressions on the basis of how they feel. Their feelings are then confirmed or corrected as they assimilate the facts, which are weighed against how they feel now, and so on. During a presentation, people in the audience shape perceptions and reach conclusions as a result of a dynamic and ongoing interplay of logic and emotion. Recog-

Figure 4-1. Types of evidence in balance.

nizing this, skilled presenters blend factual evidence that appeals to the mind with emotive evidence that appeals to the heart.

Reflection Question

When you are seated in the audience, what makes a presentation believable to you?

Key Concept 28

The body of a presentation is developed from various types of evidence selected to substantiate the presenter's message.

Chapter 3 described the components of a message, the order in which they are structured, and introduced the Rule-of-3. The body is developed first. Ideally, it contains not more than three key points. An outline identifies the key points and the sequence in which they will be presented. It naturally follows that content is prepared to substantiate each key point.

Although the primary purpose of evidential material is to solidify the message, it also serves to enhance a speaker's credibility. The presenter who cites evidence, and moves through the various forms with ease, is perceived to be someone who knows and cares about the subject. The most credible presenters develop convincing content using a combination of:

- Statistics and research results
- Examples and verbal illustrations
- Comparisons and contrasts
- Quotations
- Audiovisual aids
- Audience participation

Descriptions and examples of these various forms of substantiating material follow.

Statistics and Research Results

Statistics substantiate a point with concrete, quantitative evidence. Represented numerically, survey findings are intended to furnish factual proof. Census data, market research, product test results, and scientific measurements (such as measuring annual precipitation for weather statistics, tracking the occurrences of a particular illness, or counting the numbers in an animal population) are common examples. When related in a meaningful manner, statistical data can impress upon an audience the veracity of a point and validate a speaker's view, as indicated by the following excerpt from a presentation.

Speaking on the subject of total quality management in the fall of 1992, a presenter cited the following statistics to substantiate the value of achieving zero-defects.

> "To accept a standard of 99% quality means that we would accept:
> - 20,000 drug prescriptions filled incorrectly each year.
> - 2 unsafe landings at Chicago's O'Hare Airport each day.
> - 50 newborn babies dropped at birth by doctors each day.
> - 16,000 pieces of mail lost each hour.
> - 22,000 checks deducted from the wrong account each hour."*

While some statistics may be startling, facts and figures take on even greater meaning when they are related specifically to people in the audience. In the foregoing example, the speaker might have added:

> "If 99% quality is acceptable, hopefully you or a family member are not planning a flight to Chicago. Hopefully, one of those lost pieces of mail isn't an overdrawn notice from your bank. If you do discover that your account is overdrawn, hopefully it's because someone else's check was deducted from your account in error."

There are two important aspects to translating statistical evidence into meaningful terms. First, it is imperative to reduce large numbers to smaller equivalents to make it easier for the audience to assimilate the information. In the case of 22,000 checks each hour, the figure could have been stated as "more than 192 million checks a year." However, figures in the millions and billions and trillions have little meaning for most people. On the other hand, the figure "22,000 checks an hour" could be reduced still further to "more than 360 checks every minute." (Although the actual figure is 366.66, it is clearly preferable to communicate figures in round numbers if doing so doesn't sacrifice the integrity of the data.)

Secondly, a presenter should never assume that people in an audience will automatically make the connection between the data and their own experience. The presenter must state specifically how the statistics apply to the audience. It adds even more meaning to suggest (if there were, for

---

* Rhoda Fukushima, "Total quality management takes hold," *The Fresno Bee* (Oct. 26, 1992), p. E1.

instance, 60 people in the audience), "360 checks every minute amounts to 6 checks from the account of every person in this room." As with all types of evidence, statistics are most convincing when a presenter drives the point home by tailoring the information to the audience.

Statistical evidence need not be presented in detail. It is often referenced in summary form and embedded in the narrative of the message. For example, in a seminar on customer service, the speaker pointed out that a study by the Forum Corporation found that up to 40 percent of customers who claimed they were satisfied changed to different suppliers. The "40 percent" statistic is a recap of survey data.

This example raises another consideration when citing statistics. Percentages may be meaningful to mathematicians, but they are not to many lay people. When people are seated in an audience hearing numerous facts and figures recited, after a while the distinction between numbers fades. Percentages, especially those the presenter wants to most impress upon the audience, should be converted to whole numbers. In the situation described above, the speaker reiterated the point in this way: "40 percent. That's 4 out of every 10 customers who do business with you—today. Will they still be doing business with you tomorrow?" The percentage is invested with meaning, and the point is made more striking, when the number is translated into human terms with which the audience can identify.

Examples and Verbal Illustrations

The nineteenth-century English statesman, Benjamin Disraeli, asserted, "Experience is the child of Thought, and Thought is the child of Action." A presenter who seeks to prompt people to think, and ultimately to act, will incorporate in the content of a message evidence that is based on experience. Such evidence is found in examples and verbal illustrations.

An example can be thought of as an "expressed sample" that refers to a person or event as evidence of the validity of a point. A **verbal illustration** is a more extensive, embellished form of example. As the term aptly implies, a verbal illustration is a *word picture*. It describes a situation a presenter intends the audience to envision. Presented well, verbal illustrations are effective in that they tap into the visual channel of communication (which, as you may recall from the first chapter, has the greatest impact in face-to-face communications).

Examples and verbal illustrations may be drawn from one's own experience or the experience of others. Examples from one's own experience can help establish commonality with an audience. They inject a personalized, relational quality into a presentation. Reference to the experience of others adds variety and can heighten audience attention. Examples of recognized leaders or experts on a subject lend authority to a message, while illustrations that describe ordinary folks in everyday circumstances are ones with which a majority of people can relate. A skilled presenter will incorporate different types of examples from different sources to balance and broaden the appeal of a message.

Examples and verbal illustrations may be factual or hypothetical. As evidence intended to substantiate a point, factual examples are preferable to hypothetical ones. However, hypothetical illustrations are useful for two purposes: to project into the future and to draw the audience into the picture, so to speak, and so evoke a response. In either case, the hypothetical example is introduced (and thus distinguished from factual references), with words such as "Suppose . . . ," "Imagine . . . ," and "What if . . ."

Hypothetical situations are, by definition, not true—but they must be believable. A convincing hypothetical illustration describes something that could realistically occur. A far-fetched hypothesis will do nothing to advance the presenter's point of view, but will instead undermine one's credibility.

Like statistics, examples may be detailed or summarized. Some presenters display a tendency to develop every point with elaborate examples and illustrations. However, the use of short and simple references should not be neglected. The contrast between the simplicity of an abbreviated example against the backdrop of a fully descriptive narrative can serve to highlight a point. It provides a variation in style that helps to sustain audience attention. Moreover, abbreviated examples are useful when time constraints are a factor in a presentation. Factual examples that refer to persons or situations with which an audience would likely be familiar are the most appropriate to present in summary fashion. Whether factual or hypothetical, detailed or abbreviated, examples and illustrations are developed to support, clarify, illuminate, or personalize the points of a message.

Statistical evidence and research results are considered "hard" proof. Numbers are quantitative and, to the concrete thinker, represent the "bottom line" that underlies the verbiage of a presentation. Examples and illustrations, on the other hand, are qualitative. They are the circumstantial evidence that furnishes "soft" proof or clarification. For conceptual thinkers, they add perspective to concrete data and enliven a presentation with "human interest" situations.

Contrasts and Comparisons

An audience may be moved to recognize and accept the veracity of a point when the point is set in contrast against or compared with something else.

A contrast highlights the distinct difference between two things. Juxtaposing opposites accentuates the differences and can heighten the effect of a point, such as contrasting rich and poor, low revenues and high expenditures, educated as opposed to illiterate, automated versus manual. For example, to emphasize the value of caring for customers, a presenter related an incident of bad service in contrast to an incident of excellent service. Another speaker presented a hypothetical verbal illustration in contrast with a factual example. He described, hypothetically, what conditions would be like if the country were operating with a budget surplus as opposed to the facts of operating under a deficit. The effect was startling. The impact on the audience was far greater than it would have been had the speaker simply recited statistics in the trillions of dollars or rehashed the problems resulting from a budget deficit.

While a contrast focuses on the difference between two things, a comparison identifies similarities and/or differences between two or more items or issues. Sales presentations exemplify the use of comparison to influence the way people view something. A carefully researched or well-developed comparison can be convincing because it suggests the audience assess or reevaluate an item or idea on the basis of:

- *A comparison with a like item or idea.* Salespeople, for example, commonly compare the advantages and disadvantages of products of the same or similar type.

- *A comparison of differing degrees or circumstances,* such as comparing rates, locales, time frames, occurrences, amounts, and the like. A presenter might make a point more persuasively, for instance, by comparing the benefits of owning a product with the drawbacks of doing without it, the cost of an item compared to competitive items, current rates compared to previous rates, features in this location compared to other locations, or a minimum order compared to quantity discounts.

Another form of comparison is an **analogy**, which highlights the likeness between two things that are otherwise unlike in structure or function. An analogy operates like a mathematical equation in that it first establishes the value of "X" (as being true or untrue), then relates an aspect of "X" to a comparable or similar aspect of "Y." An analogy thus supplies evidence on the premise that if this is true (or untrue) of "X," this must likewise be true (or untrue) of "Y." (In this explanation, comparing an analogy to a mathematical equation is an analogy.)

Analogies are useful devices. A well-conceived analogy is creative and intriguing, and so invites attention from the audience. By presenting a fresh perspective, an analogy can clarify a vague concept or help to promote an unpopular one. An analogy developed for the theme of a presentation can unify the message, the analogy being the common thread that ties the key points together. These facets of an analogy are demonstrated by the following examples.

- Winston Churchill drew an analogy between politics and war when he observed, "Politics are almost as exciting as war." In what respect are the two different endeavors alike? Both entail fighting for what you believe; in both, opponents engage in conflict. The comparison appeals to the curiosity of the audience. What is the speaker getting at? Churchill explained, "In war you can only be killed once, but in politics many times." The point is: political life is brutal. Use of an analogy makes the point in an unexpected manner with a humorous twist.

■ A training professional, presenting a workshop on a recent change unpopular with many employees in the audience, developed an analogy between organizational change and the change by which a caterpillar advantageously transforms itself into a butterfly.

■ Business leader Max De Pree, author of *Leadership Jazz,* suggested in the book that an organization is analagous to a jazz band. De Pree introduced the analogy by pointing out likenesses between the two. "Jazz-band leaders must choose the music, find the right musicians, and perform—in public. But the effect of the performance depends on so many things—the environment, the volunteers playing in the band, the need for everybody to perform as individuals and as a group, the absolute dependence of the leader on the members of the band, the need of the leader for the followers to play well."* The comparision is striking and illuminates many points relating to organizational leadership. Moreover, since it is referenced at various points throughout the book (which is a presentation in print), the analogy reinforces the theme and adds cohesiveness to the message.

As interesting and useful as they are, analogies need to be developed and applied with caution. An analogy is presumptive in nature: the presenter presumes that the audience will accept the premise of the comparison. Thus, analogies do not furnish proof beyond a reasonable doubt. The likeness a presenter draws by analogy must be clear, acceptable, or forceful enough to offset the differences in the things compared. Otherwise, the audience may perceive the presenter is stretching the point. Skeptics or critics will find in a weak analogy an opportunity to reject or object to the message. Since analogies are more subjective than objective in nature, they are best suited to substantiate or elucidate concepts or ideas. Analogies are less useful as support for issues or proposals that require concrete evidence for approval.

Quotations

The popular eighteenth century English author, Dr. Samuel Johnson, suggested, "Every quotation contributes something to the stability or enlarge-

---

* Max De Pree, *Leadership Jazz* (New York: Doubleday, 1992), p. 8.

ment of the language." Quotations can also contribute to the stability of a presenter's message, provided they are selected and used with care. To use quotations with care means, first, that a speaker "give credit where credit is due" and cite the originator or source of the quotation. It also means that a person's words are never quoted out of context. Presenters who value their integrity, and their reputation with the audience, are guided by honesty when quoting others. Misquotes, partial quotes (similar to half-truths), and quotes presented out of context are abuses of a presenter's role and influence. They also make a presenter suspect if members of an audience recognize that material has been quoted or applied incorrectly. Finally, quotations should be used sparingly. To repeatedly quote others can suggest that the presenter lacks originality or adequate evidence of other types to substantiate the message.

Quotations furnish the greatest degree of substantiation when they are from recognized and respected authorities on a subject or known leaders in a field. Such quotes are then testimonials to the validity of a point. They are intended to prompt the audience to conclude, "If *she* said it, it must be true" or "If that's what *he* thinks, I'll think it, too." Quoting a person who is unknown to the audience offers little in the way of support. When a presenter is uncertain if the audience will recognize the name of the person quoted, the quote should be prefaced with a brief reference to the person's credentials or authority. For example, the preceding paragraph began by quoting Dr. Samuel Johnson. Since the great lexicographer (quoted often during his own lifetime) is someone with whom many people today may not be familiar, he is identified as "the popular eighteenth century author."

Audiovisual Aids

Points in the body of a message are often best substantiated or clarified with audiovisual aids. As vocal and visual forms of evidence, they can influence an audience more than words alone will do. The creation and use of effective audiovisuals are discussed in detail in Chapter 6 "Supporting Material."

Audience Participation

A technique often overlooked by presenters, inviting the audience to take part in a presentation can supply evidence for a point. Three methods are useful for this purpose.

1. *Survey.* The presenter poses a question to audience members, in the manner of conducting an informal, on-the-spot survey. Their expected response proves the presenter's point. For example, on the subject of retirement planning, a financial consultant made the point that social secu-

rity payments were not keeping pace with cost-of-living increases. He asserted this was cause for concern and then asked the audience, "If I could see a show of hands, how many of you are concerned about not having sufficient income for your retirement?" Almost every person in the audience raised a hand.

2. *Demonstration.* The presenter asks a person(s) in the audience to assist in a demonstration, the outcome of which substantiates a point. In a seminar on writing procedures, a presenter used this technique to convey that procedures must be thorough and explicit. She asked people in the audience to write a procedure for a simple task: preparing a peanut butter and jelly sandwich. Placing on the head table the requisite supplies (a loaf of bread, a jar of peanut butter, a jar of jelly, and a knife), she asked for two volunteers from the audience: one to read the procedure they had written, the other to follow along as the procedure was read and make a sandwich accordingly. In addition to injecting humor into the presentation, the demonstration quickly proved the speaker's point.

Inviting members of the audience to take part in a product demonstration is a useful technique in sales situations as well. Giving prospects a "hands-on" experience can enhance their comfort level with a new product, instill a "sense of ownership," and add a further stimulus to influence a buying decision.

3. *Exercise.* Activities that give people the opportunity to practice a skill or technique, exercises are common in instructional presentations. They can also be used in other types of presentations, including speeches. For example, in a motivational message on building self-esteem, the presenter made a point about visualization. To clarify the point, he talked the audience through an exercise in visualization.

Each of these techniques must be applied with caution. The situation a speaker sets up should have a predictable outcome. To ask a question that may elicit an unexpectedly unfavorable response would defeat the purpose of inviting audience participation to substantiate a point. A cautious presenter will also consider if using a certain technique is appropriate to the presentation event. To ask for volunteers from the audience to take part in a demonstration would, for example, be inappropriate in a formal setting.

The Value of Variety

The foregoing descriptions of the various forms of evidence attest to the many options a presenter has for developing the body of a message. A speaker can (and should) express and elucidate key points through a combination of different types of substantiating material. Variety is not only the

spice of life, it is the spice of a presentation. Combining concrete information and conceptual ideas increases the probability of reaching everyone in
an audience. Presenting factual evidence together with that which appeals
to feelings builds meaning on both levels of comprehension, and thus helps
make a presentation more memorable. An audience will quickly tire of a
presentation that consists entirely of abbreviated statistics or of long, drawn-
out examples. Alternating the forms of evidence used helps sustain interest
and build believability.

Reflection Questions

Would you describe yourself as someone who thinks more in concrete
terms or more conceptually? What types of evidence appeal to you? What
about some of the people with whom you work or to whom you present?
What types of evidence do they need to hear to be convinced?

Key Concept 29

*The opener is prepared from one or a combination of different
forms of expression that best capture audience attention.*

After the body, the opener is the next component of substance to be prepared. (Of the five components of a presentation, you may recall that the
preview and review are the second and third to be prepared. However, since
they are synopses of the key points, they are not considered part of the *substance* of a message. You will find an example of a preview and a review in
the sample situation at the end of this chapter.)

Different forms of expression can be used to develop an opener.
Although some are the same as those used for the body, it is preferable to
use an abbreviated form for the opener. A speaker who elaborates at length
at the very beginning of a presentation risks losing the attention of the
audience, which defeats the purpose of the opener.

An opener is prepared from any one, or a combination, of these forms of
expression:

- Anecdote
- Quotation
- Declaration

- Definition
- Rhetorical question
- Scenario
- Audiovisual aid

A description and examples of the various types of openers follow. For comparison, all of the examples are related to the subject of "Leadership." As you review them, bear in mind that a strong opener reflects originality and foreshadows the theme of the message. It is expressively stated. A sense of purpose is implicit in a strong opener. From the moment the speaker voices the first few words, the audience perceives they will receive value because they perceive the presenter has a purpose in mind and means to get down to business. Frequently, the best openers are the result of composing a number of alternatives, then selecting the one that will have the greatest effect.

Anecdote

An **anecdote** describes an incident that draws the audience into the message through the quality of the narrative. It may be dramatic, amusing, a reference that establishes commonality with the audience, biographical or autobiographical, or a combination of several of these qualities. An anecdote is synonymous with a verbal illustration or a story. As such, when an anecdote is delivered with feeling, it can inject into the very beginning of a presentation the benefits of a well-told story (covered in Chapter 5).

A speaker related this anecdote as an opener to his presentation on the subject of leadership.

It was 1931. The country was plagued by the Great Depression. I was 16 years old and went scrounging for work that summer. I found it all right! aboard a cargo ship bound for South America. As the ship sailed out of San Francisco Bay, my heart pounded in anticipation of adventure. I was not disappointed. Working as a lowly deckhand in those days was no picnic, but I soon discovered the lure and a love of the sea. I'll never forget one experience in particular: an afternoon, brilliant with tropic sunlight, when a wide-eyed boy watched in wonder from the railing as our ship slipped through the Panama Canal. Thirty years later I was back: no longer a wide-eyed boy, but the officer in command of all military port operations. You see, there was something else I discovered during those first months and many more years at sea: something of what it takes to be a leader. A ship needs a sure course, a steady crew, and a strong captain. So does an organization.

Quotation

Although quotations were discussed under the previous Key Concept 28 as a form of evidence, two factors are especially important when using a quotation as an opener. First, in order to spark interest or arouse curiosity, the name of the person quoted should be recognizable. It may be a prominent business leader, athlete, entertainer, politician, celebrity, best-selling author, or someone known to be an expert in the field. In addition, whereas a quotation as evidence is specific to the point it supports, a quotation as opener must be general enough to embrace the overall theme of the message.

A training professional, addressing a group of senior managers in a leadership development seminar, opened her presentation this way.

> General George Patton, who successfully led troops under his command to many victories during World War II, observed: "Wars may be fought with weapons, but they are won by men. It is the spirit of the men who follow and of the man who leads that gains the victory."

(To relate the quotation to the purpose of the seminar, she continued.)

> Today, we are fighting another kind of war—a war to regain our leadership on economic fronts. We will win only if we practice the spirited leadership that fosters a winning spirit in the men and women who work for this company.

Declaration

A declaration is a statement of a fact or an assertion that is based on sufficient evidence to be perceived to be fact. To cause an audience to sit up and take notice, a declaration must be succinct and expressed emphatically, with confidence.

Addressing a local community conference of business and professional people, the keynote speaker opened his presentation with the following declaration.

> American business is in danger. It is in danger because of a lack of leadership. And you and I, ladies and gentlemen, are largely responsible.

(The presenter then went on to explain his contention and suggested solutions to the problem.)

Definition

Defining a term can be an effective opener if the term is used in an unexpected way, or if the definition is unusual, surprising, or thought-provoking. For instance, Denis Waitley, recognized worldwide as an authority on human potential, offered a unique perspective on the definition of *opportunity* in his presentation of "Seeds of Greatness." Waitley pointed out that the Chinese symbols for the word *crisis* are identical to those for the word *opportunity*. The message then relates how, by viewing crises as opportunities, people can better adapt to change and move on toward success.

In a course on leadership for continuing education students, the instructor used an etymological definition in the opener to the first class meeting. (A comprehensive dictionary indicates the etymology, or derivation, of many words.) This example indicates how combining forms (in this case, a definition, rhetorical question, and declaration) can enhance the effect of an opener.

> Successful leaders demonstrate many attributes—one of which is discipline. The word *discipline* is derived from the Latin word *discipere,* which translates *to grasp.* What does grasping have to do with discipline? Just this. In order to grasp the opportunities to advance to a position of leadership, you must be disciplined: to complete assigned tasks, tackle tough problems, and persist through difficult situations.

Rhetorical Question

A rhetorical question is asked for effect, not to elicit information or a response. A rhetorical question engages an audience because it prompts people to reflect on how they would answer the question. Well-stated rhetorical questions can be a striking way to open a presentation because they stimulate interest and imply involvement of the audience. Questions may also preview the points the presenter will address, thus setting the stage and preparing the audience for the message.

To open a seminar on leadership development, a speaker posed the following rhetorical questions.

> What constitutes "leadership"? What personal qualities and professional skills do you look for in a leader? How does one develop the nature of a leader who can meet the business, social, and political demands of this decade?

Scenario

A **scenario** is synonymous with a verbal illustration in that it creates, through the use of words, a *scene* in the minds of people in the audience. According to the literal definition of the term, a scenario is an outline of a play, opera, motion picture, or theatrical work. This original definition suggests a quality that distinguishes scenarios from verbal illustrations. A scenario is inherently dramatic. It describes a tragic, comic, suspenseful, or stirring situation. Like verbal illustrations, a scenario may be either factual or hypothetical.

The president of a community action agency opened his presentation at the annual meeting of the board of directors with the following scenario.

> Two young boys who lived in a small country town were out playing one afternoon. They played kick-the-can for awhile; went down to the pond and skipped pebbles across the water; but it wasn't long before they grew bored with their usual games. So, as young boys (and sometimes grown boys) will do, they set out to create some mischief. They decided to go tease the old man who lived on the edge of town. On their way, crossing a field to his house, they came upon an injured bird lying on the ground. One of the boys picked up the bird and cupped it in his hands. When they arrived at the old man's house, they found him seated on his front porch. The one boy held out his hands and said to the old man, "I've got a bird in here. Can you guess: is it alive or dead?" The old man was wise to their tricks. He looked the boy square in the eye and replied, "Well, now, that depends on you." "What d'ya mean?" the boy asked. The old man answered, "If I say it's alive, you can crush that bird between your hands and kill it. But if I say it's dead, you can open your hands and nourish it back to life. So you see, whether that fragile creature lives or dies is up to you." Ladies and gentlemen, whether this organization dies or thrives depends on you and the kind of leadership you are willing to contribute to this community.

Audiovisual Aid

An audiovisual aid can be a creative and unexpected way to open or to augment the opener to a presentation. A speaker demonstrated the effectiveness of audiovisual openers when she began her presentation with colorful photographic slides.

> Accompanied by rousing inspirational music, the slides featured in quick succession: a football team, a military unit, a dance troupe, a group of assembly line workers, little league baseball players, and an orchestra (to name a few). As the slide presentation drew to a close, the presenter addressed the group. "In every field of endeavor," she declared, "the quality of leadership guides the performance of the team."

Characteristics of an Effective Opener

Function is more important than form. After preparing a form of opener, a presenter should ask, "How well does this opener function?" If the answer is "yes" to at least one (and preferably two or three) of the questions listed below, the opener *may* be effective.

- Is it piercing?
- Is it startling?
- Is it dramatic?
- Is it humorous?
- Is it suspenseful?
- Is it challenging?
- Is it thought-provoking?
- Is it emotive?
- Is it a familiar reference with which the audience will identify that will be of interest to them?

The preceding paragraph emphasized: the opener *may* be effective if it exhibits some of these characteristics. An additional and significant factor that determines how well an opener works is the manner in which it is communicated by the speaker. The opener is to a presentation what the kick-off is to a football game. It should be so well-rehearsed that the speaker can deliver the opener without faltering. It must be presented with ease, expressiveness, conviction—and without referring to notes.

Ineffective Openers

There are two types of openers a presenter should refrain from using: the commonplace introduction and the unnecessary joke.

Commonplace Introduction.   A speaker steps to the front of the room and says something like this: "Good morning, my name is Jan Smythe. I appreciate the opportunity to speak to you today. I have just a few comments I want to make that I think are important." Nothing the speaker has said thus far would capture attention, spark interest, or build anticipation on the part of the audience. Furthermore, the repeated reference to "I" detracts from the message because it implies that the speaker is more concerned with self than with the audience. With respect to the opener, a presentation is like a horse race: it's crucial to make a fast start out of the gate and immediately give the audience a glimpse of what they came for.

Jokes.   For numerous reasons, beginning a presentation with a joke is ineffective—especially in business and professional presentations. Many speakers lack the ability to deliver a joke with the comedic inflection and timing that might make the joke funny. What is amusing to some people may not be amusing to others. Some jokes are in poor taste; others have sexist or ethnic overtones. The presenter who uses them risks offending persons in the audience. Too often, a joke is one the audience has heard before; worse, it has no relevance to the subject of the presentation. Bad jokes, or good jokes badly told, produce an effect contrary to that which a presenter wants to achieve with the opener. Considering the many other ways in which a speaker can open a presentation, resorting to jokes is unnecessary and should be avoided.

Reflection Questions

Recalling presentations you have attended, what openers have you heard that caught your attention? What kind of openers did not?

Key Concept 30

An effective close asks the audience to do that which will satisfy the speaker's objectives.

Although it is composed last, a substantive close echoes the aspect of a presentation that was (or should have been) prepared first: the objectives. In effect, the close brings a presentation full circle by asking the audience to act in response to the message in a manner that will satisfy the objectives. The concluding appeal must be explicit. A presenter who understands anything about human nature will not leave it to the audience to translate the message into action. A speaker should never assume that the audience will make the effort, or will correctly surmise what they are supposed to do next. A guiding question for a speaker to ask when preparing the close is, "What, specifically, do I want this audience to do?"

There are, basically, three types of closes: a reminder, an application, and a request for approval. Informational presentations (especially those of an instructional nature that occur in a series of sessions) may make use of the first two types. Promotional presentations use the last type to secure approval for the product, service, or issue presented. The selected form of close is communicated after the speaker relates a summary review of the key points of the message. The review is stated in such a way that it bridges naturally to the close. Each type of close is described here.

Reminder

A reminder closes the message by reiterating, with emphasis, a crucial or dominant point of the message. As such, it may be derived from the core concept. It reflects the supporting objective of bringing the audience to understand or accept. As an example, a speaker closed his presentation on the subject of leadership by stating:

> Remember, like the captain of a ship, *you* stand at the helm of your department. You must chart and steer a sure course, and then see that it is carried out by giving responsible direction to the employees who make up your crew.

Application

As the term implies, an **application close** suggests specifically how the presenter wants the audience to apply the message. It directs the audience to take a *next step* following completion of the presentation. An application close is identified by words like *try, practice, write, read,* and *reflect.* For example, after reviewing the key points, a presenter closed her message in this manner:

> During the next month read at least one book on leadership. Then, to integrate into your management style the techniques successful leaders practice, each week select one idea you will put into practice, too.

Request for Approval

As previously mentioned, this form of close is used with promotional presentations. There are two variations of the request-for-approval close. The version a presenter uses depends on the nature of the promotion as to whether it is subtle or overt.

Some promotional presentations are conducted ostensibly for the purpose of advising or informing people. This is frequently the case with seminars presented for the public by professionals (accountants, attorneys, stockbrokers, realtors, cosmetics consultants, and the like) or public and community relations presentations. Although the audience may have one reason for attending, the presenter has another objective in mind. The presentation is intended as a vehicle to promote the firm, a product, a service, or an issue. In this more subtle form of promotional presentation, the speaker closes with a suggestion. The phrases "I encourage you to . . . ," "I urge you to . . . ," "You'll find value in . . . ," and "You will benefit from . . ."

suggest what the presenter wants the audience to do, such as, "I encourage you to enroll in the BestWays course on Leadership for the 21st Century."

In other cases, namely sales situations, the presentation is unmistakably for the purpose of promoting a product or service. Both audience and presenter understand that the salesperson is presenting a proposal that the audience will approve or not. Salespeople are well-acquainted with the term *close*. In selling situations, a close translates to obtaining an order. In most cases, a sales presenter won't obtain an order without asking for it.

There are three common approaches to the close of a sales presentation.

- The *assumed* close (so called because it assumes the prospect's approval) states something like, "If you'll sign here, we'll get this on order for you right away."

- The *options* close presents two or three options, and asks a question that prompts the audience to choose, such as, "Would you prefer this with or without feature X?"

- A *scheduling* close asks, "When would be the best time to schedule delivery of the product?" (or start-up of the service).

With the options and scheduling closes, a smooth transition is afforded by the phrases "Based on what you've seen (or heard)," or "In view of what we've discussed." For example, "Based on what you've heard, would you prefer that we start the service on the first or at the end of the month?"

Presentations done for fund-raising or project approval, although not usually referred to as such, are situations in which the presenter is (or should be) selling. In such cases, either of the two types of request-for-approval closes could be used. A planning department analyst, for example, might close with the statement, "I urge you to give your unanimous approval to this project." A fund-raiser might ask the closing question, "Given the need you've heard about today, would you prefer to make a donation at the sponsor or at the contributor level?"

A Concluding Question
for the Presenter

An audience is more apt to respond affirmatively to the close when the content that precedes it has "paved the way." In other words, the content provides appropriate and sufficient reason for the audience to do what the close asks or suggests. After preparing the close, review the narrative of the presentation and ask, "Will the substance of this presentation activate *this* audience to do what I'm asking them to do?"

Key Concept 31

Countless resources are readily available for finding material from which to prepare the substance of a presentation.

The point has been made that people are inundated with data. The current Information Age creates a need for skilled presenters—people adept at distilling and communicating information and ideas. The Information Age creates a challenge for presenters: to discover and employ means to capture audience attention and improve retention. A third aspect of the Information Age is a singular advantage for presenters. Today, to an extent previously unimaginable, it is relatively inexpensive and easy to locate material on virtually every subject. Whether a presenter is seeking hard evidence to substantiate a key point or looking for a quotation for an opener, a wealth of information is readily available from a vast array of resources and research tools.

Types of Sources

Material can be found by checking three sources: internal, external, and personal. Internal sources of information are those which can be found within the organization for which a person works. External sources are found outside of one's organization. A presenter's own experience, knowledge, and creativity are a personal source of information and ideas.

Using material from all three sources provides balance and can infuse into a presentation a quality of originality and a greater degree of credibility. A presentation that relies entirely on statistics from an organization's research department, or one which refers exclusively to personal experience, is not likely to maintain as much interest as a message that alternately refers to various sources. The substance of a message might include, for example, statistics obtained from an external agency, a comparison from an internal survey, a verbal illustration from personal experience, or a quotation from an external publication.

Specific resources for researching and locating material are listed here, under the categories of "conventional" and "contemporary." Conventional resources include items with which most people are familiar, and are typically manual forms of information. Contemporary resources are those which have developed (and which are expanding) coincident with the Information Age and make use of high-speed computer and telecommunications technologies. Not all of the resources listed would be applicable to every presentation. A speaker would narrow the list and select resources on the basis of the nature of the presentation event, the subject, and the audience.

Many of the conventional resources could be included under the broad heading "publications." However, they are listed separately as a reminder of items that are often overlooked. A person who is in the habit of reading a newspaper every day, for example, might neglect to view it as a resource for presentation material. Someone who reads for pleasure may miss picking up from books quotations or anecdotes that would be ideal for use in a presentation.

Conventional Resources

- Annual reports
- Audio and video programs
- Budgets and financial statements
- Books
- Brochures and catalogs
- Interviews
- Journals
- Magazines
- Newsletters
- Newspapers
- Reports
- Research results
- Transcripts (e.g., of meetings, public hearings, television broadcasts)
- Television (in particular documentaries, speeches, and news programs)

In addition to the preceding resources, information can be obtained from organizations which conduct or acquire research on a regular basis. Many local community agencies, government departments, business and professional associations, and technical groups furnish requested material free of charge or for a nominal cost.

Contemporary Resources

Rapid advancements in technology, coupled with consequent changes in the marketplace, make any list of contemporary resources subject to change from one day to the next. Currently, the primary ones include:

- Computer software programs
- Database research services
- Information brokers

Computer Software Programs. With respect to preparing the content of a presentation, software programs are available that help a presenter generate ideas, outline a message, find quotations, and speed research. Some programs are featured on floppy diskettes. Others are available exclusively on CD-ROM (Compact Disk-Read Only Memory). CD-ROM technology has increased the density of data storage to the extent that many research and reference documents are contained on a single compact disk (encyclopedias, legal citations, dictionaries, classical literature, climatic data, maps, and satellite imagery, to name a few). Using a personal computer, a presenter can now take advantage of immediate access to the equivalent of a university library. Details about programs that are currently available can be obtained from retail outlets, computer consultants, distributors, computer industry publications, user groups, and software producers.

Database Research Services. A **database** is a collection of related records of information stored and organized on computer for rapid retrieval. Database research services maintain massive libraries on mainframe computers and function as service bureaus to computer users who subscribe to the service. Subscription fees and rates for accessing libraries vary. From a personal computer equipped with communications capability, subscribers have on-line access to four kinds of research databases: full text, bibliographic, real-time, and computer information.

Full text libraries contain both numerical and textual data: financial and demographic statistics; newspaper, magazine, and journal articles; technical reports; and extracts from reference books. Bibliographic databases furnish citations only (as opposed to the full text), of book titles, book reviews, government publications, dissertations, articles, patents, conference papers, congressional publications, and the like. Real-time data is ephemeral in that it is updated and replaced by new information that is continuously incoming, such as stock market and weather reports. Computer databases, as the name implies, feature computer software information, helps, and user bulletin boards.

The value of database research lies in the facility with which users can locate current and accurate information on virtually every field of inquiry (even the most esoteric). The use of simple key words narrows years of study and volumes of data to a list of specific references. In a matter of minutes, proficient database users can produce in-depth, up-to-date material on subjects that might otherwise take weeks or even months to explore. Since there are hundreds of research databases from which to choose, many users find it more cost-effective to use a research annex such as *IQuest* (available through CompuServe Information Service), which features over 800 publications and databases, with helps for computerized searches.

Information Brokers.   Often referred to as "electronic librarians," information brokers offer an alternative to doing one's own research. They are especially useful when finding substantive material for a high-stakes presentation that would entail a laborious, time-consuming effort, or when conventional research methods yield only inadequate or outdated information. Information brokers can be located by consulting The Association of Independent Information Professionals (which has more than 400 members) or The Burwell Directory of Information Brokers (which lists more than 1200 brokers). The directory is available in many libraries.

Reflection Question

Of the resources listed above, which one or two that you have not previously used do you think may prove helpful to you in the future?

Key Concept 32

Selection guidelines help a presenter determine which material to choose and how much to use for a given presentation.

With the staggering volume of information that is readily available, even a cursory search of resources often yields more material than is needed for a given presentation. How, then, does a presenter choose between what to use and what to discard (or reserve for another occasion)? The four "tests" outlined below provide guidelines for selecting material. Each one lists criteria that help determine inclusion (or exclusion) of an idea or item of information.

The "Yes" Test

In the process of distilling information for a presentation, this is the first filter through which material must pass. No item should be considered for inclusion unless the following questions can be answered "Yes."

Is this item (information or idea):

- Correct? Are the statistics accurate? Is the example a true picture of the situation? Is the author quoted correctly?

- Current? Is the concrete evidence up-to-date? If conceptual material (verbal illustration, anecdote, quotation) is dated, is the concept up-to-date? Does the material address a current issue, interest, or concern?

- Consistent with the conclusion? Is there any disparity between what this material conveys and the conclusion I want the audience to reach? Does the underlying message of this information or idea coincide with the overall message of this presentation?

In addition to being viewed in terms of consistency with the conclusion, material should also be considered in terms of whether it contributes to the conclusion. Some presenters exhibit a tendency to try to do and say too much—more than is necessary or more than is feasible within the allotted time frame. Accomplished speakers identify what points require evidence, and then ask, "Does this item furnish proof or clarification? Does it augment the message?" In other words, is it necessary?

The "Spice" Test

Selecting and mixing material for a message can be likened to preparing a stew. Ingredients that pass the first "Yes" test are the meat and potatoes of the recipe. However, meat and potatoes alone don't make for a very enticing meal. A recipe that pleases people (and leaves them wanting seconds) adds spices. The following questions help a presenter ascertain if an item will add spice to the message. It is unlikely and unnecessary that every question would be answered "Yes" for each piece of material. It will add to the import of a message if, for each item, the answer is "Yes" to at least one of the questions.

Is the item (idea or information):

- Interesting? Is this something people want to know? Will it arouse curiosity? Is it an "eye-opener" that will help sustain attention?

- Invigorating? Will it stimulate the audience to think? Will it enliven, add strength, or contribute to the energy of the message?

- Inspiring? Will this induce a good, uplifting feeling in people? Is it hopeful, stirring, encouraging?

- In good taste? For each item considered, the answer to this question should be a resounding "Yes." Nothing should be included in a business presentation that is not in good taste.

The "Litmus" Test

The term **litmus test**, derived from chemistry, refers to a test that indicates the composition of a substance. It is a decisive test. With respect to the substance of a presentation, it is the final test by which a speaker ultimately decides whether material should be included or not. This test questions those factors (depicted in Figure 4-2) which are decisive in determining the success of a presentation. When the content of a message has been well developed, every one of the following questions will be answered "Yes."

Audience.   Does the content of this message accurately aim at the people to whom it will be delivered? Will it "speak" to this audience?

Subject.   Is every idea and item of information related to the subject? Is the subject effectively addressed through a balanced mixture of concrete and conceptual evidence?

Objectives.   Is the content of the message sufficiently substantive to support achievement of the objectives?

Setting.   Is the message appropriate to the setting?

Time Frame.   Can the content be presented within (or under) the allotted time frame?

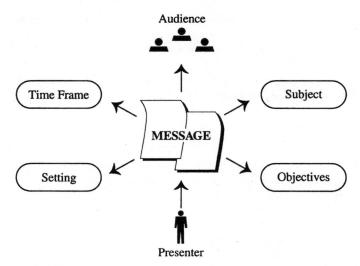

Figure 4-2. Decisive factors.

Business leader, best-selling author, and speaker Max De Pree observed that "the unexamined message is not worth giving."* It is not worth giving a presentation that has not been examined in terms of the audience, the subject, the objectives, the setting, and the time frame. The point is reiterated throughout this course because every aspect of a message—verbal and nonverbal alike—must be considered in relation to these factors in order to produce a presentation that will prove effective.

The "Time" Test

Among the factors depicted in Figure 4-2 is time frame. Familiar with the adage "to err is human," most people forgive (or simply don't notice) many of the shortcomings that may appear in a presentation. Most people do notice, and few react kindly toward, a presentation that exceeds its allotted time. Therefore, when compiling the content of a message, it is imperative to consider how much time to allocate to each segment and to select material accordingly.

In addition to the time-frame considerations discussed in Chapter 2 ("Planning Your Presentation," Key Concept 15), follow these guidelines:

- The opener and preview together should not exceed two minutes.
- The summary and close together should take no more than one or two minutes.
- Discounting time for audience interaction or a question-and-answer period (if applicable), the remaining time should be relatively evenly distributed among the two or three key points of the body of the message.

In the case of a 30-minute presentation, the time might be estimated as follows:

Opener and preview:	2 minutes
Summary and close:	1 minute
Questions at end:	5 minutes
Body of message:	22 minutes

Assuming the message consisted of three key points, approximately 7 minutes of content would be developed for each key point. In actuality, one key point may be addressed in 6 minutes, the next in 5, and the third in 8: a total of 19 minutes. This example raises two points. First, 19 minutes falls

* De Pree, *Leadership Jazz*, p. 31.

3 minutes short of the total of 22 available. If this were the case, the presenter may finish ahead of schedule—a fact most audiences would appreciate. The greater likelihood is that the total time would be used because speakers have a tendency to ad lib, to elaborate examples, or to take longer than anticipated to communicate a point. Thus, care should be taken to ensure that the amount of material selected will not exceed the amount of time allocated for the presentation. Once the content is prepared, it is essential to rehearse the presentation to time it. Simply proofreading prepared text typically takes less time than when it is actually presented aloud to an audience.

The second point raised by the foregoing example relates to balance. Many presentations are flawed because a disproportionate amount of time is spent on the first key point. The effectiveness of a presentation is jeopardized when, for example, a speaker devotes 15 minutes to cover the first point in detail, comments on the second point in a cursory manner in 5, and then hurriedly skims over the last point in a minute or two. An audience will perceive the imbalance. The presenter may be considered disorganized. If the points have been sequenced to build to a climactic conclusion, the effect will be lost. The second and third points may be presented with insufficient evidence to be convincing.

Summary

A believable presentation is based on substantive content that is developed from a balanced mix of concrete and conceptual evidence. Various types of evidence and material are used to compose the body, the opener, and the close of a presentation. Ideas and information are found by searching conventional and contemporary resources. Inclusion of material in the content of a message is determined by applying selection guidelines.

Sample Situation

Presentation Content

According to a study by AT&T and Stanford University, effective speaking before a group is the primary predictor of upward mobility. After reading about the study, Nancy Hoskins joined a speakers' association. Several weeks later, she was offered the opportunity to make a 5-minute presentation on a topic of her choice at the group's next meeting. Since Nancy would be addressing people who had career aspirations, she decided it would be appropriate to speak on the subject of goal achievement. She prepared a presentation entitled "Go For The Goal." As you review the content of the message, identify: (*a*) the components of a presentation and (*b*) the various types of material used to make the content convincing.

In his best-selling book, *The 7 Habits of Highly Effective People,* author Stephen Covey contends that one way to put ourselves in control of our lives is: *"set a goal* and work to achieve it." For those of us who want to take control of our careers, it merits our attention to focus on these two essential factors: goals and the grit it takes to achieve them.

How important is it to define your goals? A study by Yale University suggests the answer. An initial survey of graduating seniors found that only 10 percent had specific, written goals. The majority—9 out of 10—were going out into the world of work with no specific goal in mind. The real significance of these findings was revealed in a follow-up study 20 years later. Compared to the majority of people who neglected to set goals: those few who had specific goals were measurably more productive professionally, better off financially, and expressed greater satisfaction personally.

In recent weeks, such findings have been vividly demonstrated. Many of you have probably watched televised broadcasts of this summer's Olympic competitions? If you have, you've seen and heard the evidence yourself. Every world-class, winning athlete testifies to the value of setting goals.

They also testify to the second aspect of goal achievement. It isn't enough to just set a goal. You have to go for it.

The popular American actor and humorist, Will Rogers, pointed out: "Even if you're on the right track, you'll get run over if you just sit there." Goal achievers aren't sitters. They are doers. And they do with determination and grit. Grit is the fortitude and endurance it sometimes takes to accomplish your aims.

Grit is exemplified by football players. What's at the end of a football field? A goal post. How does a player make a goal? By advancing the ball—sometimes with agonizing effort—into the end zone. On rare, very rare occasions, someone may get unusually lucky and complete a "Hail Mary" pass. But in most cases, it takes training, practice, showing up for every game, and toughing it out the full length of the field. A winning football player invests—time, talent, energy, skill, judgment, and experience—in the gritty endeavor of scoring goals.

Olympic athletes and football players aren't the only goal achievers with grit. Imelda Quintanar has grit, too. I mention Imelda Quintanar because she is someone whose name you probably don't recognize. Imelda Quintanar is just a regular person, like you and me. She is twenty-three years old, the first of six children to graduate from high school. Imelda was born and raised in a congested, decaying, gang-infested neighborhood in East Los Angeles. She lives in an area known as Los Barrios. For the past six years, Imelda attended college. For her, that meant making the tiresome commute between her home in Los Angeles and California State University in Long Beach. For her, that meant taking a couple of semesters off to make ends meet financially because Imelda had to support herself through school.

Recently, Imelda Quintanar became the first in her family to graduate from college. When she was asked what advice she would give other people, she answered in the Spanish language she first learned as a youngster: "y adelante con muchas ganas," which translates "Go forward with much desire." Early on, this young woman clearly set a goal: to graduate from college. It took grit and six years of hard work, but Imelda Quintanar achieved her goal.

What does it take to take control of your career? A goal and the grit to persistently pursue it. I encourage you: if you haven't defined your career goal, take some time this week to write it out, together with the plan of work you will follow to reach your goal.

Comprehension Check

The answers to the following appear on page 333.

1. A verbal illustration is _____.
   a. a concrete form of evidence
   b. a word picture
   c. a resource for information
   d. a statement of objective
   e. a channel of communication

2. An audience is more readily persuaded by a presentation that is _____.
   a. short
   b. emotive
   c. contemporary
   d. quantifiable
   e. believable

3. "Is every idea and item of information related to the subject?" is _____.
   a. a litmus test question
   b. a factor that builds believability
   c. a database research question
   d. an example of an opener
   e. an issue motivational speakers don't have to consider

4. In a presentation on child abuse, a speaker cited the number of cases that had been reported in the county during the previous year. The statement that represents the best way to convey the statistic is _____.
   a. almost double the number reported the previous year
   b. 19,345 cases last year
   c. too many for local agencies to handle
   d. 53 children abused every day—that we know of
   e. a 34 percent increase over cases reported three years ago

5. In the space provided, list the five "litmus test" factors that must be considered in order to produce an effective presentation.

_____

_____

_____

_____

_____

To Do

For the presentation you are preparing during this course, note some of the ideas and information you will use for substantiating material.

1. The body of the message. For each Key Point, write out one piece of concrete evidence and one of conceptual material.

Key Point 1:_____

Concrete_____

_____

Conceptual_____

_____

Key Point 2:_____

Concrete_____

_____

Conceptual_____

_____

Key Point 3:_____

Concrete_____

_____

Conceptual_____

_____

2. Opener. Write out two or three different forms of opener. Review the alternatives in relation to the questions listed under "Characteristics of an Effective Opener." Then, place a checkmark next to the opener you will use.

3. Write out the statement or question you will use to close your presentation.

4. Referring to the selection guidelines listed under Key Concept 32, review the material you have prepared thus far for the content of your presentation. Does it pass every test?

5

Style: Forms of Verbal Expression

Before embarking on a journey across a treacherous desert, a sultan consulted with his fortuneteller. The fortuneteller, hoping to assure the sultan of his safe return, said, "Sire, you will live to see all your family dead." Enraged, the sultan called for the executioner and ordered the fortuneteller led away. The next day, another fortuneteller was summoned to the palace. "Sire," he told the sultan, "you will be blessed with a long life. You will outlive your family." Delighted, the sultan rewarded the fortuneteller with a treasure chest filled with gold.

Both fortunetellers delivered essentially the same message. The outcome in each case was dramatically different because of the difference in an element crucial to presenting: style. Of the four stages to preparing a presentation (shown in Figure 3-1), the two discussed thus far—structure and substance—may be thought of as the "what" of a message. Style is the "how." Audience reception and response are influenced not only by what is said, but also by *how* it is said.

Style is critical to the success of many endeavors. In figure skating, for example, skaters give attention to the two criteria by which their routines will be evaluated: technical merit and artistic impression (style). Similarly, presenters must attend to the technicalities of structure and substance, as well as to the artistry of crafting a winning style. Like championship skaters, the most persuasive and dynamic presenters skillfully develop both the technical merit of the message and the impression they will create by the style with which the message will be delivered.

There are two aspects to a presenter's style: verbal and nonverbal (previously introduced in Chapter 1 as the channels of communication). Since they are expressed when the message is actually presented, vocal and visual

145

(nonverbal) elements are covered in Chapter 8. Continuing the discussion of stages to *prepare* a presentation, this chapter deals with the verbal element of style that is expressed through the content of a message.

Objectives

To understand the components of verbal style; to recognize the characteristics of effective verbal expression; and to be able to make use of various techniques to develop an appropriate and appealing verbal style.

Key Concepts

33. A presenter's use of language constitutes the verbal style of a presentation.

34. An effective verbal style is founded on four fundamentals: the language must be clear, correct, concise, and well-considered.

35. To influence and persuade, a presenter must use verbal expressions that reflect the attributes of an effective presentation.

36. Impact, interest, and variety are added to the verbal style of a message through the use of literary techniques, figures of speech, stories, and humor.

37. It is imperative to refrain from forms of expression that detract from the appeal of the presenter and/or the message.

Key Terms

To get the most from these concepts, it is essential that you understand the following terms:

Style	Reversal phrasing
Verbal expression	Assonance
Tone	Catchword
Pace	Hyperbole
Gobbledygook	Onomatopoeia
Denotation	Parallelism
Connotation	Figure of speech
Implication	Imagery
Synonyms	Metaphor
Euphemism	Simile
Emphatic word, emphatic phrasing	Personification
Antithesis	

Key Concept 33

A presenter's use of language constitutes the verbal style of a presentation.

Style is the manner in which a message is conveyed. It is the composite of choices a presenter makes, beginning during the planning stage and culminating in the face-to-face presentation to an audience. Some choices related to style are deliberate; others occur by default, typically when a presenter is unaware of or unconcerned with matters of style. A haphazard disregard for style can produce a haphazard result. To produce an intended result from a presentation, a speaker must consciously attend to choices of verbal style while preparing the content of a message.

Such choices pertain to a speaker's use of language. Language is the fabric from which the verbal style of a presentation is fashioned. Information and ideas are communicated through various forms of **verbal expression**, a generic term for the elements of language: words, phrases, sentences, and figures of speech. Thus, verbal style is composed of vocabulary, sentence structure and length, grammar and syntax, and techniques used for expressing the message.

Verbal Style Generates Tone

One factor that makes verbal style an important consideration when preparing content is that it accounts for the tone of a message. **Tone** is the feeling or impression an audience derives from a presentation. Although the two terms—style and tone—are sometimes confused, they are not synonymous. Tone is a result of style. Style is what the speaker conveys; tone is what the audience perceives. From one style, an audience will favorably perceive a tone that is courteous, confident, genuinely concerned, friendly, enthused, encouraging. A different style will produce the unfavorable effect of a tone that is brusque, bureaucratic, condescending, detached, demanding.

The tone of a presentation is, of course, affected by vocal and visual cues, but it originates with a presenter's use of language. The following examples suggest how differences in verbal style generate differences in tone.

> SPEAKER 1: Comprehensive analyses and assessments of departmental and interdepartmental operational strategies and procedures have determined the existence of conflicting organizational paradigms.
>
> SPEAKER 2: We have a problem here. You people need to shape up!
>
> SPEAKER 3: How many of you would like to improve communications and teamwork?

From the language they hear, people perceive a presenter's attitude toward the audience and the subject—and how comfortable the speaker is presenting.

Pace Is a Factor of Verbal Style

The term **pace** refers to the rate of movement or speed with which a presentation progresses. Although pace is set primarily by vocal and visual means, word choices and sentence structure affect the pace of a presentation. As the previous examples indicate, shorter words and sentences create a crisp pace; longer ones can slow the pace. Some presentations move along at a lively pace, using language that is easy to listen to. Others use language that requires a determined effort to listen to. If the language is laborious, people won't listen for long.

After drafting the content of a message, it is helpful to read the narrative aloud, paying particular attention to the pace of the language. Slowing to pronounce multisyllabic words, or gasping for breath before a sentence is finished, are clues that the pace may be too tedious. An audio recording of the message is useful for checking pace. If you find it tiresome to listen to the language of your presentation, it is probable the audience will, too; in which case the verbal style should be corrected before the message is presented.

Key Concept 34

An effective verbal style is founded on four fundamentals: the language must be clear, correct, concise, and well-considered.

Mark Twain found, "A powerful agent is the right word. Whenever you come upon one of those intensely right words . . . the resulting effect is physical as well as spiritual, and electrically prompt." What is an "electrically prompt" word? In colloquial terms, it is a "zinger"! It is a word that strikes mind and emotion with lightning-like effect. It illuminates meaning and jolts the audience to respond.

In the millions of presentations that occur every day, few of the words used are zingers. Still, many presentations are effective. Language need not be continuously powerful in order to influence and persuade. (If it were, it would probably exhaust the audience.) Although an effective verbal style does not require *intensely* right words, it does require words that are *right*. Right words are:

- Clear
- Correct
- Concise
- Well-considered

The content of a message should be prepared using language that reflects these fundamental qualities.

Clear

When the language a presenter uses is clear, the audience is more likely to interpret the message as the presenter intends. Explanatory material (such as examples and verbal illustrations) can help make a message clear, but word choice is the point at which clarity begins. Verbal style should be clarified for much the same reason that butter is clarified: to filter out impurities.

The "impurities" that muddy the meaning of a message include ambiguity, gobbledygook, jargon, and acronyms or abbreviations that may not be understood by everyone in the audience. To promote clear meaning, a presenter refrains from using such forms of expression.

Be Specific. The language of business communication is riddled with ambiguity. For instance, "substantial savings" and "satisfactory performance" are ambiguous phrases. How much is "substantial"? What is meant by "satisfactory"? Such expressions are not clear. An audience can understand them to mean something very different from what the presenter intends. By "substantial" a salesperson may mean a 10 percent savings while the prospect hearing the presentation may interpret "substantial" to mean 50 percent. When a manager speaks at a meeting on the matter of employee performance, what does the manager mean by "satisfactory"? What do employees interpret it to mean?

Omit Gobbledygook. The term **gobbledygook** applies to language that is long-winded, pompous, or so abstract as to be unintelligible to many listeners. Gobbledygook usually contains more than two syllables and is often (although not always) found in bureaucratic or institutional settings. Shown below are just a few examples of gobbledygook.

Ameliorate

Conceptualization

Facilitate

Manifestation

Paradigm

Proliferate

Ramifications

Veracious

Presenters who use gobbledygook to sound impressive or to appear more sophisticated neglect a chief principle of effective presentation: present from the perspective and for the benefit of the audience. With every decision related to a presentation—including the use of language—the rule-of-thumb is "when in doubt, don't." It is doubtful that gobbledygook will be *clearly* understood. As a case in point, use of the word "paradigm" has become popular in business circles in recent years, yet a survey of seminar participants found that only two or three out of every one hundred people could correctly define the term.

Eliminate Jargon.   Similar to gobbledygook, jargon is terminology that is part of the language of a particular occupation or profession. Jargon can be confusing to those outside of the profession. The use of special terminology should be restricted to only those words that will be clearly understood by everyone in the audience. All forms of legalese, medicalese, financialese, technical terms, and the like should be eliminated or replaced with words familiar to laypeople.

Explain Acronyms and Abbreviations.   Acronyms and abbreviations peculiar to an occupation or organization are a type of jargon. As science and technology have expanded, acronyms have increased in number. They are often used as a substitute for lengthy terminology (such as saying LAN rather than Local Area Network). One prominent technology company publishes an in-house directory of acronyms that employees might come across in their work. It contains more than 150 pages of acronyms—and is not an all-inclusive list. As with jargon, unless everyone in the audience will clearly understand the meaning, an acronym or abbreviation should only be used if its meaning is first explained.

In addition to the foregoing points, clarity also depends on choosing words that correctly convey what the presenter means to say.

Correct

Meaning is influenced by denotation, connotation, and implication. **Denotation** is the literal definition of a word. **Connotation** is a meaning suggested in addition to the literal definition. The connotation of a word may be derived from meaning that has evolved over time, a widely held historical or cultural reference, or the context in which the word is used. **Implication** refers to the meaning a presenter adds to a word or phrase, usually by means of descriptive adjectives or nonverbal cues. The following example illustrates how a literal definition (denotation) may differ from the understood meaning (connotation) of a word.

The primary literal definition of the noun "subordinate" is "a person lower in rank." In the past, the word was commonly used to denote employees who held positions that appeared lower on an organization chart than positions held by upper-level managers (who were often referred to as "superiors"). Over time, the term "subordinate" acquired negative connotations. When referred to as "subordinates," some people interpreted the word to mean that they were *not as good as* someone in a position higher up the organizational ladder. As to implication, favorable meaning might be added with the use of an adjective like "valued" (valued subordinate). Negative meaning might be implied by tone of voice, facial expression, or gesture. Since "subordinate" now conveys negative connotations (even when none are intended), the word has been replaced in many organizations with more neutral terms like "associate," "employee," "staff member," or "personnel."

Correct word choice and correct use of language requires consideration of the following points.

Politically Correct.   In recent years, the use of language that is "politically correct" has become increasingly popular. Politically correct language uses "low-risk" words—words like euphemisms (discussed under Key Concept 35), which have the least potential to offend or upset anyone in the audience. Candor is sometimes sacrificed for the sake of this type of "correctness." To what degree should a speaker be concerned with politically correct language? The answer depends upon what the speaker has at stake in terms of position and/or potential liability.

Correct Word Choice: New Words and Changing Meanings.   In mid-1992, a new edition of an English language dictionary was released. Of its 200,000 entries, 16,000 were words added since the previous edition of 10 years before (an average of 1600 new words a year)! In addition to new words, the updated edition reflects changing definitions. For example, it is now correct to use the word "anxious" to mean "eager." Originally, "anxious" (related to "anxiety") meant "nervous, worried, or uneasy."

As the means by which people in a culture communicate, language changes as the culture changes. Some new words, such as "infotainment" and "junk bonds," are created. Others, such as "guru" and "tsunami," are adopted into the English language from other languages. Definitions are changed by popular usage. When a word is widely used incorrectly over time, the incorrect use gains acceptance. It is estimated that, in view of the rapid pace of change, dictionaries will be updated every five to six years. For a message to be understood correctly, a presenter's verbal style may need to be updated, too.

Synonyms.   With a vocabulary almost twice that of any other language, the English language contains many **synonyms**: words that have the same or similar meaning as another word. When synonyms are available, the correct word is that which best denotes and connotes (according to current usage) exactly or most nearly the meaning the presenter wants the audience to receive.

Grammar and Syntax.   In oral presentations, pace and vocal inflection may mask certain errors in grammar and syntax. Some rules of grammar are relaxed for a conversational style of speaking, allowing more latitude than would be acceptable for formal or written presentations. However, in any presentation, the adage "better safe than sorry" applies. Correct grammar is not so important for the sake of strict adherence to rules as it is for the sake of what an audience perceives. From poor grammar an audience may perceive that the presenter lacks education or intelligence and therefore lacks credibility.

Syntax is the way in which words or phrases in a sentence are arranged to indicate their relationship to one another. Errors in syntax can result in mistaken meaning. A manager addressing a staff meeting meant to say that employees should do their best to serve customers, the people who spent their money with the business. Instead, he said, "Since they spend their money with us, employees should do their best to serve customers."

Correct Statements.   One definition of "correct" is "true." A verbal style that expresses points in a manner that people will perceive to be true qualifies statements when it is appropriate to do so. Unqualified statements use words like "no one," "never," and "nowhere" or "everyone," "always," and "everywhere." Examples of unqualified statements are shown here:

No one in the company follows procedures as they should.

Our competitors will *never* beat our price.

Nowhere in this region will you find better conditions.

Everyone here wants to improve teamwork.

Customers *always* complain about service.

All working men and women *everywhere* support deregulation.

Although unqualified statements are often used to emphasize a point, they imply that there is not a single exception to the rule. Believing that to be untrue, many people in an audience will reject the statement as being untrue. Qualifying words that temper a point can make a message more acceptable. Qualifiers are words like "few," "rarely," "unlikely," "many," "most," "often," and "highly probable."

An additional form of statement that lacks correctness because it is confusing is the nonstatement. A nonstatement leaves people shaking their heads with bewilderment. A classic example of a nonstatement is attributed to Yogi Berra: "When you come to a fork in the road, take it." As amusing as the expression is, it doesn't say anything. What is correct and true about a nonstatement? Who knows?

Malapropisms. In the jargon of professional speakers, a malapropism is a misspeak: a word spoken in error. It is the inappropriate (malapropos) use of a word that is similar in sound but different in meaning. Often, a misspeak is voiced because the presenter is nervous or excited. However, misspeaks confuse an audience or convey that the speaker lacks command of the language. One salesperson, presenting to a group of prospective buyers, mistakenly said, "Our competitors charge an exuberant price for this same product." (The salesperson meant to say an "exorbitant" price.)

In many cases, forms of expression that detract from a clear and correct verbal style can be avoided by using language that is concise.

Concise

Thomas Jefferson, chief author of the Declaration of Independence, suggested that "the most valuable of all talents is that of never using two words when one will do." The point describes a concise verbal style, which expresses a great deal of meaning with few words. Concise language reflects the principle of KISS—meaning "Keep It Short and Simple."

Shorter words and phrases are easier for a speaker to say and easier for an audience to listen to. They produce a livelier pace. A word with a one- or two-syllable sound is preferable to a multisyllabic word—if the meaning is essentially the same (and if the shorter word satisfies the considerations discussed under the next Key Concept 35).

Simpler words are characteristically clear and correct. It is less likely they will be misunderstood. Presenters are sometimes reluctant to use simple words, thinking that "simple" equates to "simplistic." It does not. Simple words are "simplified": refined to make the message clearer and thus easier for the audience to absorb.

The value of being concise is illustrated in the lists on the next page. Compare the words in the column at the left (the list of gobbledygook) with the synonyms at the right.

Gobbledygook	Short and Simple
Ameliorate	Improve
Conceptualization	Idea
Facilitate	Ease, help
Manifestation	Act, showing
Paradigm	Pattern, system
Proliferate	Grow, spread
Ramifications	Results, offshoots
Veracious	True, truthful

A further advantage to using concise language is that it lends a conversational tone to a presentation. An audience usually responds more favorably to a congenial, conversational tone than to one that is stilted and formal.

When developing verbal style, presenters have many options from which to choose. Consider, for example, how many different words could be used to communicate the idea "create." (A partial list appears at the end of this chapter immediately before the comprehension check.) Which would be the best word to use? The preferred choice would be that word which is most clear, correct, concise—and well-considered.

Well-considered

As with every aspect of a presentation, verbal style should be developed in relation to the decisive factors depicted in Figure 4-2. First and foremost, the language of an effective presentation is appropriate to the audience. In addition to knowing about the particular audience to be addressed, a presenter must be aware of and sensitive to cultural conditions. In many cases, the composition of an audience reflects the composition of the community (the term "community" used in a generic sense to refer to an organization, neighborhood, city, state, or nation). As the demographics of a population change, audience composition changes. In the United States, for example, presenters must be responsive to current trends: declining literacy, increasing numbers of people for whom English is a second language, and the rise of vocal "special interest" groups. These trends affect how people receive and respond to the verbal style of a presentation, making it more crucial than ever to use language that is clear, correct, and concise.

The verbal style of a presentation should also reflect the subject and the setting—and the person presenting. A presentation will be more effective and enjoyable—for audience and speaker alike—when there is consonance between the language of the message and the presenter's natural style.

Reflection Questions

In what ways is your current verbal style clear, correct, and concise? In what ways might you make it more so?

Key Concept 35

To influence and persuade, a presenter must use verbal expressions that reflect the attributes of an effective presentation.

Introduced in Chapter 1, the attributes of an effective presentation are attention-getting, meaningful, memorable, activating, and balanced. An effective verbal style reflects these same attributes by using language that is appropriately:

- Expressive
- Emotive
- Evocative
- Encouraging
- Emphatic

A dull, dreary, or diffident verbal style dilutes the potential impact of a message. To be effective, a presenter must communicate with language that *touches* people, that impresses the message on hearts and minds and stirs the audience to act.

Expressive

Some words and phrases are more expressive than others. They convey in a striking way the sense or nature of the thing described. A verbal style is expressive by reason of its use of emotive and evocative language. Those two qualities (described next) can be better understood by first considering two verbal forms that are *not* expressive.

Overworked Adjectives Are Not Expressive. An adjective (that part of speech used to modify or describe a noun) is overworked when it has been applied to so many different situations that it has become virtually meaningless. Overworked adjectives include these words: awful, crazy, cute, fine, funny, good, lovely, neat, nice, sweet, swell, terrible, wonderful. There are others, and the list changes according to current language usage.

Cliches Are Not Expressive.   A cliche is a phrase worn out by overuse. A phrase becomes a cliche because it was vividly memorable when first expressed. People used (and some continue to use) such phrases repeatedly, as exemplified by these cliches:

A can of worms	Give the green light to
Armed to the teeth	Hands across the sea
Agree to disagree	Leave no stone unturned
Calm before the storm	Take the bull by the horns
Fickle finger of fate	Viable alternative

Many phrases that are cliches today were originated by powerful communicators. Harry Truman cautioned, "If you can't stand the heat, get out of the kitchen." Theodore Roosevelt advised, "Walk softly and carry a big stick." As meaningful as these expressions were when first voiced, their effectiveness has been dulled by repetition. A verbal style characterized by cliches does not capture audience attention, nor is it memorable. Furthermore, the presenter who indulges in cliches may be perceived as lacking in originality.

Emotive

Emotive expressions appeal to feelings to elicit an emotional response. People whose emotions are stirred are more likely to act on a message than people who feel indifferent to one. Verbal expressions may be "flat" or "feeling." Feeling language is more emotive than flat language, as is evident from this comparison:

Flat	Feeling
find	discover
happy	delighted
leave	abandon
look into	explore
on fire	ablaze
sad	sorrowful

Emotive language is often sensory; it appeals to the senses. It uses words that convey something of what it is to see, hear, touch, smell, taste. A presenter who uses flat language would say, "The *noise* in the office is disruptive." A presenter who uses feeling language would say, "The *clamor* in the office is disruptive." You can *hear* clamor in a way that you do not hear *noise*.

Evocative

Evocative language evokes a response from people, prompting them to act. Emotive language is evocative. So, too, is language that cuts through to the crux of an issue with candor. It is honest, forthright, impassioned—and powerful!

Euphemisms Are Not Evocative.   Concern with being "politically correct" has resulted in a trend to replace evocative language with euphemisms. A **euphemism** uses mild or evasive wording. In the list that follows, euphemisms are compared to their more candid counterparts.

Euphemistic	Candid/Evocative
account executive	salesman/saleswoman
downsize/rightsize	cut back, lay off
military engagement	battle, hand-to-hand combat
sanitation engineer	garbage collector
special-interest advocate	lobbyist
substance abuser	drunk, junkie

The use of euphemisms is often deliberate. A company spokesperson who announces a reorganization may intentionally use a term like "rightsizing" to avoid evoking the response that would result from using the term "layoffs." The drawback to euphemisms is that people grow suspicious of presenters who speak in evasive or diluted terms. The audience hears but doesn't trust—the words or the person speaking them—because experience suggests the message is not straightforward or honest.

Hackneyed Phrases Are Not Evocative.   To prepare a presentation as quickly as possible, some speakers resort to hackneyed phrases instead of taking the time to think of more evocative words. Like cliches, hackneyed phrases are expressions that have been used so often they are commonplace. As a result, they fail to evoke a response from people. Any reader who has attended at least three business presentations will likely recognize some of the hackneyed phrases listed here:

The bottom line is . . .

Challenges and opportunities

Compete in the global marketplace

The competition is fierce

Gain the leading edge

It's not over 'til it's over

A new paradigm for the '90s

Strategies that will take us into the twenty-first century

Success depends on you

80 percent of the sales come from 20 percent of the sales force

The name of the game is . . . (choose one: customer service, teamwork)

Phrases such as these do not reflect the attributes of an effective verbal style. People begin to tire of an expression they have heard more than a dozen times.

Encouraging

People in an audience sit up and listen, find a message personally meaningful, and are more inclined to act on it when they are encouraged. William Arthur Ward expressed responses that are common to human nature when he said, "Flatter me, and I may not believe you. Criticize me, and I may not like you. Ignore me, and I may not forgive you. Encourage me, and I will not forget you." The presentations of the most memorable presenters—Winston Churchill, Franklin Roosevelt, Martin Luther King, Jr., John F. Kennedy, Billy Graham, Elizabeth Dole, to name a few—ring with encouragement.

A presenter encourages an audience by the use of positive, rather than negative, language. The popular speaker, Leo Buscaglia, could have said, "Don't choose the way of death. Don't choose the way of hate. Don't choose the way of neglect . . ." Instead, he chose to say, in a positive, encouraging manner, "Choose the way of life. Choose the way of love. Choose the way of caring . . ." In most cases, negative terms can be easily converted into positive phrases, as the following comparison shows.

Negative	Positive
I see no alternative but . . .	Clearly, our plan of action is . . .
If you/we fail to . . .	If you/we choose to . . .
We can't possibly	We can, We will
Don't	Do, Refrain from

Of the examples that appear in the next section (under Key Concept 36), many illustrate the manner and the value of phrasing a message in encouraging terms.

Emphatic

The term **emphatic** has two definitions that apply to presenting. The first definition relates to words. An **emphatic word** is forceful. It stresses a point in no uncertain terms. Emphatic words are described as "hard" as opposed to "soft." (Soft words express sentiment or an oversensitive concern for audience reaction. They are tentative.) Hard words are typically terse, firm, and bold. Emphatic language often borrows from sports and military vocabularies, using terms like *hard ball, punch, smash, attack, explode.*

Forceful language can awaken an audience and spur them to action. Emphatic words can add meaning to a point and energy to a presentation. Although emphatic language does inject power into a presentation, it should be appropriate to the point, applied with discretion, and only used occasionally. Repeated use of forceful words will lessen their intended effect.

The second definition of emphatic applies to phrasing. **Emphatic phrasing** structures wording in a manner that is especially noticeable or striking. Two techniques make use of emphatic phrasing: antithesis and reversal phrasing.

Antithesis.   An **antithesis** poises contrasting ideas in a balanced construction. The first point is introduced, immediately followed by the counterpoint. The familiar and memorable expression, "to err is human; to forgive, divine," is an example. "Forgive" and "divine" appear in contrast to "err" and "human." The second clause balances the first. Two other examples illustrate the effectiveness of antithesis. The first, from George Bernard Shaw:

> You see things; and you say, "Why?" But I dream things that never were; and I say "Why not?"

The second example (source unknown), which conveys a similar idea, makes memorable use of imagery and humor.

> Most people looked at Goliath and said, "He's too big to fight." David looked at Goliath and said, "He's too big to miss!"

Reversal Phrasing.   Similar to antithesis, this technique presents two points in two parts. A subtle difference is that in a **reversal phrasing**, the second point is a reversal of the first. It turns to an opposite premise. Football coach Vince Lombardi used reversal phrasing when he said, "When the going gets tough, the tough get going."

This particular statement exemplifies a number of aspects of verbal style. The language is clear, correct, and concise; the tone is conversational (no gobbledygook or bureaucratic formality here). The word "tough" makes use of "hard" language. It expresses a "let's get on with it!" attitude. The phrasing is striking, in part because it expresses something unexpected. Presenting an idea in a surprising or unusual manner heightens audience attention and makes the point memorable. That it does often leads to the drawbacks that follow. When a statement is (or has been) notably effective, it is repeated . . . and repeated . . . and repeated. It then becomes a cliche, a hackneyed phrase that no longer conveys the power of "hard" language or the unexpected. "When the going gets tough, the tough get going" has been voiced by so many business leaders and sales managers in countless presentations that the second clause no longer needs to be said. People in an audience are by now so familiar with the statement they can "fill in the blanks," so to speak. An expression that, at one time, may have strengthened a speaker's verbal style now detracts from it. When this happens, presenters should look for fresh expressions—or create their own.

Reversal phrasing was mastered by John F. Kennedy (or his speech writers), as the following statements show.

> Forgive your enemies, but never forget their names.
>
> . . . ask not what your country can do for you, ask what you can do for your country.

Refrain from Redundancy

Although widely used, the following phrases (to name a few) are redundant.

Absolutely essential

Basic fundamentals

Definite decision

Desirable benefits

Final conclusion

The first word that modifies the second word is unnecessary. By definition, if something is essential it *is* absolute; a fundamental *is* basic; a decision *is* definite (or it would not yet be a decision); a benefit *is* desirable; a conclusion *is* final.

There are times when using the modifying word in a redundant phrase is intentional. A presenter may say "*absolutely* essential" or "*definite* decision" to add emphasis. Redundancies of this type are permissible in oral presentations—provided they satisfy two conditions. First, the modifying word must be stated with vocal intonation that conveys emphasis. Second, even redundancies of this type should be used sparingly. Emphasis, like any form of verbal expression, loses impact if it is overworked.

A Balanced Verbal Style

Striking a balance between the various forms of expression is a challenging aspect of developing verbal style. It is an invigorating and gratifying exercise to select and compose clear, correct, and concise language that is expressively (and alternately) emotive, evocative, encouraging, and emphatic.

The style a presenter develops indicates whether the person is a passive, assertive, or aggressive communicator. The list below identifies some of the telling characteristics of the verbal style of each "type." (Vocal and visual characteristics are covered in Chapter 8.)

Passive	Assertive	Aggressive
tentative	declarative	abrasive
uncertain	confident	combative
apologetic	encouraging	threatening

To assert is to state or to declare as true. An assertive style is the most honest and expressive. It is also (as the preceding comparison suggests) a balanced verbal style, and thus the most persuasive.

Reflection Questions

Would you describe your verbal style of presentation as passive, assertive, or aggressive? What ideas have you gained from Key Concept 35 that will help you add balance to your verbal style?

Key Concept 36

Impact, interest, and variety are added to the verbal style of a message through the use of literary techniques, figures of speech, stories, and humor.

This section identifies various forms of verbal expression that can enhance the narrative of a presentation. After each is defined, an example or two is given as a "model" of the method. You will find that many of the examples quote men and women noted for their position, education, and/or influence. Notice how, in every case, the language is clear, concise, and conversational in nature. The examples reinforce that an effective verbal style is pure, precise, and to the point. It is *not* pompous, pedantic, or ponderous.

At each example, read the quotation aloud as you would if you were making a presentation. By doing so you will hear the sounds of words and phrasing as an audience might. The tonal quality of certain words and the rhythm of sentence structure are often what lend added meaning and impact to a message. Do an exercise in developing your own verbal style: after reading the example(s), try composing a statement or two that uses the technique described.

Literary Techniques

Literary techniques are so called because they are methods of communication originally borrowed from literature. To reach their listeners, presenters can take advantage of the same techniques used by writers to reach their readers.

Assonance.   **Assonance** refers to a resemblance of sound in words or syllables. It can make a statement easy and pleasant to listen to and more memorable because of the recurrence of like sounds. The following statements make use of assonance.

> What the mind of man can conceive and believe, the mind of man can achieve. (Napoleon Hill)
>
> If you can dream it, you can do it. (Walt Disney)

In the first example, the "eive" sound is repeated; in the second the consonant "d" creates assonance with "dream" and "do." Not only is assonance pleasing to the ear; it also triggers an association of ideas. Achieving becomes associated with conceiving and believing. Doing is associated with first dreaming about what you can do.

Catchword.   A **catchword** is a phrase that "catches on" because it is clever. Frequent reference to a catchword makes it memorable. Many advertising slogans, such as "be all you can be," become catchwords. In the context of business, catchwords are created by stating an observation that is amusing or commonly held to be true. Many of the catchwords in business are named after their originator. In a business presentation, a speaker who makes mention of "Murphy's Law" can be almost certain people in the audience will understand the reference. A few catchwords that apply to organizations are listed here:

> Cap'n Jack's Law: People who are good at what they do get all the work. People who are really good get rid of it.
>
> Murphy's Law: If anything can go wrong, it will.
>
> Peter Principle: People are promoted to their level of incompetence.

Hyperbole.   An **hyperbole** is an exaggerated statement intended for effect and not meant to be taken literally. Hyperbolic expressions must be used with caution. To ensure that an audience does not misunderstand, the statement must be clearly an exaggeration. As with any technique used for effect or to emphasize a point, hyperbole should be used sparingly or the presenter's credibility may be called into question.

Presenting to a staff meeting, a product manager stated (hyperbolically), "When we entered this market we were surprised to find that our competitors were as numerous and threatening as a swarm of bees."

Onomatopoeia. **Onomatopoeia** refers to words that sound like what they mean: buzz, humm, hiss, splash, bang, and clang, for example. The poet Edgar Allen Poe made use of onomatopoeia when he created the word "tintinnabulation" (as in "the tintinnabulation of the bells"). Although the technique has limited application for business presentations, it is effective when the vocal quality will reinforce the verbal word.

A motivational speaker uses onomatopoeia to emphasize the value of reading and listening to positive messages. With reference to the catchword "GIGO" (Garbage In, Garbage Out), the speaker suggests, "If you take garbage in, you will *spew* garbage out" (pronouncing *spew* in a manner that makes it sound very undesirable).

Parallelism. A **parallelism** uses the same grammatical form with each expression of an idea. The wording or sentence structure (or both) are, in effect, *parallel*. With characteristic wit, Benjamin Franklin made use of parallelism when he said:

Who is wise? He that learns from everyone. Who is powerful? He that governs his passions. Who is rich? He that is content. Who is that? Nobody.

The message is structured so that each idea is presented in a coordinated manner: first a question, "Who is . . . ," followed by a statement, "He that . . ." The value of parallelism is evident from the comparison that follows. The first paragraph makes use of parallelism; the second does not.

We look forward to a world founded upon four essential human freedoms. The first is *freedom* of speech. The second is *freedom* of every person to worship God in his own way. The third is *freedom* from want . . . The fourth is *freedom* from fear. (Franklin D. Roosevelt)

compared to:

We look forward to a world founded upon four essential human freedoms. The first is free speech. Next, people should have the opportunity to worship God as they choose. Relief from want is essential . . . Fear is also a condition from which people are to be extricated.

Parallelism, with its reiteration of wording and rhythm in sentence structure, adds strength and clarity to the expression of a point.

Figures of Speech

A **figure of speech** is a form of verbal expression in which words are placed in a context other than the literal meaning of the words would suggest or in which words are combined in a striking manner to add force or aesthetic feeling to a point. Figures of speech are emotive, evocative, and/or emphatic.

Imagery.   Using language that paints a mental picture, **imagery** verbally appeals to visual perceptions. Imagery can advance in a subtle but powerful manner a profound or thought-provoking point, as the following examples indicate.

> There are two ways of exerting one's strength: one is pushing down, the other is pulling up. (Booker T. Washington)
>
> You cannot shake hands with a clenched fist. (Golda Meir)

The next example not only uses imagery, but also appeals to all three channels of communication: verbal, vocal, and visual.

> When the eagles are silent the parrots begin to chatter. (Winston Churchill)

Imagery is often employed in the figures of speech described next.

Metaphor.   A **metaphor** conveys a comparison between two things that are *not ordinarily* associated. The emphasis is on *not ordinary*—the very reason that a metaphor makes a point in a striking manner. Creative metaphors use inventive imagery. Both these examples liken one thing to another in terms that give fresh expression to timeworn ideas:

> Beware of little expenses. A small leak will sink a great ship. (Benjamin Franklin)
>
> War is a poor chisel to carve out tomorrow. (Martin Luther King, Jr.)

Like other forms of expression discussed in this chapter, the use of metaphors can be abused. One abuse is overuse that turns a metaphor into a cliche. Another abuse is mixing metaphors. A mixed metaphor combines, in an incompatible and often nonsensical manner, wording from two or more familiar metaphors. The need to exercise caution when expressing a point metaphorically (especially when borrowing from established metaphors) is made clear by the following examples.*

---

* Richard Lederer, *Anguished English* (New York: Dell Publishing, 1987), p. 115.

> That snake in the grass is barking up the wrong tree.
>
> The idea was hatched years ago, but it didn't catch fire until two months ago, when the co-directors jumped in feet first.
>
> It's time to swallow the bullet.

Mixed metaphors are confusing rather than clarifying. The result is often laughable when the presenter may have meant to be taken seriously.

Simile.   The term **simile** is related to the word "similar." Like a metaphor, a simile implies a comparison between two things. What distinguishes a simile from a metaphor is the word "like." As these examples point out, a simile states that one thing is *like* another.

> A man without a purpose is like a ship without a rudder. (Thomas Carlyle)
>
> Business is never so healthy as when, like a chicken, it must do a certain amount of scratching for what it gets. (Henry Ford)

Personification.   **Personification** describes an inanimate object or issue in terms that would normally be used to describe a person. Henry Kaiser made use of personification when he said:

> Problems are only opportunities in work clothes.

Stories

Historically, storytelling has been a prominent form of conveying information. Before the development of written language, knowledge was communicated by word-of-mouth. Events and ideas were passed on—from one community to another, from one generation to the next—primarily through stories because they were easy to remember.

In recent years, storytelling has regained its popularity largely because of the following factors.

- Lecturing has been found to be the *least* effective form of presentation.
- Television (a media rich in storytelling) has influenced people's expectations.
- Storytelling has been rediscovered as one of the *most* effective forms of presentation.

Stories are a means by which people share experiences and build relationships. In a culture that is becoming dominated by interaction with technology in lieu of person-to-person communication, storytelling restores the "human factor." Stories are more memorable than facts and figures. Children learn the lessons of life through stories. Likewise, adults often learn the lessons of business and professional life through stories.

Dr. David Boje, editor of the Journal of Organizational Change Management and a professor of management at Loyola Marymount University, has taught and studied storytelling extensively. He observed that better leaders are more skilled storytellers and that "the best way to pass on a company's cultural themes is by telling stories."

Of the types of substantiating material discussed in Chapter 4, anecdotes, verbal illustrations, and scenarios are forms of storytelling. Stories not only serve as evidence to support a point. The way they are told is indicative of a speaker's verbal style. Thus, the factors discussed throughout this chapter also apply to storytelling. A story should be clear, correct, concise, and well-considered. It should be told using emotive, evocative, encouraging, and occasionally emphatic language.

In addition, a story will only be effective if it is communicated *naturally*—with enthusiasm, appropriate inflection, pauses, and a varied pace. A story that is read from notes or recited from memory will sound more like a lecture than a story. The presenter must have, in a manner of speaking, "ownership" of the story. If a story is not from a speaker's own experience but has been adopted from some other source, it should be read and reread and practiced and rehearsed until it is woven into the speaker's experience. Then, it can be presented with the ease and expressiveness that are trademarks of memorable stories.

Humor

In surveys of the traits people most look for in a romantic partner, humor commonly ranks first or second. Sitcoms (situation comedies) are among the most popular programs on television. In recent years, medical science has confirmed that humor has health benefits. Laughter has been found to reduce pain and relieve stress. If an audience includes people who are romantically inclined, people who watch television, or people who experience stress, humor will appeal to them.

Humor that is appropriate to a business presentation is always good-natured and in good taste. Sarcasm or humor that is critical or malicious in intent is *never* acceptable in a professional presentation. Jokes, if enfolded in the body of a message, should be used sparingly (for the reasons mentioned in Chapter 4 on the subject of openers).

Good-natured humor mirrors some amusing aspect of human experience. There are numerous advantages to injecting humor into the verbal style of a presentation.

- Humor satisfies a fundamental human need to laugh and feel good.
- Humor supplies comic relief to a serious subject.

- Humor provides a change of pace.

- Humor sparks interest and, by their laughter, involves the audience members in a presentation.

- Humor can relieve an awkward situation or dispel a controversy.

- Humor keeps a presenter from developing a style that is too somber.

- Humor exhibits wit, a pleasant disposition, and a willingness to laugh at one's self, all of which make a presenter more appealing to an audience.

- Humor builds a bond between audience and presenter. According to Victor Borge, "Humor is the shortest distance between two people."

- Humor conveys meaning in a refreshing and sometimes unexpected way. George Bernard Shaw correctly assessed the value of humor. "When a thing is funny," he said, "search it carefully for a hidden truth."

Reflection Questions

What story have you heard during a presentation that made an impression on you? What made the story meaningful or memorable?

Key Concept 37

It is imperative to refrain from forms of expression that detract from the appeal of the presenter and/or the message.

Early in this course, the point was made that the chief purpose of a business presentation is to influence and persuade. To accomplish that purpose, presenters must refrain from using language that is demeaning, derogatory, discriminatory, and/or distracting.

Demeaning, Derogatory, and Discriminatory Language

Demeaning language denies the dignity of a person(s) or group. Derogatory statements belittle a person or convey in unfavorable terms a lowly opinion of a group or thing. Discriminatory language expresses partiality or prejudice.

All are unacceptable in business presentations and should be eliminated from a presenter's vocabulary. Mindful that an audience is made up of a mix of people, a respectful presenter shows respect for every person.

An effective verbal style communicates respect through the use of bias-free language, particularly with regards to the factors outlined next.*

Gender.   A respectful presenter refrains from language that implies a bias on the basis of gender (male or female). Generic (inclusive) terms are used in place of gender-specific references. Salesperson or sales representative, for example, is used instead of salesman or saleswoman.

Ethnic Background.   A respectful presenter refrains from language that conveys bias on the basis of race or culture. When a point must be made with reference to race or culture, terminology currently preferred by the ethnic group(s) referenced should be used. For example, the term "Asian" has replaced use of the word "Oriental."

Position.   A professional presenter refrains from language that communicates bias related to position or socioeconomic status. Adjectives that imply comparison (such as "lowly" versus "superior") are omitted.

Physical/Mental Condition.   A professional presenter refrains from language that expresses bias with respect to physical or mental condition. Non-judgmental language is preferable to wording that may be interpreted as unkind. The word "slim" would be used, for instance, instead of "skinny." References to disabilities should not equate a person and the disability, nor imply limitation. For example, to say a person *has* a disability is acceptable. To say a person *is* disabled is not. It is appropriate to state that a person *uses* a wheelchair; inappropriate to describe a person as *confined* to a wheelchair.

In every case, a presenter should eliminate language or references that are unnecessary, inappropriate, irrelevant, or that perpetuate stereotypes. An acceptable and appealing verbal style gives equally respectful and equally favorable consideration to people of every description. Adhere to the Golden Rule of presenting: communicate to and about others as you would want others to communicate to and about you.

Distracting Language

Language that distracts (and detracts) from the content of a presentation is identified in the following paragraphs.

---

* A booklet entitled "Guidelines for Bias-Free Publishing" is available from McGraw-Hill. It contains suggestions that apply equally well to the verbal style of a presentation.

Anything in Poor Taste.   Although they may not voice their objections, many people are offended by obscenities, profanities, and off-color jokes. Any point that is not in good taste calls attention away from the message and signals a lack of professionalism on the part of the presenter. Unless its use will clearly appeal to the audience, slang should also be omitted from a presentation, At one time, slang expressions like "awesome," "rad," and "not" were popular among teenagers. However, using such words (or whatever slang is currently popular) is inappropriate in a business presentation.

Apologetic Language.   An apologetic style is a trait of a passive communicator. An audience wants to hear what a presenter has to say, not that the presenter is "sorry."

Abbreviated forms.   An effective verbal style expresses words correctly and fully. The city is "San Francisco," not "Frisco." A developer builds "condominiums," not "condos." An organization is a place of "business," not "the biz." Savings are "maximum," not "to the max." People should be offered "congratulations," not "congrats." Some abbreviated forms of expression are objectionable because they sound very like slang.

"I" language.   If you listen to popular professional speakers, you will find that they rarely use the word "I." Phrases like "I think," "I want to cover," "I would like to make the point," and "I want to thank you for the opportunity" are, in most cases, unnecessary. Such phrases should be reworded or omitted altogether. For example, rather than say "I think" or "I want to say," simply state the point—assertively. "I want to tell you about . . ." should be amended to "We'll focus on . . ." or "Let's consider . . ." "I want to thank you" is more effectively phrased, "Thank *you*"—with the emphasis on the audience.

An Affirmative Style

In most situations, the verbal style that most appeals to an audience is one that is affirmative. It is positive in manner. An affirmative style uses language and forms of expression that:

- Affirm the value of the people in the audience
- Affirm the significance of the message
- Affirm the professionalism of the presenter

An affirmative verbal style is the hallmark of a skilled communicator.

Summary

Language creates the verbal style of a message, which produces the tone and affects the pace of a presentation. An effective verbal style uses language that is clear, correct, and concise, and that takes into consideration the decisive factors of a presentation. Verbal style is more expressive and persuasive when it makes use of emotive, evocative, encouraging, and emphatic language. A striking verbal style is developed through the use of literary techniques, figures of speech, stories, and humor. A respectful verbal style expresses esteem for all people through the use of bias-free language. It reflects a presenter's professionalism and regard for the "Golden Rule" of communicating.

Sample Situations

Situation 1: A Lesson from History

A promotional presentation is made to sell people on a product, service, position, or idea. It will succeed only if the audience can clearly understand the message.

Over 200 years ago, during the formation of the United States of America, the issue of voting rights was hotly debated. One faction contended that ownership of property should be a voting requirement. Benjamin Franklin disagreed. A group that supported Franklin presented their case this way:

> It cannot be adhered to with any reasonable degree of intellectual or moral certainty that the inalienable right man possesses to exercise his political preferences by employing his vote in referendums is rooted in anything other than man's own nature, and is, therefore, properly called a natural right. To hold, for instance, that this natural right can be limited externally by making its exercise dependent on a prior condition of ownership of property, is to wrongly suppose that man's natural right to vote is somehow more inherent in and more dependent on the property of man than it is on the nature of man. It is obvious that such belief is unreasonable, for it reverses the order of rights intended by nature.

Powerful communicator that he was, Franklin presented a more convincing argument. He said:

> To require property of voters leads us to this dilemma: I own a jackass; I can vote. The jackass dies; I cannot vote. Therefore the vote represents not me but the jackass.

In terms of verbal style, what did Franklin do to promote his position in a more persuasive manner than the others?

Situation 2: Getting the Point Across

Dr. Alvarez, a science professor, was preparing an informational presentation on the theory of relativity. The previous semester, some students had complained that her lectures were confusing. To see how she might clarify the information, Dr. Alvarez reviewed writings and speeches by Albert Einstein (who first expressed the theory in the mathematical equation $E=mc^2$). She discovered from the great physicist himself that even the most seemingly complex concepts can be communicated in clearly understandable terms. She revised the content of her presentation using a quote from Einstein, who explained:

> When a man sits with a pretty girl for an hour, it seems like a minute. But let him sit on a hot stove for a minute—and it's longer than any hour. That's relativity.

What techniques of verbal style did Albert Einstein use to convey information in a meaningful and memorable way?

Situation 3: The Vocabulary of Verbal Style

Craig Samuels is a senior manager with an MBA degree from one of the country's most prestigious schools of business. The company for which he works was recently restructured to reduce costs. A plant manager asked Craig to speak to employees about the reorganization. Most of those attending the meeting would be employees under the age of 20 working in entry-level positions.

Craig prepared a draft of his message (an internal/down-line presentation), using a vocabulary indicative of his advanced college degree. A sample is shown below.

> Organizational restructuring indubitably engenders transformation. Joint cooperation is essential to meet the requirement for production of optimum output with declining resources. Resolution of this conundrum is contingent upon the application of proficiencies.

Craig asked an administrative assistant to review the draft of his presentation. She suggested it should be revised, as the following sample shows.

> With reorganization, it is certain the company will change. How will we do more with less? It is a puzzling question. The answer depends on our willingness to work together and make the best use of our skills.

In addition to eliminating gobbledygook and the redundancy "joint cooperation," the revised sample uses a vocabulary more appropriate to the audience. Typically, a majority of people under the age of 20 working in entry-level positions would not yet have more than a high school education. In many geographic areas of the United States, the vocabulary of high school graduates (on average) is at a sixth- to ninth-grade reading level.

Synonyms for the Word "Create"

Build, compose, construct, design, engender, fabricate, fashion, forge, form, formulate, generate, make, mold, originate, shape.

Comprehension Check

The answers to the following appear on page 333.

1. "A bull in the hand is worth two in the bush" is an example of _____.
   a. clarity
   b. a mixed metaphor
   c. personification
   d. jargon
   e. a comparison

2. On the subject of persistence: which of the following quotations would best make a point in a clear and concise manner, using imagery and humor? _____
   a. "Success seems to be largely a matter of hanging on after others have let go." (William Feather)
   b. "I think and think for months and years. Ninety-nine times, the conclusion is false. The hundredth time I am right." (Albert Einstein)
   c. "Nothing in the world can take the place of persistence. Talent will not; nothing is more common than unsuccessful men with talent. Genius will not; unrewarded genius is almost a proverb. Education will not; the world is full of educated derelicts. Persistence and determination alone are omnipotent." (Calvin Coolidge)
   d. "He conquers who endures." (Persius)
   e. "The nose of the bulldog has been slanted backwards so that he can breathe without letting go." (Winston Churchill)

3. The main reason gobbledygook should be eliminated from a speaker's verbal style is that it is not _____.
   a. correct
   b. clear
   c. amusing
   d. visual
   e. relevant

4. One of the *most* effective forms of verbal expression is _____.
   a. a simile
   b. jargon
   c. a story
   d. a figure of speech
   e. emphasis

5. "People in professional fields often have little time to spend with their wives and children" uses language that is _____.
   a. concise
   b. well-considered
   c. metaphoric
   d. biased
   e. politically correct

To Do

1. Review the content of the presentation you are developing for this course. Is it clear? correct? concise? Is the language expressive and encouraging? If there are word choices you feel should be changed, revise the content accordingly.

2. For each key point of your presentation, write a statement(s) that uses one of the techniques from the following list.

   ▪ Catchword
   ▪ Humor
   ▪ Imagery
   ▪ Metaphor
   ▪ Simile
   ▪ Story

   For example: for the first key point, you might develop a metaphor; for the second key point, a humorous story; for the third key point, you might create your own catchword.

6
Support:
Audiovisual Aids

Throughout human history, people have communicated through visual images: from painting on the walls of prehistoric caves to putting up billboards along freeways. They have communicated through sound: beating out messages on drums or adding a theme song to a movie. In contemporary society (as a result of viewing television, movies, computer screens, and video games), people have become accustomed to receiving information and ideas through audiovisual media. In fact, they expect it.

Any business presentation that does not feature audiovisual aids is an incomplete presentation. A presenter who neglects to use audiovisual aids loses the benefits of a powerful form of communication. The right choice and proper presentation of audiovisuals can create a compelling impression that people in an audience will remember long after they have forgotten the words the presenter spoke.

Objectives

To describe the characteristics of effective audiovisual support; to assess the relative merits of various types of graphics and media for a given presentation; and to apply the guidelines for choosing, producing, and using audiovisuals.

Key Concepts

38. The purpose of audiovisual aids is to complement communication.

39. Visual aids are most effective when they are pictorial, colorful, and creative.

175

40. Numerous types of graphic representations can be used for visual aids.

41. Various media may be used to present audiovisual support.

42. Presenters find it helpful to follow guidelines for the selection and preparation of audiovisual aids.

43. To support a presentation effectively, audiovisual aids (like verbal expressions) must be clear, correct, concise, and well-considered.

Key Terms

To make full use of these concepts, you will need to understand the following terms:

Aid   Medium, media

Audiovisual aids   Graphic

Complement

Key Concept 38

The purpose of audiovisual aids is to complement communication.

By definition, an **aid** is something that helps or assists. Audio refers to sound and visual to sight. Thus, **audiovisual aids** are devices which use sounds and sights to assist in the presentation of a message. Defining an audiovisual aid may seem to be stating the obvious. However, the need to do so is suggested by the fact that in too many presentations audiovisuals are used ineffectively (or not at all).

What an audiovisual aid is denotes why it is used. The primary purpose of audiovisuals is to complement communication. To **complement** is to supply a lack of any kind, to complete what is missing. What is missing from a presentation that doesn't make use of effective audiovisuals? According to findings cited in Chapter 1 (Key Concept 4), in face-to-face communication, words alone have far less impact on people than either vocal or visual means of communicating. In a presentation without audiovisual aids, what is missing are the sights and sounds that enhance audience understanding and acceptance of a message in a way that verbal forms of expression cannot fully do. Naturally, a presenter's nonverbal style of delivery provides vocal and visual cues. However, even skilled speakers find that ideas and information are more clearly communicated when accompanied by audiovisual support.

Studies by the Wharton School of Business found that, on average, people retain about 10 percent of a presentation communicated through words alone, whereas the effective use of visual aids increases retention up to 50 percent. In surveys by numerous research and consulting firms, executives have reported spending one-third or more of their time in meetings. The Wharton study found that the addition of visual aids to a presentation could reduce meeting time by as much as 28 percent (suggesting that thousands of meeting hours could be spared every month if more presenters made good use of audiovisual support). In addition, a study by the University of Minnesota concluded that presentations using visual aids were 43 percent more persuasive than those without visual support. Clearly, audiovisual aids supply benefits that presentations without them are lacking.

What Audiovisual Aids Do Not Do

One can better understand the purpose and functions of audiovisual aids by identifying what they do *not* do.

- Audiovisual aids do *not* replace the presenter.
- Audiovisuals do *not* substitute for the presentation itself.
- Audiovisuals do *not* compensate for inadequate organization and preparation.
- Audiovisual aids do *not* mask weak content or poor presentation skills.

These are important points to bear in mind as this chapter unfolds, especially with respect to technological advancements in audiovisual support.

What Effective Audiovisual Aids Do

Audiovisual aids are included in a presentation to *support* successful communication of a message. As such, the primary purpose of using audiovisuals is to:

- Clarify concepts or data that may be difficult for an audience to grasp from a verbal explanation alone.
- Highlight the most significant points of a message.
- Reinforce verbal communication to increase audience retention.

Audiovisual aids may also be used to:

- Create interest.

- Stimulate thought.

- Inject humor.

- Vary the pace of a presentation.

- Focus audience attention.

- Suggest interpretations.

- Involve the audience in the message.

- Graphically depict, in a striking and more meaningful manner, relationships between data or ideas, comparisons and contrasts, operations, processes, and trends.

- In longer informational presentations (such as training sessions), visual aids are also useful to review points covered in one section and provide a transition to the next.

Audiovisual aids will serve the purpose for which they are intended, and add value to a presentation, only if they are effective.

Key Concept 39

Visual aids are most effective when they are pictorial, colorful, and creative.

For years, many speakers who used visual aids displayed for the audience material that contained, for the most part, words and numbers on a plain white background. Since it is relatively easy and inexpensive to write information on a flip chart or to make transparencies from typewritten copy, these were (and sometimes still are) the common forms of visual support. They do not, however, add much impact to a presentation. They do not reflect the characteristics of effective audiovisual aids. Effective audiovisuals are pictorial, colorful, and creative.

Pictorial

The literal definition of *visual* is *having to do with sight*. According to this definition, any item an audience can see could then be described as a visual aid. However, not all visuals are aids in terms of helping—either the presenter to communicate the message or the audience to grasp it. Visual aids that are truly "helps" reflect the figurative definition of *visual;* they *produce a mental picture.*

By analogy, when a passage in a novel is described as "visual," the connotation is that it calls to mind an image. Interest and understanding are sharpened by words that prompt the reader to envision a scene in the "mind's eye." Such passages are the most memorable. Presenters have an advantage over novelists. They do not need to rely on words alone and hope that the audience "gets the picture." Using a visual aid, a presenter can give the audience an actual picture; and, to coin a familiar phrase, "a picture is worth a thousand words."

Pictorial visual aids make a message more memorable. Many people remark that they never forget a face, but admit to having trouble remembering names. Pictorial visual aids give a "face" to points in a presentation. Often, people find their way to a place by spotting landmarks along the way. Pictorial visual aids are like "landmarks" in a presentation. Many people can flawlessly describe a scene from a movie, even one they saw years before, but they can't recite the lines the actors spoke. Pictorial visual aids present "scenes" for the audience to view and help to make a message more memorable.

Colorful

The introduction to this chapter pointed out that people have come to expect information and ideas to be communicated through audiovisual media. They have also come to expect that what they view will appear in color. People photograph memorable moments—in color. They read newspapers that, once printed in black ink on white newsprint, now make use of color. Black-and-white television is a thing of the past. Monochrome monitors on computers are fast following suit.

With the technology that is currently available, it is relatively easy and inexpensive to prepare colorized visual aids. Certain models of photocopiers have the capability to reproduce in color; some can add color to copies from black-and-white originals. Many computer printers also produce copy in brilliant colors.

There are several advantages to using color on visual aids. Color heightens interest and makes a message more memorable. On advertising copy, color was found to increase readership and retention by as much as 80 percent. There is no reason the same shouldn't hold true for visual aids. Color affects the mood of an audience. It can add to the persuasiveness of a presentation. Marketing and scientific research has revealed that colors affect emotions, evoke responses, and motivate people to buy. Furthermore, color adds meaning to a message. The appropriate use of color reinforces the points depicted on visual aids because people associate colors with certain qualities, conditions, and events.

Color Associations. The meanings most commonly associated with the primary and secondary colors, and with black and white, are described next.

Red. Red is a stimulating color. It conveys passion, love, and fulfillment. In a business context, red connotes power and speed; used in excess, red may be perceived as overbearing or intimidating. Red can convey a negative message, reminding people of red-ink corrections on school papers and the expression of indebtedness, "in the red."

Yellow. A brilliant "highlight" shade of yellow is a stimulating color. It conveys confidence, esteem, and optimism.

Blue. Blue is both a soothing and a strong color. It connotes peace, assurance, faith, and truth. Dark blue signifies authority, while light blue suggests sincerity.

Violet. The dark shade of violet referred to as "royal purple" expresses the association of violet with dignity. Violet is also a conservative color and suggests economy or frugality.

Orange. Orange is a warm color. Dark orange expresses action, aggression, or valor. Brown-hued shades of orange (commonly described as earth tones) are associated with friendship and harvest.

Green. Green signifies hope or prosperity. It is associated with growth, youthfulness, health, and leisure.

Black. Depending on the context in which it occurs, black can be either a striking or a morbid color. It conveys authority, loyalty, strength, and a sense of mystery. Black is also commonly associated with death.

White. Traditionally, white signifies cleanliness, virtue, and holiness. It is a color associated with professionalism.

Color Combinations. Certain combinations of colors evoke memories because of their association with events. Red and green combined are, of course, reminiscent of the Christmas season. Orange and black are reminders of Halloween. In the United States, the combination of red, white, and blue is associated with patriotism.

According to a color preference study by Pantone Color Institute and Cooper Marketing Group, the color favored by most people is blue. The least popular color is a yellow-green shade like the color of sulfur. According to a Gallup survey of color preferences by gender, a majority of men best remember violet, dark blue, olive green, and yellow (in that order); most women best remember dark blue, olive green, yellow, and red.

Naturally, it is preferable to choose colors which best match the points presented on a visual aid, giving consideration to color preference and retention factors. It is also useful to apply the following guidelines.

Number of Colors.   Keep color choices few and simple. The number of colors on any one visual aid should be limited to two or three different colors. Too many variations in color will create a visual aid that looks more like a piece of abstract art. A visual aid is intended to make a point, not to make a presentation "pretty." The point will be lost if too many colors compete for meaning. To distinguish among several different factors, variations in shades of one color can be used. If a bar chart features six different bars, for example, the bars may be depicted in light, medium, and dark shades of two different colors, or light and dark shades of three colors.

When using two or three colors, choose colors on the basis of associated meaning and for contrast. When visual aids are projected (especially if they appear at a distance from the audience), people will not be able to clearly discern the difference between dark red against dark purple, or dark blue on a black background.

Contrast.   Use contrasting colors to identify contrasting ideas or major changes. To call attention to dominant points, use bright or intense colors which are "active." For minor points, use pale or "passive" hues. Important material belongs in the foreground of a visual aid, offset from the background with a contrasting color. White provides a striking contrast for most darker, dominant colors. It also provides relief from a potentially overwhelming use of color.

Complementary Colors.   Colors that appear opposite one another on the color wheel are referred to as "complements." Complementary combinations are red-green, yellow-violet, and orange-blue. Shown in complementary colors, components of a visual aid remain distinct because of the contrast in color. Placing red and green side by side should be avoided, however, because one in ten people cannot clearly distinguish between them.

Consistency.   Apply the use of color consistently. If a number of visual aids feature the same element (a graphic, symbol, or label), it should appear in the same color on all visuals. The color green, for instance, may be selected to represent revenues (because of its association with growth and prosperity). On every visual with an element that signifies revenue, the element would appear in green. Consistency reinforces meaning.

Labels.   Titles, headlines, key words, and captions appear sharpest in black print. Dark shades of blue, green, red, or purple may also be used provided they appear in sharp contrast to other colors. Colorized text, which appears smaller than text printed in black, should be enlarged so that it can be clearly read.

Armed with this color information, a presenter can prepare striking visual aids that will serve to imprint the message in people's minds. Colorized visuals support a presentation far more effectively than nondescript black-and-white visual aids.

Creative

The chief challenge presenters face when addressing an audience is how to gain people's attention and then sustain it throughout a presentation. The techniques for making a message more meaningful, memorable, and activating count for nothing—unless a speaker first has a group's attention. As soon as a speaker displays the first ordinary visual aid, many people in an audience are inclined to "tune out." What is an "ordinary" visual aid? It is a form of visual that audiences have seen hundreds of times before: a flip chart with words written on it with black marking pen, a black-on-white transparency filled from top to bottom margins with lines of typewritten information. Viewing ordinary visual aids is like watching the same movie replayed over and over again. After a while, an audience just doesn't want to watch anymore.

On the other hand, people tend to sit up and take notice of what is creative: a visual that is different, imaginative, intriguing. Creativity in audiovisual aids is essential:

- The longer a presentation runs.
- The more serious or tedious the subject.
- The greater the need to persuade.
- The more one wants to distinguish oneself from the norm.

Creative visual aids are always graphic and colorful, and they present information in an unexpected way. They offer an audience a fresh perspective on a point. Ideas for creative visual aids typically occur to presenters who practice creative-thinking techniques (see Chapter 1, Key Concept 6), and who take the time to consider, "In what unique, attention-getting way can this point be portrayed?" It is also helpful to observe striking magazine and television advertisements, which can trigger ideas for conveying a message creatively.

Reflection Questions

Of the presentations you have attended, what visual aids have made an impression on you? Which ones did not? What do you remember about the visual aids you liked in contrast to those that did not appeal to you?

> # Key Concept 40
>
> *Numerous types of graphic representations can be used for visual aids.*

A dictionary lists several definitions for the term **graphic**. Graphic is used for words that produce the effect of a picture. It refers to descriptions that are vivid and lifelike. Graphic denotes diagrams, drawings, paintings, engravings, etchings, handwriting, and graphs. In short, the term *graphic* applies to anything that creates an artistic or visual impression.

Types of Presentation Graphics

In the context of business presentations, there are four categories of graphics. Shown in Figure 6-1, they are charts, graphs, pictographs, and illustrations. The nature of the information to be depicted on a visual aid determines the type of graphic(s) used.

Charts. This category of visual aid includes (but is not limited to) bar charts, pie charts, flow charts, organization charts, and Gantt charts. Both bar charts and pie charts depict numeric data. Flow charts visualize processes or procedures. Organization charts picture an organization's functions and the relationships between them. Gantt charts indicate time-lines for task, project, and program scheduling.

Graphs. Graphs plot numeric data. They are typically used to depict trends, cycles, and relationships between variables.

Pictographs. A pictograph is a diagram, chart, or graph that represents statistical data in pictorial form. Symbols of an oil well, for example, might be used to show changes in the price of crude oil. In recent years, newspapers and business publications have increasingly featured pictographs. That they are growing in popularity confirms the value of pictorial visual aids.

Illustrations. Illustrations are types of visual aids most commonly used to convey ideas, operations, locations, or humor. Illustrations include drawings, photographs, diagrams, maps, and cartoons.

Each type of graphic described above translates alphanumeric data into a form an audience can visualize. Doing so makes it easier for people to grasp, interpret, and assess information and ideas. All types of graphics benefit from the use of color. In addition, pictographs and illustrations can

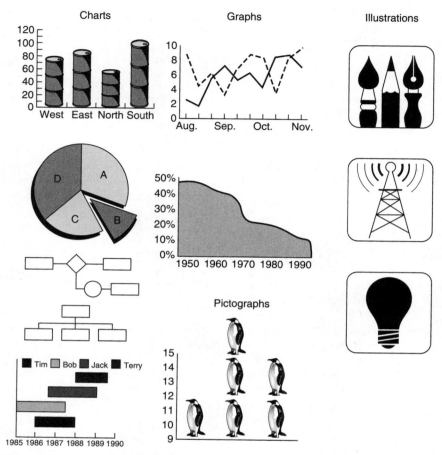

Figure 6-1. Types of presentation graphics.

make creative use of shapes and symbols. As with color, shapes and symbols should be selected to reinforce the meaning of the information displayed and the feeling the presenter wants to convey.

Using Shapes and Symbols

Like color and graphic representations, shapes and symbols appeal to viewers in an audience and some convey meaning as well.

Shapes. Boxed and squared shapes are "hard" forms, best used to depict concrete numeric data (pie charts being an exception). Circles and arched shapes are "soft" forms, appropriate for picturing conceptual ideas. The

Figure 6-2. Examples of symbols.

shape of an oval has almost universal appeal, suggesting as it does a rectangle with rounded corners. A combination of squared and rounded shapes on one visual aid (when appropriate to the information pictured) will help to appeal to both concrete and conceptual thinkers.

Symbols. Representing ideas as they do, symbols are a pictorial form of visual aid. Symbols, especially widely recognized ones, augment the point a graphic illustrates and make it more memorable. What, for example, is signified by a circle with a diagonal slash through it? This symbol is almost universally understood to mean "NO." (The item or activity pictured within the circle is prohibited.) Such symbols are powerful communication tools. Many visual symbols common to a culture are invested with so much meaning that they are a message in and of themselves, as indicated by the symbols pictured in Figure 6-2. (What meaning do the symbols in this figure convey?)

A *logo* is a form of symbol that represents a product or an organization. When delivering a presentation to a specific group, adding the logo to visual aids is an effective technique for customizing the presentation. The logo and other symbolic "shapes" (such as the organization's type style, a rendering of its headquarters, and the like) associate the presentation with the organization. The technique is especially useful for sales presentations.

Key Concept 41

Various media may be used to present audiovisual support.

The term **media** is the plural of **medium**: a substance or agent through which an effect is produced. From the standpoint of business presentations, media are the tangible means by which visual aids are shown. Presentation media are described in terms of the following categories:

- Manual
- Projected

- Specialized
- Computerized

Each medium has relative advantages and drawbacks. Some media are more appropriate for use with small groups; others are better suited to large audiences. There are types of media that are preferable in interactive settings, such as presentations in which members of a group overtly and vocally participate. Other types of media limit, or eliminate altogether, interaction with an audience. Some media are relatively inexpensive and readily available; others entail costly equipment and special setup. Operation of media equipment ranges from simple to complex. The point is: there is no one medium that is inarguably the best for all situations. Presenters should be acquainted with the options that are available, become sufficiently skilled with the use of various media, and then select the option(s) best suited to a given presentation.

Manual Media

This category includes flip charts, chalk boards, and visual boards. In most situations, the presenter writes on the media as the presentation proceeds and so manually creates the visual aid. Relatively inexpensive and easy to use, manual media are best suited for use with small groups in interactive settings. To a limited degree, color can be added by using marking pens of different colors.

Flip Charts.   Flip charts are useful in interactive meeting presentations when a speaker wants to capture remarks from members of the group and retain the notes for later reference. Using drafting tape, chart paper can be posted on the walls around the room. The technique is common in planning sessions, for example, when the presenter's role is more that of a group facilitator. High-quality flip charts with colorful graphic visuals can be professionally prepared. However, in most cases, preprinted flip charts are not worth the cost. The pages become creased and dog-eared with repeated handling, and other more effective media are usually readily available.

Chalk Boards.   Chalk boards are typically a medium of last resort for presenters. Writing in chalk is messy and does not appear as clear or as readable as print on other types of media. Presenters who must use chalk boards refrain from wearing dark wool suits, which quickly become soiled with white chalk dust.

Visual Boards. Visual boards, like flip charts, provide a writing surface but not much else. Magnetized visual boards are somewhat more versatile; prepared visual pieces can be placed and rearranged on them. One speaker made clever use of a magnetized board to present the steps in a design process. As he presented each step, the speaker placed on the board color-coded cutouts with magnetic strip tape on the back, creating a flow chart of the process as he went along. In recent years, another variation of the visual board has appeared in meeting rooms: the electronic visual board. Similar in size to a standard flip chart, electronic visual boards offer the capability of printing photocopies of material that has been written on the board.

Projected Media

In a sense, all visual aids are "projected"—from the media to the audience. However, as a term used to describe a type of media, "projected" refers to media which rely on projector equipment: namely, transparencies, slides, films, and video.

Transparencies. Transparencies are displayed from an overhead projector, and are appropriate for use with either small groups or larger audiences (provided the projected image is sufficiently enlarged to be clearly seen by people seated farthest away). Many presenters have never taken advantage of the variety of visual images that can be projected from transparencies. Consequently, transparencies are often associated with the worst of visual aids: the plain black-on-white alphanumeric text. However, transparencies have untapped potential. They are easy to prepare, easy to use, easy to transport, and relatively inexpensive.

When taped to cardboard frames or enclosed in plastic flip-frame protectors, transparencies hold up well with repeated use. Key-word notes can be written in the margins of the frames. Since transparencies can be produced on many photocopiers from an original print, they can be customized, colorized, and graphic. In interactive settings, blank transparencies can be used as a writing surface. An advantage to transparencies over slides, films, and videos: transparencies can be viewed without having to turn off the lights in a meeting room. However, images from colorized, pictorial transparencies do not appear as sharp or as bright as they would on good-quality slides or film.

Slides. Conventional 35mm slide presentations require a slide projector. Like transparencies, slides are appropriate for use with either small groups or larger audiences. They are also easy to transport and can be used repeatedly. High-quality slides are usually more expensive than transparencies because they are (or should be) professionally produced. For that reason, slides often are perceived to be a more professional medium for business presentations. The quality of the image projected from slides is superior to that of transparencies, provided the lights are turned off in the meeting room—suggesting that slide presentations should be brief.

Films and Videos. The factors that apply to slides also apply to films and videos. Quality films or videos produced professionally can be relatively expensive. However, the cost may be justified if the media will be used repeatedly. Films and videos offer the distinct advantage of adding audio to moving visual images. Thus, well-chosen films and videos are a dynamic, action-oriented media. Since the media is dynamic, presenters who use films or videos must be equally or more dynamic in their delivery—or the audience may experience a letdown when the speaker resumes the presentation after a film or video is shown.

Specialized Media

This category includes poster boards, sales presentation binders, props, and audio aids. These media are considered "specialized" because, in most cases, their use is limited to special situations.

Poster Boards. Usually about the same size as a standard flip chart, poster boards are appropriate for smaller groups and are often used in sales situations. For a quality appearance, poster boards should be professionally prepared. They can display material in text or graphic form with colors. A distinct disadvantage to using poster boards is that they are bulky, making it cumbersome to transport them and to handle them with ease during a presentation.

Sales Presentation Binders. Best suited for use when presenting to two or three people in a sit-down situation, sales presentation binders are sometimes referred to as "sales kits." When a sales representative is seated at a desk or table across from a prospect, a well-designed sales binder is a convenient and more personalized way to add visual support to a message. For a quality appearance, presentation binders should be professionally prepared or computer-generated. For impact, they should feature the benefits of colorful, pictorial, graphic visuals.

Props. A prop is any tangible item that can be related to the point the prop is intended to convey. Provided the object is visible to everyone in the audience, props can be used with small or large groups. Props that are familiar objects can be very effective in providing a "memory hook" for the message. Author and speaker John Bradshaw, for example, makes creative and memorable use of a prop: a mobile made up of symbols that represent members of a family. An assortment of articles have been used by presenters as props: balloons, footballs, coins, hangers, playing cards, and batteries, to name a few. As with all aspects of a presentation, the chief consideration in selecting an article appropriate for a prop is relevance.

Audio Recordings. Until the advent of multimedia systems (discussed next), audio aids were the "neglected species" of presentation media. This has been an unfortunate oversight since sound can be a powerful means of introducing a message or supporting a point. The eighteenth century English dramatist, William Congreve, suggested that "music has charms to sooth a savage breast." Selected music also has qualities that can stir in an audience a sense of energy and anticipation. As a preface to a presentation, speakers have played inspirational theme songs from popular movies to enliven the atmosphere in a meeting room or to imply an association between the theme of the music and the message.

Sound has been used creatively in other ways as well. A consultant who presented seminars on interpersonal communication skills used audio recordings of conversations between clients to validate his points and to prompt participation from the audience. Presenting to prospective customers, a sales representative compared two audio recordings: one of street noise heard in an office, another on which the noise was noticeably absent because of sound-reduction window coverings the salesperson sold. The audio comparison was very persuasive.

Computerized Presentation Aids

Technological advancements in computer software and hardware have revolutionized presentation media. There are two facets to computerized presentation aids: computer-generated presentation graphics and computer-driven presentation showings.

Computer-generated Presentation Graphics. Using a desktop or personal computer, presentation graphics software enables a proficient user to prepare high-quality visual aids in a fraction of the time that it takes to prepare comparable visuals manually. A number of software programs also generate speaker notes and copy for handouts. Among the types of graphics that can be produced are line drawings, illustrations, clip art, two- and three-dimensional graphs, maps, symbols, and slide presentations. Graphics can be output on a color printer for colorized visuals, and reproduced to other media like transparencies or slides. Computer files for slide presentations can be telecommunicated to a service bureau, processed and returned within a matter of days. Some service bureaus offer expedited turnaround within 24 hours.

Computer-driven Presentation Showings. The term *showings* denotes an exhibition or performance. It applies to computer-driven presentations which, through the use of multiple media, can exhibit a combination of slide presentations, prerecorded or live video inserts, digitized still photography, and animation—all to the accompaniment of voice and music. A multimedia presentation is truly a performance. From a purely technological standpoint, multimedia systems have obsoleted conventional media.

For multimedia presentation showings to small groups, the computer or a television monitor may be adequate for viewing. For larger audiences, large-screen projection is required. Multimedia systems take time to learn and skill to use proficiently. It is preferable to have a skilled technician operate the system, leaving the presenter free to do what presenters are supposed to do—relate to the audience. Preoccupation with the operation of equipment will distract both presenter and audience, and will detract from the effectiveness of the presentation.

As versatile as multimedia systems are, there is a danger to viewing the technology as a panacea for business presentations. The danger is in letting the technology *be* the presentation. It is important to bear in mind: the more attention the media (any media) attract, the less attention an audience pays to the presenter. The more prominent the electronic production, the less visible the presenter. The more gadgets there are, the greater the risk of goofs.

Don't trust technology to do your job. Use computer technology for what it is intended: as a tool that can lend audiovisual *support* to the presentations *you* deliver. Electronic wizardry—no matter how impressive— cannot replace the value that a live (and lively) human being can bring to other human beings. At its best, presenting is a process of building relationships through communication. People in an audience still look to a person—the presenter—as someone who relates to them and as someone to whom they can relate in turn.

Choosing Computerized Presentation Aids. Anyone considering presentation graphics software or multimedia hardware will find dozens of options available. Technological advancements and new product announcements occur almost daily. To become better acquainted with the software and systems currently on the market, it is helpful to read computer-user publications or attend meetings of computer-user groups. Before purchasing computerized presentation aids, it is advisable to follow the three steps outlined here:

1. *Clarify.*   Clearly identify the features and functions you need for the presentations you do (and expect to do in the future). Determine how much money you will invest in a total system, including software and hardware. Clarifying your buying criteria and budget will narrow the options.

2. *Consult and compare.*   Consult with at least two reputable dealers or computer consultants. Compare the price-performance (price relative to system performance) of the various options that are within the scope of your buying criteria and budget.

3. *Confirm.*   Before making a final decision, talk with at least three users to confirm actual performance. Ask about training time and learning curves, service and ongoing support, and the users' experience with the functions and limitations of the product.

When you have purchased a system, invest the time to learn how to use it or provide sufficient training for the person(s) who will operate the system.

Key Concept 42

Presenters find it helpful to follow guidelines for the selection and preparation of audiovisual aids.

Some people invest four, six, eight, or more years to prepare for their careers; yet they are reluctant to invest eight hours to prepare for a presentation that can establish (or destroy) their credibility in minutes. In some fields, professionals invest hundreds, sometimes thousands of dollars for opportunities to compete for business; but they are reluctant to invest a few days to prepare for a presentation that could secure new business. The advantages audiovisuals add to a presentation warrant the time it takes to prepare quality audiovisual materials. The following guidelines describe the steps to follow and factors to consider to prepare effective audiovisual aids.

Select the Points Needing Audio or Visual Support

Review the content of the presentation. Identify and make a list of points that will benefit from audiovisual support. In some situations, it is appropriate to include visual aids for the title, preview, and review, and to introduce key points.

Select the Media

Choose the media best suited to the presentation event. It is preferable to limit to two the number of media used during a presentation (except, of course, for presentations that employ computer-driven multimedia systems). For example, a presenter may use an overhead projector and a flip chart, or a slide projector and a prop. The use of too many different media can create a confusing or carnival type of atmosphere. The following questions address factors that should be considered when determining the type of media to select. The answers to the first two questions may influence every other consideration.

- *R.O.I.:* Assuming the presentation is successful, what is the potential "Return On Investment" (investment including the time, money, and human resources that will be spent on preparing the presentation and accompanying audiovisual aids)?

- *Resources:* What resources are available in terms of budget, time, human resources, and media production services?

- *Audience:* Is the presentation for a small or large group? Will this audience respond most favorably to a formal, professional, or casual approach? Will it be advantageous to use a visual aid on which comments from the audience can be noted?

- *Subject and points in the presentation:* What media will best serve the needs of this presentation? Would this particular point be supported best by audio? visual? or both? Would it be beneficial to customize the audiovisual aids?

- *Facility:* In what kind of facility will the presentation be given? Is the meeting site confined or spacious?

- *Lighting:* What lighting factors need to be considered? Can the lights be dimmed? Where are windows located and can they be adequately covered?

- *Frequency of use:* Will the audiovisual aids for this presentation be used only once or repeatedly?

- *Portability:* Will the presentation be done at an on-site or off-site location? Will it be transported to many locations? If so, is the medium portable or readily available in other locations?

- *Equipment:* Does the medium being considered require special equipment? If so, is the equipment readily available?

- *Skill:* Does the medium being considered require special skill to operate? Does the presenter have the requisite skill? If not, is a technician available with whom the presenter can work to rehearse presentation of the audiovisual aids?

Design and Produce the Audiovisual Aids

To gain the benefit of well-designed materials that truly contribute to a presentation, audiovisual aids should be developed in three stages: design, proof, and produce. It is not uncommon for a presenter to lack the objectivity, or the artistic and technical skill required, to design and produce quality audiovisuals. It is, therefore, common to enlist the help of others (such as graphic artists, typesetters, and photo processing labs) to design or produce support materials.

1. *Design.*   Once the points of a presentation that need support have been identified and listed, sketch a visual for each point. (For presenters who are proficient in the use of presentation graphics software, this first stage can, of course, be done on a computer.) Materials should be designed to reflect the characteristics of effective visual aids. In addition to the factors discussed earlier in this chapter (notably under Key Concept 39), attention to the following details will improve the design of visual aids.

   - Each visual aid should concentrate on a single major point, with no more than six or eight lines of subpoints included on the same visual (provided the number of lines in the type size used does not detract from the clarity).
   - To the beginning of lines of text add bullet points, boxes, or arrows to distinguish between points.
   - For labels and text, use key words only.
   - Select type styles (fonts) for clarity. Sans-serif type is preferable for headlines, serif type for captions or key-word text. Limit the use of ALL CAPITAL LETTERS (except for very short, key-word titles), as the individual characters are difficult to distinguish from one another when projected on a screen. Refrain from the use of italics, shadowed, or outline styles. They do not project as clearly as straight-line type, especially on colorized visual aids.
   - When appropriate, make use of visual aids that are layered or that can be displayed progressively in stages. When the point to be supported by a visual aid is composed of several subpoints or segments, it may be more clearly or emphatically presented by showing only one part at a time. For example: using a layered transparency, a speaker displays and speaks about the first point on the transparency. Subsequent points are covered until the speaker addresses each one in turn. In a similar manner, diagrams or charts shown on slides can be presented in stages. One slide depicts the first segment, the following slide the next, and so on. The technique serves to direct audience attention to a single item at a time, and can be effective to build anticipation and interest.

2. *Proof.*   Proof and test the effectiveness of the audiovisual aids prepared in the design stage. To obtain objective feedback on the effectiveness of the audiovisual aids, do a walk-through presentation for two or three coworkers. Invite comments and suggestions from the group. An audiovisual aid that makes sense to the presenter (who knows the point to be made) may not make as much sense to others who are not familiar with the presentation.

Each item of support material should be assessed in terms of the following considerations.

- Is this visual aid readable?
- Is the material understandable?
- Is it professional? Does it project a quality image (or quality sound)?
- Is it necessary?

3. *Produce.*   The time, cost, and steps involved in the production process vary, depending on the media used. Producing a customized computer-driven multimedia presentation, for example, entails more than the production of overhead transparencies. The lead time required to produce audiovisual aids should be considered when planning for a presentation.

Key Concept 43

To support a presentation effectively, audiovisual aids (like verbal expressions) must be clear, correct, concise, and well-considered.

Chapter 5 pointed out that an effective verbal style is composed of language that is clear, concise, correct, and well-considered. The same criteria apply to audiovisual aids.

Clear

Clear visual aids are those an audience can clearly understand. Information (whether printed or handwritten) must be legible and large enough to be clearly readable from every seat in the meeting room. Audio recordings should be clear as well: free of static and loud enough to be heard, but not so loud as to be deafening. Although presenters know (or should know) why they are using a certain audio or visual aid, the audience may not. Therefore, a presenter should provide a clear explanation of each audiovisual aid.

The placement of media affects the clarity of visual aids. Media equipment (chart stands, boards, projectors, screens, or computer terminals) should be placed to furnish to every member of the audience a clear and unobstructed view. When projecting visuals onto a screen, the screen should be set at a right angle to the center line of projection to avoid distortions of the image. For presentations to large groups, the screen should be elevated, with the bottom edge at least four or five feet above the floor to provide a full view to those seated at the back of the meeting room. It may also be necessary to move the screen back or to rearrange seating to allow for a clear view from seats situated at the sides of the room. All details relating to equipment setup should be checked *prior* to a presentation. Fiddling with audiovisual equipment during a presentation distracts the audience and detracts from a speaker's credibility.

The presenter should also check to ensure that visual aids are clearly in focus and appear in sharp contrast for easy readability. This may mean adjusting the lighting in the room. Overhead track or spot lights that shine directly on visual aids should be shut off, and windows covered to eliminate glare. The darker a room, the sharper visual images appear. However, for some people in an audience, total darkness can be a temptation to nap. Worse, a speaker's presence in connection to the audience is diminished when the speaker is not clearly visible. The solution is to dim the lights sufficiently to sharpen the clarity of visual aids, while retaining enough light for the speaker to remain in full view of the audience. These points raise a further consideration with respect to visual aids: the placement of the presenter.

An effective presenter always maintains a position at the front of the meeting room so as to face toward and to focus on the audience. A presenter wants to be seen by the audience, and needs to be able to see audience reactions to the points presented. To remain in clear view of the audience and simultaneously present visual aids in a clear manner, observe the following techniques.

- Never fully turn your back to people in the audience. Learn to write on flip charts and visual boards standing sideways so as to remain at least partially turned toward the audience. When showing slides, stay at the front of the room, standing to one side. A presenter who stands behind the audience when delivering a slide presentation becomes little more than a disembodied voice.

- Refrain from leaning against or over equipment. A flip chart is not a crutch. An overhead projector was not designed for showing shadow figures of a speaker's hands. When using transparencies, after placing the transparency on the projector, step away from the equipment and refer to the image on the screen. Avoid staring fixedly at the transparency that is on the glass of the projector, and avoid the appearance of being permanently attached to the equipment.

- Refrain from walking in front of a screen when a visual aid is displayed on it.

- For both verbal message and visual aid to be clearly understood, they must occur in sync. An audience can be confused when a speaker goes on to address another point while a visual aid of the previous point remains displayed. When finished addressing the point that appears on a visual aid, turn to a fresh page on the flip chart, erase the visual board, shut off the light on the overhead projector, and turn off the slide projector.

- Use visual aids for reference—to clarify or emphasize. Bear in mind that visual aids are *support* to a message, not the message itself. Do not read verbatim every word or number that appears on a visual aid. If the visual aid is clearly designed, the audience will clearly get the message.

Correct

The material on a visual aid, such as graphics and colors, must be correctly matched to the information or ideas that the visual is intended to support. Data must be correct in terms of accuracy. The accuracy of the information should be validated by noting the source, either verbally or as a footnote on the visual aid. Consistency with the verbal message is equally important. For example, if a presenter verbally expresses numeric data in percentages, figures on an accompanying visual aid should likewise be shown as percentages. Effective visual aids are also correct from the standpoint of being bias-free and in good taste.

An additional consideration is the correct number of visual aids to use for a given presentation. Chapter 5 pointed out that overuse of a verbal expression will reduce its meaning and impact. The same principle applies to visual aids. Presenting too many visuals one after another can frustrate rather than focus an audience. Too many visual aids can supplant the presenter rather than support the presentation.

Speech and communication consultants differ in their opinions of how many visuals to use. Some recommend not more than one visual aid for every minute of a presentation; others suggest not more than one for every two or three minutes. When deciding on how many visual aids to use, follow the rule-of-thumb, "When in doubt, don't." When in doubt about whether a visual aid contributes to the meaning of the message, don't use it. When in doubt if a presentation is dominated by visual aids, it probably is. Don't use them all. A second rule-of-thumb applies to the use of audiovisual aids: "Everything in moderation." Moderate use of audiovisuals avoids the risk of overwhelming a message with media.

Concise

Visual aids are flawed when they appear crammed with too much information for viewers to assimilate at a glance. Too much text or data on a single visual aid will confuse rather than clarify. The same principle that applies to verbal expressions applies to audiovisuals, too: KISS—Keep It Short and Simple.

Concise also applies to the coverage a presenter gives any one audiovisual aid. Brief is better. Leaving the same audio or visual aid on for too long will slow the pace of a presentation and begin to bore the audience.

Well-considered

Of the many types of audiovisual aids and media available, not every type is appropriate to all situations. How does a presenter determine what to use? You may recall the decisive factors of a presentation (pictured in Figure 4-2). The same factors should be considered when choosing and using audiovisuals. Effective audiovisuals are appropriate and relevant to the audience, setting, subject, objectives, and time frame.

Well-considered use of audiovisuals also takes into account the equipment and supplies that will be needed for a presentation. In addition to the items listed on the "planning checklist" (included at the end of Chapter 2), the well-prepared presenter will have the following items available for "back-up": extra working light bulbs for projection equipment, an extension cord, and (if applicable) duplicate diskettes for a computer-driven presentation.

Reflection Question

What pointers have you picked up from this chapter that you will put into practice in order to make more effective use of audiovisual aids?

Summary

The purpose of audiovisual aids is to support a presentation by making use of images and sounds that clarify, emphasize, or in other ways enhance audience understanding and interest. Visual aids that are pictorial, colorful, and creative are most effective, and can be presented in various graphic forms on different types of media. The potential benefits of audiovisual aids merit attending to the selection, preparation, and use of audiovisuals that are clear, correct, concise, and well-considered.

Sample Situations

Situation 1: Creating a Graphic on the Spot

Many presenters feel that manual media limit them to visual aids that consist entirely of words and numbers. With some creative thought and practice, presenters discover ways to add graphics to manual media.

Addressing a group of managers in a meeting on the subject of workplace incentives, a presenter had only a visual board available in the conference room. To support one of the points of her message, in a matter of seconds she drew a vertical line down the left side of the board and a horizontal line across the top. The lines were joined at the upper-left corner. Across the horizontal axis she wrote the numbers 1-2-3-4-5. Down the vertical axis, using colored marking pens, she sketched three symbols: a green dollar sign to represent money, a blue ladder for success, a yellow "happy face" to signify job satisfaction. She posed the question to the group, "What is your primary motivator on the job?" As members of the audience responded, she created a bar chart. When the results were depicted graphically, the effect was far more striking than it would have been in words and numbers.

Situation 2: A Creative Use of Photographic Visual Aids

A representative of an electric utility company that served a major metropolitan area was asked to make presentations to commercial users on the subject of energy conservation. She reviewed pages of statistical data that compared increasing demand against declining resources. Although the information was useful, she determined that busy professionals would soon tire of a visual aid that displayed so much detail. She prepared a handout and included the detailed data in it for reference.

For her presentation, she produced two photographic slides. The first depicted the city skyline at night, with many of the buildings ablaze with lights. The second slide pictured the same skyline, but in this one the buildings were barely visible against the night sky. No lights appeared to relieve the dark image. She opened her presentation with the slides, pointing out, "If we continue to do this" (the first slide suggested a wasteful use of energy), "we will end up like this" (the second slide depicted the result of the first).

Situation 3: Creating a Prop from Material at Hand

Seated across the desk from a prospective buyer, a salesman for a worldwide telecommunications company presented a proposal for long-distance services. As he brought his presentation to a close, the salesman picked up a sheet of paper and crumpled it into a ball. Subtly, he opened his hand and extended it toward the prospect, saying, "Using our long-distance service is like having the world in the palm of your hand." The prospect eyed the paper orb for a moment, picked it up, and then signed the order.

Comprehension Check

The answers to the following appear on page 333.

1. The most effective visual aids _____.
   a. display 3-dimensional graphs
   b. are multimedia presentations
   c. include symbols
   d. are graphic, colorful, and creative
   e. include audio

2. The primary purpose of visual aids is to _____.
   a. write down input from the audience
   b. support the message
   c. add color to a presentation
   d. interpret statistical data
   e. make a presentation more competitive

3. One advantage to using visual aids is that they _____.
   a. increase audience retention
   b. develop the key points of a message
   c. compensate for a poorly organized message
   d. minimize questions from an audience
   e. demonstrate the presenter's graphic skill

4. The size of the audience is one factor to consider when deciding _____.
   a. how to customize graphics
   b. the type of media to use
   c. the use of presentation graphics software
   d. how much to invest in media
   e. the colors to be used on visuals

5. Creative audio or visual aids _____ .
   a. distract an audience
   b. are usually spontaneous
   c. rarely make use of graphics
   d. distinguish a presenter from the norm
   e. always add a professional look to a presentation

To Do

In this "To Do," you will begin to prepare audiovisual aids for the presentation that you are developing during this course.

1. Indicate the medium or media you will use to present audio or visual aids.

2. For each key point, sketch at least one visual aid you will use to support the point. Indicate the colors you will use on each visual. (If you are currently using presentation graphics software, you may opt to prepare the visual aids on your computer system.)

Presenting: Building Relationship and Response

The preceding chapters concentrated on the "mechanics" of planning and preparing a presentation. The result is the "raw material" of a message, ready to be delivered to an audience. Delivery entails three interrelated aspects: (1) the way a presenter relates to the audience, (2) what a presenter conveys to the audience, and (3) how a presenter responds to questions and comments. Relating to the audience is the subject of this chapter. (The second and third aspects are discussed in Chapters 8 and 9 respectively.)

The degree to which a presenter is successful in relating to people is determined by the material in the message and by techniques employed when presenting. Therefore, some of the points discussed in this chapter pertain to content, others to communication skills. Both relational content and relational skills are essential to influence and persuade people.

Objectives

To describe the value that relational attributes add to a presentation; and to incorporate relational techniques when preparing and presenting a message.

Key Concepts

44. Relational content and skills balance a presentation and help convert a resistant audience to a receptive one.

201

45. Effective presenters relate to an audience in terms of what people need and want.

46. People want to know what to expect.

47. People want to be recognized.

48. People want to be a part of the presentation event.

49. People want to know how a message applies to them.

Key Terms

To apply the key concepts, it is essential to understand the following key terms in the context of business presentations:

Relational	Proactive
Information-bound	Interactive
Relevant	Open question
Direct reference	Recall
Affirm	Value statement
Self-disclosure	

Key Concept 44

Relational content and skills balance a presentation and help convert a resistant audience to a receptive one.

The term **relational** applies to that which suggests a connection or describes an affinity between persons or groups. Through a relational presentation, a speaker builds an alliance with the audience. Listening, people are moved to respond, "I can relate to that point" or "I can relate to this speaker." The more relational a presentation is, the more likely the audience will be drawn into agreement with the presenter.

Depending on the subject and the composition of the audience, people will be, to varying degrees, either resistant or receptive. (Some remain undecided, which is a form of resistance.) Audience resistance commonly occurs as a consequence of any one or a combination of the following factors:

- Conflicting values
- Different experience or frame of reference
- Apathy

- Doubt or distrust
- Unfavorable perception of the presenter

To successfully persuade an audience to one's point of view, sources of potential resistance must be overcome. Resistance can be overcome by applying the skills described in this course, paying particular attention to relational techniques that build a bridge, so to speak, to the audience. Unless people in an audience personally relate to the material presented, and understand how it relates to them, they are inclined to reject the message. Unless people relate favorably to the presenter and perceive that the presenter is genuinely interested in relating to them, they are inclined to reject the messenger.

Beware of Being an Information-bound Presenter

Some speakers mistakenly assume that if they present sufficient amounts of factual data, an audience will be persuaded to accept the message. Many professionals who have attempted to persuade people in this manner—and failed—could attest to the fact that nothing could be further from the truth. Information alone does not persuade people.

Typically, an audience does not respond favorably to information-bound presenters. A presenter who is **information-bound** relies primarily on facts and figures as the means to express a message. Information-bound presenters, preoccupied with data, appear to an audience to be more concerned with their connection to the podium than with connecting to the people seated in front of them. Information-bound presenters rely heavily on note cards and scripts, their attention focused on an overhead projector or teleprompter. They tend to neglect the most decisive factor in any communication situation: relating to people. As a result, information-bound presenters often encounter resistance from an audience.

Build a Balanced Presentation

Effective presenters recognize that a persuasive presentation relies on striking a balance between informational and relational elements, as shown in Figure 7-1.

INFORMATIONAL		RELATIONAL
What	▲	Who

Figure 7-1. Informational and relational in balance.

Relational attributes add balance to a presentation. They "soften" an audience to be more receptive to the information, ideas, and insights a presenter offers. Presenters who have the greatest influence see in front of them not an autonomous audience, but *people*. They do not attempt to impose their views on others, but rather seek to draw their listeners into a kind of partnership of information exchange. They strive to build the affirmative relationship with people that engenders an affirmative response.

A positive relationship with an audience is built on a foundation of the following principles (discussed earlier in this course).

1. A presentation is *person-to-persons communication*. (Chapter 1, Key Concept 4; see Figure 1-1.)

2. An effective presentation incorporates material and techniques that "speak to" the *nature and needs of the audience*. (Chapter 2, Key Concept 13.)

3. An *approach* that is fitting to the audience is essential. (Chapter 3, Key Concept 21.)

An audience is more apt to be receptive to a presentation that exemplifies these concepts.

Presenter Attitude + Actions = Audience Response

An audience is also more apt to be receptive when they perceive that *they* are the presenter's chief concern. As Figure 7-2 illustrates, audience response to a presentation is determined in large part by the presenter's attitude and actions toward the audience.

Generally, what presenters give *to* an audience is what they will get *from* an audience. There are, of course, exceptions: the bull-headed individual who persists in preserving a biased point of view or the person who is argumentative or apathetic by nature. However, such personalities that

Figure   7-2. Relationship and response.

doggedly resist the appeal of a relational presenter tend to be in the minority. Even the best speakers do not please all of the people all of the time, but all speakers can realistically aim to make a difference with many people much of the time.

An affirmative response is fostered by an "audience-oriented" attitude. Speakers who are primarily concerned with themselves convey an "*I* am here to tell you . . ." attitude. Relational speakers, on the other hand, convey an attitude that underscores the audience: "*You* are here, giving me the value of your time." In turn, relational presenters seek to give the audience the value of a meaningful and memorable message. An audience is far more likely to be favorably disposed toward the presenter who concentrates attention on them.

An "audience-oriented" attitude has a further advantage as well. Frequently, anxiety about speaking before a group is the result of being unduly *self*-conscious. Such anxiety is alleviated when a speaker is more *audience*-conscious. "I" as the speaker am not the center of attention; "you" are. Viewing the audience as the center of attention can help to relieve the pressure some speakers feel.

Key Concept 45

Effective presenters relate to an audience in terms of what people need and want.

The point of this concept was first introduced in Chapter 3 (Key Concept 13). It has been reiterated throughout this course because it is *the* key to reaching people. A business presentation may be done *about* a subject, *in* a certain setting, *within* a scheduled time frame, and *by* a speaker who presents a message to achieve an objective. First and foremost, however, a presentation is done *for* the audience. To successfully influence or persuade people, a presenter must appeal to what people in the audience need and want.

A presentation is to a speaker what a widget is to a manufacturer, what a book is to a publisher, what a building is to an architect. It is a product. Time, thought, and care may go in to producing a presentation; as with any product, though, people will not be interested in it unless it satisfies something they want.

Human wants and needs have been considered from different perspectives. Three with which presenters should be acquainted are summarized next.

A Marketing Perspective on Needs

Marketing and advertising expert Jay Conrad Levinson determined that people respond to a product offering when it appeals to one or a number of the following needs:*

- Convenience
- Comfort
- Love
- Friendship
- Security
- Style
- Social approval
- Health and well-being
- Profit
- Savings or economy

A Behavioral/Motivational Perspective on Needs

Many people who have studied management or psychology are familiar with the work of the behavioral scientist Abraham Maslow. Maslow identified five basic needs that people are motivated to satisfy, described as a "Hierarchy of Needs." Listed in ascending order, they are:

- *Survival:*   the need for air, water, food, clothing, and shelter to sustain physical life.
- *Security:*   the need to feel safe and secure from fear or threat.
- *Social acceptance:*   the need for love and a sense of belonging.
- *Self-esteem:*   the need for self-respect and regard from others.
- *Self-actualization:*   the need to grow, to be involved in work or an activity that fulfills one's potential.

A Presenter's Perspective: What an Audience Wants and Needs

An audience will be more responsive to a message when their needs are met in terms of the four relational attributes outlined below. As indicated, these attributes echo a number of the needs identified by Levinson and Maslow.

---

* Jay Conrad Levinson, *Guerrilla Marketing* (Boston: Houghton Mifflin Company, 1984), p. 59.

Expectation. An audience wants to know what to expect. Knowing what to expect creates a comfort level that satisfies the need for security.

Recognition. People in an audience want to be recognized. Recognition satisfies the need for friendship, social approval, and a sense of well-being.

Participation. An audience wants to feel they are a part of the presentation event. Participation satisfies the need for a sense of belonging and self-esteem. Some presentation events also provide opportunities for self-actualization.

Application. An audience wants to know how a message applies to them. Depending on the subject of a presentation, application of the message might satisfy any one or a number of needs.

The key concepts that follow describe techniques for integrating these four relational attributes into a presentation.

Key Concept 46

People want to know what to expect.

When a presentation begins, the audience is at first uncertain about what will transpire. When the subject is controversial or potentially unpleasant, some people may be guarded or uneasy. If the presenter is unknown to the group, the audience may be curious or skeptical. If they have just returned from lunch or if they have attended meetings "like this" before, they may be waiting for an opportunity to nap. Meanwhile, the presenter hopes the audience will give their full attention to the message. To stir interest in a presentation, a presenter must provide an indication of what is coming.

Letting the audience know what to expect at the outset of a presentation helps put people at ease and readies them to listen to the message. The need to know what to expect is initially satisfied when a presenter relates the opener and preview. Later in a presentation, transitions serve to let the audience know what point to expect next.

In addition to the verbalized opener and preview, nonverbal cues suggest to an audience what they might expect. Is the presenter composed? organized? smiling or somber? Is the speaker wearing appropriate attire? A presenter conveys countless nonverbal cues (discussed in the next chapter), from which an audience forms expectations.

First impressions are critical. Before presenting it is beneficial to double-check the opener, the preview, and a mirror. A speaker can gain useful insights by considering the following question:

> Based on what they initially see and hear, what will people in the audience expect?

For effective presenters, the answer will be: the audience will expect the key points of a meaningful and memorable message delivered by a confident and credible professional.

Key Concept 47

People want to be recognized.

Giving people what they want and need from a presentation is deceptively simple. It has little to do with subject matter or how articulate the speaker is. It has everything to do with human nature. In addition to the various human needs identified by Levinson and Maslow (listed under Key Concept 45), there is another. It is a universal need. It is attention. People want attention. An audience will be more responsive to a presenter who pays attention to them than to one who does not. Presenters demonstrate attention to an audience by recognizing who is in the group and what is important to them (insights gained from planning).

A presentation will not be effective unless it is **relevant**, meaning that it bears upon or is connected to the matter at hand. In a presentation, the "matter at hand" is the audience. Relevance is the essence of a relational presentation. It signals to people in an audience that the speaker recognizes them. To relate in a relevant manner and thereby build a winning relationship with an audience, a presenter must:

- Adapt the message
- Address the message
- Affirm the audience

Adapt the Message

A presentation that is adapted to a particular situation reflects the presenter's interest in the audience. A message on any subject can and should be altered to fit the profile of the audience. One way to adapt a message is to tailor the approach (discussed in Chapter 3, Key Concept 21). Other aspects of a presentation that should be adapted to the audience include:

- Language and terminology
- Types of evidence and examples used
- Audiovisual aids
- Applications of the message

Address the Message

A presentation is like a letter. If it is addressed incorrectly, it will not be received. An audience is inclined to "return to sender" a presentation that is not addressed to them. For a presentation to be well received, it must be specifically addressed to the audience for whom it is intended. A message is addressed to an audience with the use of the following techniques.

Pronouns.   Sprinkle a presentation with personal pronouns. The audience-oriented pronoun "you" or the inclusive pronoun "we" are preferable to "I." For example, "you will find" appeals to an audience more than "I have found . . ." "We experience success when we . . ." is preferable to "I experience success when I . . ." Addressing an audience using "you" and "we" conveys a sense of talking *with* people rather than talking *at* them.

Names.   In presentations to small groups and in interactive settings, addressing people by name helps to build relationship with them. Presenters who speak in such settings should master the ability to learn and remember names. Most people appreciate being referred to by name. It signals that the presenter recognizes them individually.

When a speaker addresses a group for the first time and is not acquainted with people by name, name tags or tent cards should be supplied. A more professional impression is created by having name tags or cards printed in advance (when the situation allows), with lettering large enough for the presenter to read. It also creates a favorable impression when a speaker arrives at a presentation event early and makes the effort to become acquainted with at least a few people by name. If the situation calls for participants to introduce themselves at the beginning of the presentation, their names will be easier to remember if repeated. For example, after one person says, "I'm Jan Smith, Director of Human Relations," the presenter would restate the name, saying something like, "Jan, it's a pleasure to have you here."

Direct References.   As the term implies, a **direct reference** refers directly to some characteristic that people in the audience have in common. The following phrases are examples of direct references.

For managers like yourselves . . .

Instructors who use this technique . . .

Most salespeople find . . .

The more direct a reference, the more the audience will infer that the message is related to them. For example, in a sales presentation, a representative who cites testimonials from satisfied customers might say something like "Customers who use this product . . ." The term "customers" is generic. A more specific reference will have greater appeal, such as "Building contractors who use this product . . ." When the audience is so diverse that a single direct reference would not apply, a combination of specific and generic terms may work. A presentation may be addressed, for example, to "Business owners, managers, and technical professionals like yourselves . . ."

Affirm the Audience

The literal definition of **affirm** is to declare something as true, to validate it. With the growth in the human potential and self-esteem movement, the term has assumed additional meaning. It refers to that which is positive (as opposed to negative); it connotes building up rather than putting down. In the context of presenting, to **affirm** an audience means relating in a positive manner that validates people. With few exceptions (and there are, unfortunately, some), most people in an audience are more receptive and responsive to a presenter who makes them feel good. Affirmation satisfies the human need for recognition—to be recognized as having value.

A presenter affirms an audience by both attitudes and actions. An affirming attitude fosters a positive and pleasant atmosphere in which people in the audience feel welcome, comfortable, and secure. Affirming actions include the language, gestures, posture, and the full array of nonverbal cues by which a presenter relates to an audience. The combination of vocal and visual forms of communication send the audience a "message within the message." It should be a positive one.

One popular and very persuasive presenter carries a note card as a reminder. It reads:

Don't preach.

Don't patronize.

DO personalize.

The three points summarize the type of approach that affirms an audience, expressed further in the following suggestions.

Care. A relational presenter embodies an attitude of caring about people and so deals with all people as peers. Refrain from displaying a condescending attitude. An audience is inclined to resist (if not altogether reject) a presenter whom they perceive to be a self-proclaimed expert who talks down to them. Relationships are not built on the basis of a "superior" speaker who lectures to listeners as though they were "inferior."

Refrain from making disparaging remarks. Disparagement is the opposite of affirmation. When a speaker makes comments that slight or belittle—a person, a particular group, or competitors—the audience may infer that the speaker would just as readily disparage them, too.

Self-disclose. Develop an affiliation with the audience through appropriate self-disclosure. By **self-disclosure** a presenter reveals to an audience something of a personal nature from the presenter's experience. Self-disclosure may express a fact, a feeling, or an opinion. For example, to say, "As a teenager, I was the tallest and skinniest kid in my class," is a disclosure of fact. "I was unhappy about my appearance," would be a disclosure of feeling (one with which many people in an audience may relate). "Teenagers need to know that outward appearance is not a true measure of a person's value," is a disclosure of opinion. Self-disclosure is really a form of substantiating material. In some situations, a personal anecdote or an example from personal experience is the most relational, meaningful, and memorable way to express a point.

Self-disclosure is also a means of building a responsive relationship with an audience. Unless a presenter and people in the audience know one another, there is a distance between them when a presentation begins. The speaker is "up there." The audience is "out here," and they have little idea of what the speaker is going to say or do. Self-disclosure helps to bridge the gap. It develops in the audience a sense of getting acquainted with and thus better able to relate to the presenter.

By showing something of oneself, a presenter conveys to an audience, "I trust you." Doing so encourages an audience to likewise trust the presenter. Developing trust helps to break down audience resistance. Trust is an essential ingredient in a business presentation because people are not easily influenced by someone they do not trust.

Self-disclosure also signals an audience that the presenter is willing to relate on a personal level: not as "speaker" and "listeners," but as "persons" who share some experience. A self-disclosure can also serve as an icebreaker, especially when delivered with a touch of humor that displays the presenter's humanity.

It is important to know when and what and how much to disclose. Any self-disclosure should be relevant to the subject and the audience. It should be appropriate to the setting and the situation. What a presenter reveals should be limited to the nature and extent of disclosure that the presenter would be comfortable hearing from the audience. The guidelines (discussed in Chapter 5) regarding material that is bias-free and in good taste apply, as does the principle that "discretion is the greater part of valor."

Appear Approachable. An audience is affirmed by a presenter who appears approachable, which means dealing with people in a personable, agreeable, and pleasant manner. To be approachable is to be perceived by people in the audience as the kind of person they would like to meet and talk with one-on-one. An audience perceives a presenter to be approachable (or not) from both verbal and nonverbal forms of communication. Verbally, humor, self-disclosure, and the use of affirming techniques when responding to audience questions and comments promote a perception of approachability.

Reflection Question

In the presentations you give, what specific phrasing or techniques could you use to indicate your recognition of the audience members and your genuine regard for them?

Key Concept 48

People want to be a part of the presentation event.

An additional way to affirm people in an audience, and to make a message more meaningful for them, is to involve people in a presentation. When people take part in a presentation experience, they are far more likely to listen and respond than they are if they sit passively. A speaker who relates to people in a manner that welcomes their involvement elicits response from the audience, which signals that they, in turn, are relating to the speaker.

In many respects, a presentation is similar to a stage play. The presenter may fill the leading role of "Speaker," but in an effective presentation, it is not a solo act. Every person in the audience should be invited to play a part. Often, the role a presenter wants an audience to fill is that of "Attentive Listeners." Since many people have not learned how to listen attentively, it is not an easy part for an audience to play. Their listening attentively and responding actively improves in proportion to the prompting they receive from the presenter.

Modes of Presentation

How a presenter prompts an audience depends on the mode of presentation. Although there are many different settings in which presentations occur, they can be categorized into one of two modes: ProActive and InterActive.

ProActive. **Proactive** is defined as active in advance. It suggests that one anticipates conditions and takes appropriate steps to promote a certain outcome. While all effective presenters might be described as proactive, when used to describe the mode of presentation the term refers to the fact that, in the ProActive mode, the presenter is predominant. Again, by analogy with a stage play, in a ProActive mode the presenter is the protagonist—the main character who keeps the action moving forward. ProActive presentations include speeches and seminars in which the presenter is most visible and vocal.

InterActive. **Interactive** refers to occasions when presenter and audience interact, sharing speaking and listening roles. Information is exchanged. While the presenter may play the more prominent role of "group leader," the audience regularly voices comments and offers ideas. Participative workshops, classrooms (ideally), and meetings (ideally) are examples of presentations in the InterActive mode.

Participation Belongs in Both Modes

In the terms ProActive and InterActive, "Active" is capitalized to emphasize that the audience is *active* in both modes. Communication always involves two parties. It is (as depicted in Figure 1-1) a two-way process. Although listeners may not be vocally active in response to a speaker, in effective communications they are mentally and emotionally active and involved.

In ProActive presentations, the audience may seem to be passive. From a presenter's point of view, it may appear the audience is just sitting while the presenter speaks. However, throughout a presentation a presenter should query:

> "Is the audience sitting there attuned to what I am saying, or are they tuned out? Are people mentally taking part in the message, or are they mentally elsewhere?"

Every presentation—ProActive or InterActive—has an interactive dimension to it in terms of the give-and-take of message and response between speaker and listeners. When listening attentively, most people exhibit some form of reaction to what they see and hear. Although an audience may not *voice* their reactions, they do communicate response in nonverbal ways. People nod or shake their heads, smile or frown, facially express interest or indifference. According to these observable responses, alert and astute presenters adjust how (and sometimes what) they relate to an audience.

If a speaker overlooks audience reactions or fails to involve the audience, people will eventually stop listening. When people no longer listen, presenters lose their power to persuade. The question, then, is not *if* a presenter should develop an active and participative relationship with the audience. It is, rather, *how* to do so. In a ProActive mode, audience participation is implied. In the InterActive mode, it is explicit (as well as implied). In both modes, the following techniques are aimed at involving the audience.

Ask Questions

Questions draw people into a presentation. In the ProActive mode, a presenter asks rhetorical questions; in the InterActive mode, direct questions. The essential difference between the two types of questions is simply that a direct question seeks a verbalized response whereas a rhetorical question does not. Whether the answer is voiced or not, the advantage to posing questions is the same. Questions alert people in the audience to listen and to formulate an answer. A presenter who prompts the audience to mentally consider a point has people's attention. When a presenter poses a question, timing and phrasing are critical.

Rhetorical Questions. A rhetorical question must be stated with the intonation that indicates it is a rhetorical question. It is followed by a brief but meaningful pause to give the audience an opportunity to absorb the question and consider the point. The presenter then states the answer, with feeling appropriate to the point.

Direct Questions. When direct questions are posed in InterActive presentations, the pause that follows a question needs to be longer than it is with rhetorical questions. After asking a direct question, a presenter should wait for as long as twenty to thirty seconds to allow sufficient time for someone in the audience to volunteer an answer. It takes that much time for most people to hear and digest a question, mentally formulate a response, work up the courage to speak, and finally voice their answer. In many cases, presenters wait no more than five or ten seconds, then rush on and answer the question themselves. Understandably, people are discouraged from actively taking part if a presenter does not give them the chance to do so.

With both rhetorical and direct questions, it is the pause after the question that invites audience involvement. The effect questions are intended to create is lost if a presenter speaks up immediately after posing a question.

Open Questions.   In most cases, questions should be phrased in the form of an open question. An **open question** is so named because it opens up communication and response using one of the following words:

- Who
- What
- When
- Where
- How

Although "why" questions are also open, they can be perceived as testy or threatening and therefore should usually be avoided. It is preferable to ask open questions because they elicit more of a response than closed questions.

Closed questions begin with words like can, are, do, will, and have. They are called "closed" because they "close off" the listener's response. Since such questions require only a "yes" or "no" answer, people do not have to pay very close attention. The degree of participation is limited, as illustrated by the comparative examples shown here:

Open: What are the advantages of relating to people's needs?

Closed: Are there advantages to relating to people's needs?

Open: How does this point apply to your situation?

Closed: Can you apply this point to your situation?

Open: Who would most benefit from this (product, service, idea)?

Closed: Will anyone benefit from this . . . ?

Obviously, open questions are more thought-provoking than closed questions and so serve to do exactly what a presenter wants to do: provoke the audience to think about the message. As such, open questions prompt greater participation from the audience—even when they are rhetorical and the participation is only implied.

Suggest Recalls

A **recall** invites the people in the audience to call to mind something they have heard or experienced. A recall prompts people to rethink or reexperience in part an issue or a situation. A recall may refer to a previous point in the presentation or to an event.

Recall a Point.   The audience is invited to reflect on a point made earlier in the presentation. For example, "You may recall the Model Outline we used for preparing a presentation. . . ." When listeners hear such a phrase, they shift their minds into gear, so to speak, and mentally participate as they recall the point. A recall of this type not only involves the audience, it can also be used to reinforce key points and to weave together the various strands of a message for greater continuity.

Recall an Event.   Recalling an event can be useful to introduce or substantiate a point, develop an analogy, or stir an emotional response. Participation is implied as people form a mental picture of the occasion recalled. Recalls often awaken feelings associated with an event. They can be especially effective when a presenter wants the audience to feel a certain way about an issue or a point that is related through the use of a recall. The following examples suggest how the technique works.

> "If you'll recall what it was like when our troops first returned home . . ."
>
> "Remember the hurricane that devastated southern Florida?"
>
> "You may recall how customers reacted when Product X was announced . . ."

The foregoing examples also suggest that event-related recalls need to be chosen with care. They must be relevant to the subject and must refer to an event with which the audience will be familiar. If a presenter recalls an occasion outside of the experience of the audience, the recall will not serve the purpose for which it is intended. In this respect, a presenter must be sensitive to the "generation gap" or to a "cultural gap" that may exist between speaker and listeners. In one case, for example, a speaker stated, "Recalling the social turmoil of the '60s . . ." When the recall elicited little response other than blank stares, the speaker realized that most of the people in the audience were too young to recall that time or they had not yet been born.

Describe Scenarios

In Chapter 4, a scenario was defined as a "word picture" that creates a scene for the audience to mentally picture. Chapter 4 referred to a scenario as a form of opener. In addition, scenarios in the body of a presentation can be effective for involving the audience. Even a simple scenario, like the example that follows, can give an audience a sense of what it feels like to be part of the experience described.

> "Imagine: you have just been introduced to the group. You are about to present your proposal when [pause] unexpectedly the CEO walks into the meeting."

When audience members picture a situation, and feel emotions associated with it, they are a part of the presentation. To involve people, a scenario may relate a situation with which they are familiar (or could well imagine). It may be self-disclosing if the disclosure relates a circumstance that they can picture or likely experienced themselves. It may describe an incident involving someone who is known and respected by both speaker and listeners. The best scenarios suggest a connection between the presenter and the audience, and foster agreement on the point the scenario is used to support.

Activities That Engage the Audience

In small-group interactive settings, a presenter can create even more opportunities for people to take part—explicitly. People in an audience become involved to a much greater degree when a presentation includes discussion in break-out groups, problem-solving or creative-thinking tasks, role playing, workbook exercises, or team games. Such techniques are the tools of the trade for presenters who serve as instructors and group facilitators.

Reflection Question

From this discussion of Key Concept 48, what ideas have you gained that you will use to make your presentations more participative, to prompt response from the audience?

Key Concept 49

People want to know how a message applies to them.

The relational techniques discussed in the preceding concepts make a presentation more meaningful and memorable for an audience. They will not, however, ensure that a presentation is activating. To motivate people to act, a presenter must go a step further. A message must be applied to an audience in terms of value.

Generally, people are motivated by self-interest. They act on the basis of what they perceive will best satisfy their needs. An audience is more inclined to listen, accept, and act on ideas or information which they find not only relevant to them, but useful and gratifying as well. When people are convinced that a product or service will be beneficial for them, they are far more likely to buy it. The outcome of a presentation depends on whether the audience recognizes the value of what is presented, the key words being *the audience recognizes.*

Typically, presenters recognize the value of the information they present. As a result, it is easy to overlook communicating to members of the audience why *they* should act on the message. Some speakers mistakenly assume that the advantages are obvious. One should always assume that they are not—unless the presenter clearly relates value statements to the audience.

Value Statements

A **value statement** translates a point into something the audience wants or needs. The needs outlined earlier in this chapter (under Key Concept 45) provide insight into what people value. When formulating value statements, it is helpful if a presenter considers:

> "If I heard the point from the perspective of this audience, what would move me to act on it?"

Listed are examples of phrases that communicate value:

"What this means to you is . . ."

"As a result, you'll enjoy . . ."

"A significant advantage is that you will gain . . ."

"You will find this especially useful for . . ."

"You can look forward to increasing revenues by as much as . . ."

"The benefit to you is: you can reduce costs by as much as . . ."

Notice how the foregoing examples make use of words that appeal to people: meaning, enjoyment, gain, usefulness, financial benefit. Notice how each statement is phrased to address "you" (that is, the audience). Value statements may also be introduced with a rhetorical question (combining a participative technique with the application of the point). For example: "What does this mean to you? [momentary pause] Clearly, the opportunity to . . ."

For more persuasive effect, value statements are incorporated throughout a presentation: notably with or after each key point and immediately before or as part of the summary. The more specific a statement of value is, the more convincing it will be. Vague or ambiguous remarks do not make much of an impression on people (and may foster the doubt or distrust that results in resistance). A presenter should never leave it up to the audience to infer value from the content of a presentation. People may not make the effort or they may reach a conclusion different than what the presenter intended. A relational presenter states value explicitly as it applies to the audience.

Summary

Relational content and skills are woven throughout a presentation to add balance to the information, to break down possible audience resistance, and to build an affirmative response from the audience. An effective presenter relates to an audience on the basis of what people want from a presentation; namely, to know what to expect, to be recognized, to be a part of the presentation event, and to understand how a message applies to them in terms of value.

Sample Situations

Situation 1: Business Presentations as a Method of Managing Change

Since the early 1980s, many organizations have undergone sweeping changes brought about by automation, reorganization, and economic transition. Most have followed the predictable path of initiating the change at the executive level and then passively allowing the news to filter through the rumor mill that operates in every organization. For many, the result has been uncertainty, discontent, and sagging morale among employees, which endanger productivity at the very time when productivity gains are most needed. Some organizations have suffered more far-reaching consequences: distrust (sometimes outright hostility) from unions, unfavorable media coverage, a reduction in their credit rating, a decline in the value of their stock.

The executives of one corporation responded to a reorganization more creatively. One objective of their restructuring plan was to maintain good relations with entities that influenced how the company was perceived, and with those who could affect the outcome of the change. Recognizing that communication is essential to build affirmative relationships, they devised a program to conduct carefully timed and skillfully delivered presentations. Managers from various functional units were trained in presentation skills and delegated responsibility for addressing groups with which they dealt. Presentations were made to supervisors, sales personnel, administrative and clerical staff, research specialists, manufacturing plant workers, key commercial customers, major vendors, lenders, bargaining units, and the media. The presentations were adapted to address the particular audience in attendance. Information that was relevant to each group was provided, in language and with examples to which each audience could relate. People perceived that the company was paying attention to them, recognized their interests and concerns, and welcomed them to participate in the change process.

By relational presentations delivered in advance of the reorganization, the company managed how the situation was perceived and received, as opposed to having to react to exaggerations and distortions from the rumor mill.

Situation 2: Relational Techniques in a Sales Presentation

A sales representative for a software company sold multimedia interactive learning systems. She was very successful as a result of incorporating relational techniques into her presentations of the product. She focused attention on the audience, rather than concentrating attention on the operation of the system. Instead of highlighting equipment features, she presented the system as a solution *in relation to* the needs of students, teachers, and administrators—her audience and prospective buyers.

Describing a scenario, she "walked" the audience through a very different kind of classroom experience. She expressively "painted a picture" of students coming to class eager to set to work at their computer terminals; youngsters quiet and intent on a geography lesson displayed through colorful three-dimensional maps; students enthusiastically learning literature from authors featured on and speaking from the system. The scenario created feelings of "ownership" of the product, and encouraged prospective customers to visualize the positive outcomes of approving the sales representative's proposal.

Throughout her presentations, the sales representative made use of open questions to elicit immediate feedback. Such feedback helped her track the prospects' response to the product, and also prompted them to consider the practical applications and advantages of the system. At regular intervals, she asked questions such as, "How do you envision this would work in your classroom?," "What do you think your students would most like about this?," and "In what ways would you foresee this helping you to better manage classes that are becoming overcrowded?" She injected direct references to relate significant points to the audience: "I often find that teachers and administrators like yourselves are concerned with raising test scores. Is that true for you?" (Of course, the audience answered "yes," giving her an opportunity to point out how the system would help them in that respect, too.)

She built relationship with prospective buyers through self-disclosure and recalls. She would relate, for example, "When I was a youngster, I had trouble learning biology. Do you recall how frustrating it was when you just couldn't seem to get a subject, and you were afraid of maybe failing?" She would conclude a key point with a value statement such as, "What this gives to each of your students are the benefits of immediate feedback, the means to interact with the information at a level consistent with their learning ability, and regular reviews for reinforcement. What this means to you is the satisfaction of knowing that you are providing every student with a learning tool that will help them achieve their best. An added advantage is that you gain a teaching tool that reduces the time you spend preparing lesson plans."

Comprehension Check

The answers to the following appear on page 333.

1. A common cause of audience resistance is _____.
   a. poor lighting in the meeting room
   b. a tailored approach
   c. self-disclosure
   d. doubt or distrust
   e. the use of emotive expressions

2. A relational presenter is primarily concerned with _____.
   a. relating humorous anecdotes
   b. the people in the audience
   c. the sequence of the message
   d. facts and figures as evidence
   e. causes of audience resistance

3. Self-disclosure serves to build relationship with an audience because _____.
   a. it is convincing
   b. it expresses trust
   c. it is always humorous
   d. it is not boring
   e. it conveys credibility

Match. The phrases on the left are examples of the relational techniques shown on the right. Match each numbered phrase with one of the lettered terms. (A lettered item will be used only once.)

4. _____ You may remember when the company expanded . . .

5. _____ For professionals like yourselves . . .

6. _____ When I began my career, I was uncertain about . . .

7. _____ What this means to you is . . .

8. _____ What questions do you have?

a. Direct reference
b. Self-disclosure
c. Direct question
d. Value statement
e. Recall

To Do

Review the presentation you have prepared for this course, paying particular attention to relational content.

1. If you find that your presentation would benefit from the addition of relational elements, revise it to include the following:

   - Use of pronouns like "you," "your," "we," "our"
   - Direct references
   - Self-disclosure
   - A recall
   - Rhetorical questions (worded in the form of an open question)

2. Write a value statement for each key point, and a concluding value statement for inclusion in the summary. (For ideas on how to apply your message to your audience in terms of what they value, you may find it helpful to review the needs listed under Key Concept 45.)

8

Platform Behavior and Projection

Nonverbal means of communication account for as much as 60 to 90 percent of a presenter's impact on people, according to studies cited in Chapter 1 (Key Concept 4). The message itself *is* important. An audience is not inclined to accept material that lacks validity, substance, or relevance. However, even flawless verbal content does not stand on its own. It must be delivered to people. The manner in which a message is delivered—namely, through platform behavior and projection—is critical to the success of a presentation.

Objectives

To understand the importance of platform behavior and projection; to explain the elements of nonverbal style; and to identify the vocal and visual attributes that contribute to effective delivery.

Key Concepts

50. The success of a presentation is determined in large part by a presenter's platform behavior and projection.
51. Nonverbal style is the sum total of the vocal and visual cues a presenter projects to an audience. Nonverbal style has a significant impact on audience perceptions and response.
52. Vocal cues are communicated through voice qualities and speech patterns.

223

53. Visual cues are communicated through facial expressions, gestures, movement, and attire.

54. An audience is most attentive and responsive to a well-paced presentation that is delivered in an expressive, energetic, and enthusiastic manner.

Key Terms

To make full use of the key concepts, it is essential to understand the following key terms:

Platform behavior	Pitch
Projection	Speech pattern
Presence	Articulation
Modulated (vocal quality)	Fillers
Mellow (vocal quality)	Pace
Moderate (vocal quality)	

Key Concept 50

The success of a presentation is determined in large part by a presenter's platform behavior and projection.

In the context of presenting, a platform is the place from which a speaker addresses an audience. It may be the front of a conference room, the stage of an auditorium, or a chair across from someone's desk. It may be the area behind a podium or the open floor of a meeting or classroom. In a manner of speaking, a platform is the "stage" on which a presenter "acts out" a message for an audience.

In the context of presenting, behavior includes all aspects of speech and conduct by which a message is communicated. It involves how a presenter thinks and feels as well as acts, because thoughts and feelings shape actions. Thus, **platform behavior** encompasses everything a speaker does in front of and toward an audience. From the perspective of the audience, it is everything people see, hear, and sense from a presenter.

In its written form, a presentation may consist of well-organized, substantive content. The writing may reflect an effective verbal style. When the presentation is delivered "live," the speaker must then give meaning to the message through skilled platform behavior. The behaviors by which a speaker communicates are instrumental in determining the outcome of an oral presentation. An exciting topic will seem bland if delivered by a bland speaker. On the other hand, an expressive and exciting speaker can transform the most banal subject into one that interests and excites an audience.

Projection

A chief aspect of platform behavior is projection. The literal definition of **projection** is the act of casting forward or displaying. As it applies to presenting, the term refers to the ability to "cast forward" one's voice and visual behaviors from the platform out to the audience. To project is to visually and vocally express the points of a message much like a film projector transmits pictures and sounds in the showing of a movie. People seated in the last row and along either side of a theater want to be able to see and hear the movie as well as those who are seated closer to the front. In a similar manner, every person in an audience attending a presentation should be able to clearly see and hear the speaker.

Projection is more than a matter of "how"—how loudly one speaks or how expansively one moves in order to reach everyone seated in a meeting room. It also refers to "what" a speaker projects in terms of investing meaning in a message. A movie director has done a good job only if what the moviegoer sees and hears is true to the script. Likewise, a presenter does a good job only if what an audience sees and hears is true to the intended meaning of the message.

Characteristics of Effective Platform Behavior

The various factors that comprise platform behavior are described in the key concepts that follow. In every case, what a presenter projects to an audience should fit the setting, add meaning to the message, awaken the audience, be used in moderation, and appear natural.

Appropriate to the Setting. Presentation settings are formal or informal, professional or casual. Some behaviors are appropriate in one setting, but not suited to another. For example, standing behind a podium may be the norm in a formal setting. Doing so in an informal or casual setting creates an unnecessary barrier between speaker and listeners.

Add Meaning to the Message. Platform behavior should enhance the content of a presentation. Doing something solely for dramatic effect or as a gimmick does not contribute to a presenter's effectiveness. It may, in fact, diminish it by distracting the audience or confusing the meaning intended.

Awaken the Audience.   One of the criteria of an effective presentation is that it gets and keeps audience attention. The longer a presentation, the more critical it is to project in a manner that keeps the audience alert.

Moderation.   The familiar adage, "Everything in moderation," applies to presenting. Anything done to excess can be distracting. More is not necessarily better. Moderation implies balance because it avoids extremes. It is effective to project certain qualities such as emphasis, forcefulness, or humor—at appropriate points. However, any form of expression projected unrelentingly throughout a presentation will become meaningless.

Appear Natural.   Every platform behavior should appear natural, not contrived. New behaviors can be adopted into a presenter's style and practiced until they become natural. Professional speakers, for example, have discovered dynamic platform behaviors and have developed and refined them over time.

Key Concept 51

Nonverbal style is the sum total of the vocal and visual cues a presenter conveys to an audience. Nonverbal style has a significant impact on audience perceptions and response.

Every presenter projects a unique, personal style. It is the chief factor that distinguishes one speaker from another. Style is composed of verbal and nonverbal elements. Verbal style (discussed in Chapter 5) refers to the language a presenter uses. Nonverbal style comprises vocal and visual cues: the signals that communicate a "message within the message" and prompt response from an audience. Nonverbal style and platform behavior are synonymous.

Nonverbal Style and Audience Perceptions

The key concepts that follow describe components of nonverbal style and perceptions commonly associated with them. In view of the extent to which nonverbal style affects a presentation, each component should be considered with respect to the principles listed below.

- How do I want to be perceived?
- Perception is more powerful than fact.
- Nonverbal communication traits are learned behaviors.
- Cultural variations are common.

The first two principles were introduced in earlier chapters. They are reiterated at this point in the course because they are influenced by nonverbal cues.

How Do I Want to Be Perceived? Chapter 3 (Key Concept 21) suggested that an effective presenter is perceived to be credible, competent, confident, caring, and convincing. To be perceived as such, a presenter's nonverbal style must convey those attributes. Often, presenters are preoccupied with the question of "What am I going to *say*?" An effective presenter also considers, "How am I going to *sound* when I say this?" and "How am I going to *look*?"

Perception Is More Powerful than Fact. A speaker may, in fact, possess qualities which an audience does *not* perceive as a result of what they see and hear from the speaker's nonverbal style. For example, if an audience sees a presenter fumbling awkwardly with notes or visual aids, they may perceive that the person is disorganized (equating disorganization with incompetence). From certain speech habits or physical mannerisms, an audience may perceive that the presenter is not credible or confident. On the other hand, a presenter can (and many do) project vocal qualities and a visual image that convey a greater measure of credibility and confidence than the presenter actually has.

Nonverbal Communication Traits Are Learned Behaviors. The manner in which a person communicates is largely learned from parents, teachers, early-life experiences, and professional role models. An advantage of learned behavior is that, having been learned, the behavior can be reinforced or modified. Some aspects of a person's communication style are professional assets; they enhance how the person is perceived and are reinforced by continued practice. Other communication behaviors are professional liabilities; they detract from a person's effectiveness as a presenter. Such behaviors can be changed.

Before changing a behavior, a person must be aware of it. Identification is a prerequisite to modification. It is difficult to objectively evaluate one's own nonverbal style. A speaker doesn't hear the sound of his or her voice the same as an audience does. A presenter is often unaware of physical mannerisms that are glaringly evident to an audience. Therefore, it is beneficial to elicit feedback from associates or coworkers, asking for their observations and suggestions for improvement. It is also helpful to videotape presentations and review them to identify communication traits that should be modified.

In some instances, a physical condition accounts for a vocal or visual characteristic. A rasping tone of voice, for example, might result from irritation of the vocal chords. Some conditions can be corrected by medical treatment, speech therapy, or training.

Cultural Variations Are Common. Professionals who present to culturally diverse groups or in other countries must be alert to differences in the interpretation of nonverbal cues. Platform behavior considered appealing and expressive in one culture may be perceived as aggressive in another. A gesture that conveys a positive meaning in one country may have negative connotations in a different country. Before delivering a business presentation to an audience whose cultural background differs from that of the presenter, it is advisable to become familiar with the "local customs."

The Power of Presence

The term **presence** is defined as "something of a visible or concrete nature; the bearing, carriage or air of a person; a quality of poise and effectiveness that enables a performer to achieve a close relationship with an audience." Presence is an appearance of composure, of being at ease and in command of a situation. A presenter with presence attains a high degree of positive visibility and delivers a business presentation in a manner that is memorable. Presence is a powerful quality in that it attracts people in the audience to the presenter. It invites their trust, their confidence, and elicits a favorable response.

Presence is an attribute of nonverbal style which (like verbal style) is described as passive, assertive, or aggressive. From the standpoint of nonverbal style, characteristics common to each category are summarized next.

Passive. Ambivalence is typical of a passive style, which is also characteristically restrained, inhibited, meek, or timid. A passive presenter often sounds nervous and appears awkward. Eye contact fluctuates. Passive presenters convey a sense of being anxious to escape from the presence of the audience.

Assertive. An assertive style is vocally and visually expressive. Presenters who are assertively expressive are perceived to be decisive. They appear comfortable and relaxed in front of a group, and maintain steady and focused eye contact. Expressive communicators convey a sense of self-assurance that frees them to be attentive to the audience.

Aggressive.   Aggressive speakers tend toward extremes. They speak in an extremely loud or menacingly low tone of voice. Gestures and movements appear taut or angry. Eye contact is fixated. Aggressive speakers commonly convey a sense of establishing dominance over the audience.

As the discussion of verbal style in Chapter 5 pointed out, the preferred style is a balanced one that avoids the extremes of too little or too much. A passive speaker exhibits nominal presence with an audience, while an aggressive speaker displays an overbearing presence that an audience may find offensive. It is the expressive, assertive presenter who demonstrates the personal magnetism that is the essence of a powerful presence.

Key Concept 52

Vocal cues are communicated through voice qualities and speech patterns.

A voice communicates a great deal more than words alone. A presenter's voice is a potentially powerful tool. Having long recognized the impact of vocal cues, actors have worked with voice coaches. In recent years, politicians have followed suit. Professionals whose careers depend on skillful communication take seriously the need to develop positive and powerful vocal attributes.

Factors Affected by Vocal Attributes

A voice communicates meaning, an image, and a level of energy. An effective speaker projects vocal attributes that enhance both the presentation and audience perceptions.

Meaning in the Message.   A word is just a word. Words assume meaning as a result of the way in which they are voiced. A voice can express a range of feelings, signal humor, or underscore a point. A voice that lacks expressiveness will likely fail to get the message across as the speaker intends or to a degree that will have a significant impact on an audience.

Voice Image.   When addressing an audience, a presenter has an objective in mind. For the objective to be satisfied, the audience must make a judgment regarding the issue or item presented. Audience members arrive at a decision and support their judgment based, in part, on their impression of the presenter. Figuratively speaking, vocal characteristics paint a picture of what a person is like. The perceptions an audience forms may not be accurate. Nonetheless, from what they hear, listeners reach conclusions about a speaker's personality, background, education, intelligence, interest in the subject, conviction about the message, and the like. Therefore, it behooves a presenter to consider, "What does my voice say about me?"

Vocal Vitality.   Vitality is a measure of the energy a speaker invests in delivering a message. It is crucial for a presenter to project vocal vitality because without it an audience may think, "If you are not going to put any energy into this presentation, why should I?" A flat, monotonous voice lacks vitality. At the other extreme, too much vocal vitality can suggest that the speaker is overly emphatic, too urgent, or too intense. The level of vocal vitality that heightens audience interest and sustains attention conveys strength, with sincerity and enthusiasm.

Vocal Qualities

The quality of a speaker's voice is determined by four characteristics: pitch, volume, rate, and tone. An effective speaking voice is well **modulated**, meaning the pitch, volume, rate, and tone are altered to give appropriate and interesting expression to the message. A voice that is pleasing and easy to listen to is **mellow**, meaning it is rich in tone and sounds fully mature. It is **moderate**; the pitch is not too low or too high, volume is not too loud or too soft, and the rate of speech is neither too fast nor too slow.

To add to the effectiveness of a presentation, the qualities of a speaker's voice should be varied and congruent with the message. Vocal qualities should also be varied to provide contrast. In addition, since it is often perceived that the nature of a person's voice reflects something of the nature of the person, a presenter should develop and communicate with a steady, resonant, and mature voice.

Pitch.   The term **pitch** refers to the degree of highness or lowness of a sound. Every voice has a normal pitch in terms of what is "normal" for the speaker. The norm for an effective communicator is a pitch that can be raised a few levels without sounding squeaky and lowered a few levels without sounding grumbly. Such a range allows a speaker to vary pitch for contrast while maintaining a vocal quality that is pleasing to the ear.

Pitch has a notable impact on how a presenter is perceived. In every species that makes audible sounds, the young have higher-pitched voices than do grown adults. Consequently, a high-pitched voice is associated with immaturity. An excessively high-pitched voice is shrill and unpleasant to listen to for long. A person who speaks in a high-pitched voice will be taken more seriously if the pitch is lowered.

An effective presenter uses pitch changes to indicate a change in the message. At the end of a sentence, dropping the pitch signifies a statement; raising the pitch signifies a question. For that reason, repeated lifts in pitch at the end of declarative statements create an impression of a speaker who is uncertain. Occasional and appropriate variations in pitch can be used to accentuate meaning. Rapid, frequent, and meaningless changes in pitch make it difficult for an audience to listen attentively, and may suggest that the speaker is highly emotional or frantic.

Volume. Listeners want to clearly hear a speaker without straining to do so and without being blasted out of their chairs. A presenter who speaks too loudly may be perceived as bombastic, aggressive, or insensitive to listeners. On the other hand, one who speaks too softly may convey the impression of being passive or insecure.

It is commonly thought that a point is emphasized by voicing it more loudly. The reverse is true. An audience is more attentive to a point that is stated at a lower (but still clearly audible) volume. Emphasis is added by lifting the pitch, slowing the rate, and/or changing the tone of voice. (Vocal emphasis is further strengthened with appropriate visual cues.)

Rate. An average rate of speech is 140 words per minute. As with other vocal characteristics, the rate of speech should be varied during a presentation. For emphasis, a speaker may periodically slow down to less than 100 words per minute to voice a point in a deliberate manner. To elevate the level of energy or quickly convey a point of lesser importance, a speaker may occasionally accelerate the rate to more than 170 words per minute. A consistently slow rate of speech conveys fatigue or disinterest. Halting speech can suggest that the speaker has difficulty formulating thoughts. Presenters who consistently speak at a rapid rate may be perceived to be nervous, impatient, or hurried.

Tone. The quality of tone is a combination of pitch, strength, and character. Character refers to the sense or meaning a particular tone conveys. For example, a tone of voice may be described as gentle, angry, sarcastic, childish, or serious. The tone of voice with which a speaker expresses a point says more to an audience than the words themselves. As with other vocal characteristics, tone also says something to an audience about the speaker. A faltering tone of voice is perceived as timid or indecisive, a harsh tone of voice as aggressive. A nasal tone lacks the depth that adds authority to a voice. A monotone or flat tone that lacks variations suggests a lack of interest or energy.

Speech Patterns

The term **speech pattern** refers to any vocal trait that is habitual. Although usually learned behaviors, speech patterns are sometimes a reflection of a psychological or emotional condition. A person who repeatedly voices the phrase "like, you know" may have acquired the habit from a peer group, or the pattern may signal that the person is nervous when speaking before a group.

Like the characteristics of vocal quality (pitch, volume, rate, and tone), speech patterns can either contribute to or detract from a presenter's effectiveness. Some speech patterns are very pleasing and add to the clarity and meaning of a message. Others are very distracting or muddle a message. The speech patterns with which presenters are most concerned are inflection, articulation, fillers, pauses, and accents.

Inflection. Proper inflection is the practice of altering the tone and/or pitch of voice to more clearly express or magnify meaning. It is an effective communication technique that can help to sustain audience attention and make a message more memorable. Proper inflection is a speech pattern of skilled speakers who deliver each point in just the right pitch and tone that exactly conveys the essence of the information, how the speaker feels about the point, or how the speaker wants the audience to feel in response.

Meaningless or misplaced inflection is a barrier to effective communication. For instance, a sing-song (roller-coaster) effect is produced by a repeated pattern of gradually raising pitch when voicing the first phrase of a compound sentence; peaking mid-sentence at the conjunction (and, or, but); then dropping the pitch as the second phrase is voiced. It is meaningless to repeatedly begin sentences with a booming volume, then allow the volume to trail off at the end, with little or no inflection on selected words.

Articulation. **Articulation** is the skill of speaking in distinct syllables. Articulate speech is characterized by correct pronunciation and clear enunciation. More articulate speech is developed by listening to articulate speakers and emulating their speech patterns, checking a dictionary when in doubt about the pronunciation of a word, and practicing enunciation exercises. Enunciation exercises stress movement of the mouth; relaxation of the lips, tongue, and jaw muscles that are used to form words; and voicing consonants clearly and distinctly.

Mumbling is a speech pattern lacking articulation. Speakers who mumble do not convey vocal vitality, they lose the advantage that skillful inflection adds to a presentation, and they may be perceived as disinterested or timid. Articulation can, however, be overdone. Precise and obviously deliberate attention to every detail of sound and syllable suggests the speaker is making too much of an effort to speak correctly, which may sound contrived to an audience.

Fillers. One of the more distracting patterns of speech is the use of **fillers**—unnecessary words or phrases that are repeatedly interjected into a message. Expressions such as "uh," "um," "you know," "basically," and "it's kinda like" add no meaning. Fillers interrupt the continuity of communication. They signal uncertainty or nervousness on the part of a speaker who tries (often unconsciously) to fill up every silence with sound. The speech pattern of voicing fillers can be overcome by practicing the techniques listed below.

- Speak in shorter sentences. Avoid run-on sentences that string together several phrases joined by conjunctions. Speakers who make excessive use of conjunctions are more likely to develop a habit of attaching a filler to every conjunction, as in "and um" or "but uh."

- Concentrate on bringing each sentence to an end (period).

- Pause to breathe.

- Prepare. Know the message so well that the material comes to mind quickly and easily. Frequently, fillers are an attempt to "fill in" a gap between one idea and the next. A well-prepared speaker is less likely to experience mental gaps.

- Practice alternate words and phrases that can be used in place of fillers, such as "in addition," "on that point," and "however."

A speech pattern similar to the use of fillers is the repeated use of superlatives: exaggerated expressions such as "awfully," "enormously," "terrific," "amazing," and "awesome." Rather than adding meaning to a message, the frequent injection of superlatives can be distracting and may detract from the speaker's credibility.

Pauses.   At one time, a soft drink was advertised with the slogan, "The pause that refreshes." Pauses in a presentation can have the same effect. While a presenter is speaking, the audience is working at listening. A moment of silence gives listeners an opportunity to digest what they have heard. Pauses help a speaker avoid the use of fillers. They can serve to slow a too-rapid rate of speech. Intentional pauses can add import to a message. Inserted after a key point or after a particularly striking or insightful statement, a pause allows the audience a moment to reflect. "The right word," Mark Twain noted, "may be effective, but no word was ever as effective as a rightly timed pause."

Accented Speech.   Every speaker has an accent. How pronounced an accent sounds depends upon how much the presenter's speech varies from that of the listener. Some accents are pleasing to listen to. They add a distinctive flavor to a presentation and enhance how the presenter is perceived. In other cases, accented speech is difficult for an audience to understand. Accented speech is problematic only if it inhibits a person from pursuing opportunities to present, or if it interferes with the clarity of communication. Usually, an audience indicates if a message is not clear by their feedback: quizzical facial expressions, gestures that signal uncertainty, or frequent questions that ask for clarification.

Since they are regional or ethnic in origin, accents suggest something of a speaker's background. As with other vocal characteristics and speech patterns, accented speech may influence how an audience perceives a presenter. Concern about the affect of an accent on the audience is alleviated by delivering a dynamic presentation that leaves people wanting to hear more. Presence, positive vocal qualities, and articulation offset the potential drawbacks of accented speech.

Breathing Power into the Voice

The most effective presenters practice voice management. They do not assume that the voice with which they have spoken for years is necessarily their only or best voice. They are aware of their vocal traits and speech patterns and strive to improve them. They practice developing vocal power because a strong voice is associated with professional strength in terms of knowledge, authority, and decisiveness.

Since vocal power is produced and sustained by air, it is essential to breathe easily and expansively. Breathing in a manner that lifts the weight of one's chest thousands of times throughout the day can lead to voice fatigue, as the following exercise demonstrates.

> With your mouth closed, take a deep breath, inhaling through your nose. If your chest rises, you are breathing in a manner that will not provide sufficient air to sustain the vocal power you need to read this paragraph aloud—without gasping for air.

A tired voice sounds disinterested or weak. Voice fatigue often results in ineffective speech patterns: a drop in volume at the end of sentences, a slow rate of speech, a tone of voice that sounds strained.

Vocal power comes from breathing in a manner that expands the diaphragm, the band of muscles below the chest cavity. An expanded diaphragm functions like an inflated balloon, providing breath support to the voice. Diaphragm-centered breathing can be developed by practicing this exercise:

> Lie on the floor on your back. Place a book on your midsection (the area of the diaphragm). Keeping your mouth closed and inhaling through your nose, take a deep breath. When you breathe in, concentrate on expanding your diaphragm. Slowly, release air by exhaling

through your nose. As you breathe in and out, the book on your diaphragm should rise and fall. (Your chest and shoulders should not move.) The first few times you do the exercise, count to 5 as you exhale. Continue practicing, gradually increasing the count to 10. Increase the count in increments of 5 until you can do this exercise and easily count to 25 without gasping for breath.

When you speak, you should be able to breathe through your nose so that your mouth is free to articulate words while you are breathing.

Voice fatigue is also alleviated by moving the concentration of sound away from the vocal chords and into the "mask": the area that extends from behind the bridge of the nose to the lips. (The "mask" is the lower portion of the face that would be covered by a surgical mask.) When the bridge of the nose is lightly pressed between the thumb and index finger, a slight vibration can be felt when a person says "humm." By the practice of humming, a presenter can develop an awareness of concentrating sound in the "mask" area, to avoid unnecessary strain on the vocal chords.

Speakers who present frequently or at length can strain their vocal chords from overuse. When vocal chords are strained (for other than medical reasons), a speaker should avoid drinking hot or cold liquids. Warm water or warm tea with fresh lemon juice will help relieve a hoarse or raspy throat that is the result of tired vocal chords. If a vocal problem persists, a medical expert should be consulted.

Reflection Questions

When you speak, what vocal qualities and speech patterns do you hear? What do others hear? (You may want to ask a trusted friend or associate whose judgment you respect.) What, if any, vocal traits do you want to modify in order to improve how you are perceived when you present?

Key Concept 53

Visual cues are communicated through facial expressions, eye contact, gestures, movement, and attire.

People in an audience are viewers as well as listeners. They *see* a speaker before they hear the first words of a message. Speakers are their own best or worst visual aids. As with vocal cues, visual cues convey meaning, spark attention and response from the audience, and shape audience perceptions of the presenter. Skilled presenters are alert to what they communicate by facial expressions, eye contact, gestures, movement, and attire.

Facial Expressions

Standing before an audience, a presenter looks at the expressions on people's faces to ascertain audience reactions. Mentally, the presenter checks, "How does the audience feel about this point?" Likewise, an audience observes the presenter. From facial expressions, an audience derives a sense of how a presenter feels about a point—and about them. Is the presenter smiling? serious? or wearing an expression of bland indifference? Is she grim or glad to be here? Does he appear confident or uncertain? Does the presenter appear relaxed and naturally expressive or tense and restrained?

Some persons, nervous about speaking before a group, suppress their feelings in an attempt to exert self-control. The result is rigid and inhibited platform behavior that lacks expressiveness—facially and in other respects as well. It is only by expressing how one feels about a subject that a presenter can hope to instill those same feelings in others. It does not suffice to express oneself in words alone. To have the greatest impact on an audience, a presenter must express feelings visually. The excitement on a speaker's face generates excitement in an audience. An expression of concern prompts an audience to respond with concern. A facial expression that reveals anxiety causes an audience to feel anxious and uneasy.

Chapter 12 discusses techniques for overcoming the anxiety of speaking before a group. Such techniques can help a person gain confidence in presentation situations, and confidence frees a presenter to express naturally. With respect to facial expressions in particular, it is helpful to address a group as though speaking to a trusted friend one-on-one. Many people who mask their feelings when presenting are animated communicators when they "just talk," showing a range of facial expressions that would move an audience to applaud.

Eye Contact

Of all the features of the face, none has more potential for expression than a person's eyes. Making eye contact with people in an audience is important because it sends a signal that the speaker is connecting with them. Attention to eye contact forces a presenter to become sufficiently prepared so as not to be dependent on reading from notes. Meaningful eye contact distinguishes relational presenters from information-bound speakers.

To make and maintain eye contact entails more than merely looking at people. How a speaker looks at people in an audience is telling; the expression in and around a person's eyes is self-disclosing. A message and perceptions of the presenter are enhanced by meaningful and focused eye contact—meaningful in terms of being expressive, focused in terms of attentiveness to persons in the audience.

Depending on other visual cues conveyed, shifting one's eyes creates an impression of being either nervous or devious. Presenters want to avoid being perceived as "shifty-eyed," a term used to describe someone who is not straightforward. Rolling one's eyes can communicate uncertainty, frustration, or annoyance—traits that are not appealing in a professional presenter. A presenter should also refrain from fixated eye contact; that is, unrelentingly fixing one's gaze on any one point or person in the room. A speaker who concentrates on notes, the top of a podium, or on visual aids neglects the audience. Fixing one's gaze on one person can make that person feel uncomfortable.

It is easier to make focused and meaningful eye contact with everyone in a meeting room when presenting to a small group. When presenting to a large audience, eye contact is made by "sweeping" the room with the eyes (similar to the way hands sweep the face of a clock). The technique is described below.

> Picture that people in the audience are seated on the face of a clock. Periodically focus on different points of the "clock": to 12 (the back of the room), 3 (the side of the room to your right), 9 (the side of the room to your left), 6 (the front of the room nearest you). Move your glance to the center of the clock, and then sweep the room again. To avoid following a pattern that becomes predictable to the audience, alter the direction in which your eyes sweep the room.

Although the sweeping technique does not ensure that a speaker will make eye contact with every person in a large audience, it does promote the perception that the speaker is doing so.

Presenters who refer to notes must develop skill at maintaining eye contact while handling notes. A technique practiced by newscasters is useful. Notes are placed unobtrusively at waist height. The speaker glances down to check facts (but doesn't drop the head too much), and quickly resumes eye contact with the audience. When changing from one sheet of notes to the next, the top sheet (or note card) is moved inconspicuously to the side and slipped under the bottom—without lifting, waving, or rattling pages in a distracting manner. Being *very* well prepared for a presentation minimizes the need to look at notes and frees a speaker to look at the audience with focused, meaningful eye contact.

Gestures

Natural, spontaneous gestures are an asset to a presentation—provided they are consistent with the meaning a speaker intends to convey (and provided they are culturally correct). Appropriate gestures give physical expression to the spoken word. They are symbolic in nature, in that the meaning of many gestures is commonly understood among members of the same culture. What does it mean, for example, when a person responds to a question by shrugging the shoulders? In the United States, the gesture indicates "I don't know."

In a business presentation, a speaker should refrain from gesturing in ways that trigger negative responses from an audience. Pointing or wagging the index finger, for example, is impolite and potentially offensive. Pointing is perceived as parental and is often associated with scolding. Instead of pointing, emphasis can be added by gesturing, with an open hand, fingers together, palm and inner wrist turned slightly toward the audience, forearm slightly bent and extended at about a 45-degree angle to the side (not aimed directly *at* the audience). A point can also be accentuated by slightly raising the forearm and cupping the hand with fingers touching (in a manner that suggests the point is perched on the fingertips). When gesturing, fingers should be together (splayed fingers make hands appear larger and gestures more aggressive). The palm should be relaxed (slightly curved, as opposed to a flat and rigid palm).

Hands should never be used to grip a podium. Doing so inhibits gesturing and conveys tension. A speaker should refrain from placing hands on hips with arms bent at the elbow—a stance perceived as aggressive. In most situations, hands should be out of a speaker's pockets. Speakers who put their hands in their pockets often do so because they don't know what else to do with them. From nervousness or lack of awareness, they jingle coins or rattle keys and distract the audience from the message. On occasion, when the setting is casual and a speaker wants to convey the impression of being "just one of the folks," placing hands in one's pockets (briefly) can be a gesture that puts an audience at ease. However, it is a gesture that should be done intentionally, sparingly, and only when appropriate to the setting.

Gestures are more natural when arms and hands are relaxed. When not gesturing, arms may drop loosely to one's sides, or hands may be comfortably folded (not tensely clutched) in front of the body in a manner that curves the arms forward. When a presenter uses gestures to accentuate a message, arms and hands will not stay in any one position for long.

Very expressive speakers need to take care to avoid gesturing excessively. On the other hand, stoic speakers need to add gestures to their repertoire of presentation skills. When presenting to large groups, gestures need to be expressed more expansively or they will not be seen by people seated at a distance from the platform.

Movement

The influence of television has accustomed people to viewing visual images in action. A presenter is a visual image. As a rule, when a speaker remains stationary, as though locked in one place on the platform, the interest of the audience wanes. When a speaker doesn't move, people in the audience don't move—their heads, their eyes, or their position while seated. Remaining sedentary for long is tiresome, and the last thing a presenter wants to create is the impression of being tiresome.

Head Movement.   A speaker's head should move. How? In a manner that reinforces the meaning the speaker wants to convey. Nodding the head up and down communicates affirmation. Shaking the head side to side signifies disagreement. Cocking the head to the side signals uncertainty, or suggests that a person is thinking.

Body Movement.   A speaker's body should move. Body movement adds more than expressiveness to a presentation. It adds energy as well. Effective presenters make use of the entire platform available to them as a means of expanding their presence before a group. From the perspective of the audience, a speaker who remains in one spot is present on that one spot only; whereas presenters who move around the platform fill the meeting room with their presence. Movement suggests that a speaker is at ease, comfortable, and confident in the presentation environment. Movement also enables a presenter to relate to an audience more effectively. By moving alternately to both right and left sides of the platform and forward toward the audience, a speaker can better make meaningful eye contact and convey connection with the audience.

The attentiveness and energy of both speaker and audience are heightened when a speaker stands. Standing, a speaker can move and gesture more freely than when seated. Standing, a speaker can breathe more fully than when seated. A person thinks faster when standing and more easily maintains a posture that appears alert. On the matter of posture, the most becoming posture is upright (not rigidly erect), shoulders back and squared, head held up. A slouching or slumped posture suggests disinterest or low self-esteem. A presenter wants to appear at ease and, at the same time, attentive and on the ready. Good posture is an attribute that contributes to a speaker's presence.

Skilled movement avoids actions that are potentially distracting or irritating to an audience. Pacing repetitively back and forth, back and forth, from one side of the platform to the other is distracting. So is rocking on the feet or swaying from side to side. Effective presenters refrain, whenever possible, from standing behind a podium.

A podium places a barrier between a presenter and people in the audience. If a podium is required, it is preferable to place it to one side of the platform, leaving the platform open for the presenter to be "out front" and "up front" with people in the audience. The speaker can move back toward the podium to refer to notes when necessary. Placing a podium at the center of a platform increases the temptation to stay behind it, which inhibits a presenter's gestures, movements, and relationship to the audience. In formal settings, the use of podiums persists. When a presenter must speak from behind a podium that restricts full-body movement, other vocal and visual cues take on even more significance than usual.

Attire

Earlier in this chapter, the term presence was defined in part as "something of a visible nature." Few things about a presenter are as visible as attire. It is the first and most visible thing an audience sees and something they view throughout a presentation. The preferred attire, accessories, and grooming for a business presentation enhance audience perceptions of the presenter. They convey that the speaker is a credible, competent, first-class professional. Attire, accessories, and grooming should not distract from the presentation of the message. A persuasive presenter wants people thinking and talking about what was said—not about how the speaker looked or what the speaker wore. For these reasons, a presenter's attire should be clean, neat, and understated. The guidelines described below are consistent with the standards commonly accepted by successful professionals.

- Refrain from overdressing or underdressing. In a business setting, a conservatively-tailored suit of a dark color is preferable. (For women, a tailored jacketed dress is also appropriate.) For men, a white shirt remains the standard. A white, cream, or pastel blouse is preferable for women. Loud colors or busy patterns should be avoided. Clothing should be clean and pressed. Shoes should be shined and in good repair.

- Few accessories should be worn. Those that are should be relatively inconspicuous. Audience attention should be on the presentation, not distracted by large or flashy jewelry, such as glittery rings and watches or dangling necklaces and earrings.

- Hair should be clean and neatly styled. Hair that is too long, too fluffed, unkempt, or that falls across the face is distracting and detracts from a professional appearance. Fingernails should be clean, well-manicured, and trimmed to a moderate length. Pale nail polish is preferred. Very long fingernails painted in bright or dark colors can distract an audience when a speaker gestures.

- Clothing of very bold or bright colors should be avoided. Hot pink or neon green may be stylish and attractive to wear to a party Saturday night, but will not create a favorable impression during a business presentation.

Appropriate attire for a business presentation is not based on personal preference or styles that are currently in vogue for social occasions. The purpose of a business presentation is not to make a fashion statement. It is to deliver a message that the audience will take seriously. They will be more inclined to do so if the presenter looks like someone to be taken seriously.

Avoid Distracting Habits

Some behaviors do not belong on the platform of a business presentation, among them those listed below.

- Never chew gum in a business presentation.
- Never smoke in a business presentation.
- Never drink alcoholic beverages before or during a presentation.
- Refrain from fiddling with clothing, jewelry, hair, fingernails, audio-visual equipment, or in any manner that could distract the attention of the audience.

A professional's platform behavior is always governed by good manners and courteous regard for the people in an audience.

Reflection Questions

What visual cues do you project when you present? Which ones do you consider positive attributes? What visual platform behaviors do you want to develop or improve in order to enhance your style of presentation?

Key Concept 54

An audience is most attentive and responsive to a well-paced presentation that is delivered in an expressive, energetic, and enthusiastic manner.

People in an audience come into a presentation from an environment that is fast-paced and growing faster. Almost universal and increasing exposure to electronic media and real-time communication devices has accustomed people to receiving messages in short increments that change rapidly. As the most widely viewed medium of mass communication, television has virtually set the standard for what people have come to expect. A single program presents several story lines, featuring one for only a couple of minutes before changing to the next. Commercials last 30 seconds. The viewer-listener switches channels with a flick of a remote control. The audience turns off or tunes out any program that fails to hold their attention. An audience at a business presentation will do likewise, mentally, if a presentation is not well-paced.

Pacing a Presentation

In Chapter 5 on the subject of verbal style, **pace** was defined as the rate of movement or speed with which a presentation progresses. A well-paced presentation moves along at a brisk and lively clip. Audience interest is sustained by variations in delivery. In terms of nonverbal style, pace is altered, to keep the audience alert, by applying the following techniques throughout a presentation.

- Switch "story lines." Refrain from belaboring any one point for longer than two minutes. Regularly introduce different types of material to keep the message fresh and interesting.

- Physically move to different positions on the platform.

- Alternate the forms by which material is delivered. For example, provide commentary on a point, then refer to an audiovisual aid(s), engage the audience in an activity or, by the use of a rhetorical question(s), inject an intentional pause. Pick up the pace by returning to commentary delivered in a lively manner.

- Vary vocal and visual cues—change tone of voice, use a range of gestures, alter the mood and tempo of delivery.

- Occasionally inject humor to provide comic relief.

Overall and most important: enliven the pace of a presentation, and audience interest in the message, with a nonverbal style that is expressive, energetic, and enthused.

Expressive

Like the best forms of media communications, the best presentation style is animated. A skilled presenter "clothes" the words of a message in expressive vocal and visual cues. In addition to reinforcing meaning, expressiveness creates a mood in a meeting room. Research by human behavior experts has found that moods are contagious, conveyed from one person to another by subtle non-verbal cues: posture, tone of voice, facial expression, and the like. People "pick up" the feelings, interest level, and mood that the presenter expresses. A presenter who is animated will animate the people in an audience. An animated audience is more attentive and more likely to respond affirmatively.

Energetic

An animated style is energetic! From the outset and throughout a presentation, a presenter must deliver a message with energy in order to generate and sustain energy in the audience. People in an audience usually are seated. When seated (especially for any length of time), after a while people tend to slump, which diminishes their energy. People in an audience that neither perceive energy in a presenter nor feel it themselves will likely find a presentation "boooring." The time seems to drag and the audience can't wait for the presentation to be over. Such an atmosphere is not conducive to persuasion. On the other hand, energy in and from a presenter bolsters the energy of an audience. An alert and lively style picks up the pace of a presentation and conveys, "Sit up and take notice of this message! It's worth it!"

To heighten energy for a presentation, follow the practices listed here:

- Get a good night's sleep before the day of a presentation.

- Refrain from eating a heavy meal before a presentation.

- Immediately before a presentation, take a few minutes to do a "warm up" that will get the blood circulating (even if the only place to do so is in a nearby restroom). Stretch and swing the arms up, out, and around; walk at a brisk pace; shake out hands and arms (like swimmers do at poolside before a competition). Take slow, deep breaths. Deep breathing oxygenates the blood stream and also helps to calm a person.

- Unless a physical condition prevents you from doing so, remain on your feet throughout a presentation. Periodically, balance (slightly forward) over the balls of your feet. (It keeps you on your toes and puts a spring in your step.) In casual, small-group settings, resist the temptation to join the group and sit (unless specifically invited to do so). Standing and moving help a presenter stay energized.

Enthusiastic

An expressive and energetic style contributes to the third quality of a well-paced presentation: enthusiasm. Enthusiasm is not podium-pounding rhetoric, nor is it rah-rah cheerleading or a pep talk. Enthusiasm is the expression of genuine interest in a subject and in the audience. It is showing delight in what you are doing and in who you are doing it for. If you are excited by a topic, let the audience know. If not, pretend you are. Even if you present what you consider a dull or difficult subject, look for or create in it something you can be enthused about. It is unlikely people will be persuaded of the value of a message unless the message is delivered with enthusiasm. An audience becomes enthusiastic in proportion to the enthusiasm you express!

Summary

By skilled platform behavior, a presenter projects the meanings in a message out to the audience. Platform behavior, also referred to as nonverbal style, consists of vocal and visual cues. Voice qualities and speech patterns, facial expressions, eye contact, gestures, movements, posture, and attire all influence how a presenter is perceived and how an audience responds. An audience is more favorably affected and persuaded by a well-paced presentation that is delivered with expressiveness, energy, and enthusiasm.

Sample Situations

Situation 1: Presenting 2-Up

Carol took a job with a corporation where she would find opportunities to pursue her career aspirations. The company advanced promotable people to (1) first-line management in a branch office to (2) a staff position at corporate headquarters to (3) management in a regional office, and so on.

Carol gained visibility by working in positions that provided occasions to present. After a few years, she was promoted to a first-line manager's job in a branch office. Shortly after her promotion, Carol attended an area-wide management meeting. When a member of the regional management team congratulated her on her recent promotion to the region, she said, "Thank you, but my promotion was to a branch office." The regional manager clarified, "That's *this* promotion. To be promoted to the branch, you had to be considered promotable to at least two positions further up the career path."

Carol was curious. "How," she asked, "do they determine that?" The regional manager answered, "I've seen you present. By your communication skills, demeanor, and dress you've demonstrated that you are promotable 2-Up." From the conversation, Carol learned an important principle of professional success: to communicate and present, not according to who and where you are today, but according to who and where you want to be in the future.

Situation 2: A Political Blunder

Three weeks before a local election, a candidate was running 28 percentage points ahead of the incumbent (his nearest competitor) in the race for city mayor. Two weeks before the election, the candidate appeared in a televised campaign ad. The 30-second spot featured the candidate in a close-up shot, looking directly into the camera at viewers. Addressing the television audience, he said, "I have a new vision for the city. I believe that, together, we can make this a safer and more prosperous place to live." As he spoke the words, ever so subtly he moved his head from side to side in the manner that signifies "No." He lost the election. From that visual cue, voters perceived that the candidate was indicating "No"—either "I don't believe we can do it" or "I'm lying." The visual cue had a greater impact on viewers than the candidate's words.

Comprehension Check

The answers to the following appear on page 333.

1. One characteristic of effective platform behavior is that it _____.
   a. is melodramatic
   b. adds meaning to the message
   c. poses rhetorical questions
   d. is well-organized
   e. is predominantly passive

2. Platform behavior is synonymous with _____.
   a. the language of a presentation
   b. pacing
   c. the area in which a presentation occurs
   d. nonverbal style
   e. movement across a stage

3. Nonverbal style consists of _____.
   a. substantive content
   b. vocal and visual cues
   c. preparation for a presentation
   d. presence
   e. energy and enthusiasm

4. From a high-pitched voice and rapid rate of speech, an audience may perceive that the presenter is _____.
   a. nervous
   b. enthusiastic
   c. knowledgeable
   d. mature
   e. expressive

| Evaluation of Platform Behavior | | Date: _____ |
| (Nonverbal Style) | | Presenter: _____ |

Vocal Cues	Strengths	To Be Improved
Voice qualities		
Pitch		
Volume		
Rate		
Tone		
Speech patterns		
Inflection		
Articulation		
Fillers		
Pauses		
Accent		
Voice image		
Vocal power		

Visual Cues		
Facial expressions		
Eye contact		
Gestures		
Movements		
Attire, accessories		
Grooming		
Expressiveness		
Energy		
Enthusiasm		

5. Attire and accessories are very noticeable visual cues. As such, in a business presentation, they should _____.
   a. be stylish
   b. match what the audience wears
   c. be a statement of the presenter's individuality
   d. be bold and colorful to attract attention
   e. convey professionalism

To Do

Deliver the presentation you have prepared for this course to a group of friends, coworkers, or associates. Videotape the presentation. (If video equipment is not available, record the presentation on audio cassette.) A videotape recording of a "live" presentation provides a more accurate picture of what an audience sees and hears.

From the video (or audio) tape, identify characteristics of your nonverbal style. Try to view and listen to the presentation from the perspective of an audience. You may find it helpful to use a copy of the "evaluation of platform behavior" that appears on page 246.

9

Handling Questions, Comments, and Disruptions with Ease

Some people admit to feeling uneasy before giving a presentation. Many admit to feeling even more so when they relinquish control of the platform and open the floor to questions. Of greater concern than what questions might be asked is that no questions will be asked at all. Silence from an audience does not imply consent nor is it golden. On the contrary, a silent audience is an unresponsive one. Silence suggests that people have not listened attentively, do not care for or about the message, are reluctant to interact with the speaker, or have already reached a decision that does not include what the presenter proposed.

Questions and comments signal interest. They are indicators of audience perceptions and reception of a message. Often, questions and comments reflect an attempt on the part of an audience to assimilate and apply the information presented. They can reveal hidden agendas or potential barriers to the approval of a proposal. Questions and comments provide a presenter with opportunities to correct misunderstandings, clarify or reiterate key points, and relate to an audience in a participative manner.

Objectives

To apply the practice of preparing for probable questions, comments, and objections; to recognize the different types of questions, comments, and disruptions that may occur during a presentation; and to develop the ability to respond effectively to each type.

Key Concepts

55. Preparation supplies answers to probable questions and comments.

56. A presenter may invite questions and comments before, during, or after a presentation.

57. An effective response to verbal feedback involves four steps: listen, discern, affirm, and answer.

58. Questions differ as to type and content. A skillful presenter gives an answer appropriate to the nature of the question.

59. Comments from an audience differ as to type. A skillful speaker voices a reply appropriate to the type of comment.

60. One measure of a presenter's skill is the ability to deal with disruptions with aplomb.

Key Terms

To make full use of these concepts, you will need to understand the following terms:

Verbal feedback, audience feedback	Composite question
Q & A	Objection
Field	Detractor
Paraphrase	Unplugging

Key Concept 55

Preparation supplies answers to probable questions, comments, and objections.

Business presentations commonly include verbal feedback from the audience. In the context of this chapter, **verbal feedback** (or **audience feedback**) refers to questions, comments, or objections that are voiced by persons in the audience. A presenter can prepare effective responses by following the four steps outlined below.

1. Anticipate
2. Answer
3. Revise
4. Rehearse

Anticipate Probable Questions and Comments

Questions and comments that an audience is likely to raise can be anticipated by considering previous experience, common concerns, planning, and input from associates.

Experience.   If a presenter has delivered the same or a similar subject previously, it is helpful to recall the questions or objections that were raised before. If the content of the message is essentially the same, it is probable that some questions and comments will be essentially the same from one presentation to the next. For instance:

> A consultant who makes oral presentations to prospective clients is regularly asked, "How do you propose we implement this program?"

Common Concerns.   A presenter should expect questions or objections on issues that commonly interest or concern people. In broad terms, such issues pertain to time, cost, and impact. For example, people are likely to ask questions similar to those shown here:

- How much time will it take to develop, learn, implement, or gain a return?

- How much does it cost: short-term, long-term, per user, or compared to competitors?

- What is the impact if we do not act on the matter? What is the impact if we do?

Planning.   Planning for a presentation can reveal questions and concerns that may be raised. Key concepts 11 and 13 (Chapter 2) pointed out that questions guide the planning process and help a presenter gain insight into the audience. By asking questions, a presenter can identify questions an audience may ask.

> While planning and preparing a presentation for a prospective client, the consultant reflects on the following questions. Who among this group is likely to raise questions or objections? What points in this presentation are subject to question? What issues will this client be most interested in or concerned about? Are there any gaps or oversights in the message that the client will question?

Associates.   Business associates can be a helpful source for identifying probable questions and objections. Associates who have more experience than the presenter in certain areas (the subject, the audience, or a role the speaker has recently acquired) can serve as "advisors," alerting the presenter to the type of audience feedback to expect. If the presenter is as experienced as associates, it is still beneficial to solicit input from others who are likely to be more objective. An effective means of doing so is to deliver the presentation to associates who role-play members of the prospective audience and make note of questions or concerns that occur to them.

Write Out Answers to Anticipated Questions and Objections

Anticipating audience feedback does not fully prepare a presenter to respond skillfully. A presenter must determine how each question or comment will be answered. Some speakers invest considerable time and effort preparing the content and audiovisuals for a presentation. They practice their platform behavior to deliver the message effectively. Then, when a member of the audience raises a question at the end, they hem and haw and stutter and stammer in response—and sacrifice their credibility.

While preparing for a presentation, every anticipated question and objection should be written out. For each one, an answer is also written out. The best answers (like the best presentation content) will relate to the nature and needs of the audience, and will echo the core concept or a key point of the message. It is useful to prepare two options: a summary answer and an expanded explanation. In most cases, it is preferable to answer in a summary manner (especially when time is limited). However, if a summary answer does not satisfy the person who raised the issue, the presenter is prepared with a more detailed "back-up" answer.

Revise the Content of the Presentation

After anticipating questions and preparing answers to them, a presenter may find it advantageous to revise the content of the message. Doing so is recommended when a presentation is delivered repeatedly and, on almost every occasion, the same (or similar) questions and comments are raised. By rephrasing an existing point or inserting an additional point, the presenter addresses the issue before the floor is opened to questions.

Anticipated questions or concerns may be incorporated into the content by the use of rhetorical questions. The following questions are based on the earlier examples that referred to a consultant's presentation. In this example, the presenter takes the initiative and beats the audience to the punch, so to speak, by integrating the issues into the message.

"How, you might ask, would you implement this program? That's the next point we'll consider . . ."

"What impact can you expect? Understandably, many of our clients have asked that same question. They found . . ."

When anticipated questions or objections are addressed as part of the content of a message, the presenter is relieved of the pressure of having to formulate an answer on the spot. Moreover, people in the audience may perceive that the presenter is clever to have anticipated what is on their minds. They are favorably impressed when a presentation obviously is well prepared and relates specifically to their concerns.

It is *not* advisable to revise content to incorporate anticipated questions if one or more of these conditions exist:

- If doing so would interfere with the continuity of the message
- If the time available for the presentation is limited
- If the issue is potentially controversial and may not occur to an audience unless the presenter brings it up

Rehearse a Q & A Session

Q & A is an abbreviation for the question-and-answer period that accompanies many presentations. Unless a presenter is proficient in fielding questions, and the presentation is one that has been done before, the presenter should rehearse a Q & A. Although the attention of an audience may vacillate during a presentation, all eyes and ears are on the presenter as soon as someone raises a question or objection. Vocal and visual cues are especially telling when a speaker is "on the spot" responding to audience feedback. It is essential to maintain a confident presence, which is developed by practice.

In a simulated Q & A session, associates play the role of members of the audience to whom the presentation will be given. The presenter responds to questions and objections posed by associates. Rehearsing in this manner helps to develop self-assurance. In addition, it brings to light any answers that are vague, ambivalent, or that could be better worded to make a stronger case.

Types of Verbal Feedback to Anticipate

Recognizing that thinking and communication patterns differ, a presenter should be prepared for verbal feedback that ranges from conceptual to concrete. Visionary people (those who look at the "big picture") typically ask questions that are broad in scope, such as "What are the implications?" or "What are your 10-year projections?" Detail-oriented people will focus on specifics and ask questions like, "How would this apply to assembly-line workers at the Main Street plant?" or "How do your projections break down on a monthly basis per workstation?" Presenters who are inclined to be conceptual thinkers sometimes overlook preparing for detailed questions from others. Conversely, those who tend to think in concrete terms may neglect to anticipate questions of a broader nature. Both types—concrete and conceptual—should be considered.

Reflection Question

With respect to the subject(s) you expect to present in the future, what questions or comments might you anticipate?

Key Concept 56

A presenter may invite questions and comments before, during, or after a presentation.

A presenter does not have to wait until the end of a presentation before inviting questions and comments from the audience. A speaker may solicit feedback from a group before, during, and/or after a presentation. As with every aspect of a presentation, the chief consideration is, "What will work best with this subject and this size and type of audience in this setting?" The norm in public speaking has been to defer questions until a Q & A session at the end. However, as presenters recognize the value of relational skills, the norms are changing.

Inviting Audience Feedback before a Presentation

When it serves the purpose of a presentation to encourage audience involvement at the outset, a speaker can elicit questions or comments before delivering the body of the message. Audience feedback can, in fact, serve as the opener to a presentation. One sure way to capture people's attention is to get *them* talking. If the presenter has not yet delivered the message, what feedback can the audience members offer? They can voice feedback from their experience or ideas. The following example illustrates how the technique works. It is beneficial to make use of a flip chart or blank overhead transparencies to write key words of the points people raise.

In a presentation to civic leaders, an urban development specialist opened his presentation by inviting comments from the audience. "I know you're all eager to hear our proposal for redevelopment of the downtown area. Before I relate what we have in mind, I'd like to take a few minutes to hear what is on your minds." (Knowing that people are sometimes reluctant to speak up, the presenter volunteered the first comment to encourage feedback from the group.) "For example, if I were seated where you are, I'd want to know about the cost of the project. Is cost an issue some of you want to hear about?" (Of course it was and the audience nodded their heads in agreement.) "What else . . . ?"

One person posed the question, "Will your plan stimulate business in the area?" (On a flip chart, the presenter wrote "New Business.") Another member of the audience offered, "I'd like to see a plan that will add beauty to the downtown area." (The presenter wrote "Aesthetics.") In minutes, half a dozen items were listed. Resuming his speaking role, the presenter went on to say, "Thank you. These are all good points. And, as you'll soon discover, they are the very points that our plan addresses."

The foregoing example shows how a presenter can invite direct questions or comments from a group. A similar effect can be achieved with rhetorical questions if time is limited, if the audience is very large, or if the speaker is concerned about losing control of the situation.

Soliciting audience feedback before a presentation gets underway offers a number of advantages. It is very relational. From the outset, a presenter recognizes people in the audience and gives them an opportunity to participate. Recognizing people, drawing out questions and concerns in advance, and pointing out that they will be covered during the presentation are tactics that help to reduce forms of resistance such as skepticism. Latent resistance can develop into full-blown overt resistance if members of an audience perceive that a speaker is unaware of or indifferent to their needs. Inviting feedback in advance dispels (or certainly minimizes) such resistance. When presenters indicate early on that they are willing to listen to the audience, people in an audience are more likely to respond in kind.

Questions and Comments during a Presentation

To invite questions or comments during a presentation requires a sufficient time frame, a setting in which participation is an acceptable norm, and a presenter who can maintain control of the situation. These conditions occur primarily in the InterActive mode. Typically, a presenter would not invite questions from the audience during a 15-minute speech at a service club luncheon. It might be appropriate and useful to do so during a one-hour sales demonstration. It is highly recommended to actively engage the audience during a full-day seminar or a three-day training session.

There are drawbacks to inviting verbal feedback during a presentation. It can interrupt the orderly progression of the message and consume valuable time. It can disrupt a speaker's agenda, especially if an aggressive person tries to monopolize the Q & A session. Nevertheless, including the audience adds a high degree of relational value to a presentation.

When done during a presentation, the best time to ask for questions or comments is after each key point. In that way, the presenter and the audience are less likely to lose the "train of thought." Before resuming the presentation, the speaker would make a transition statement: a brief summary (of the previous point) and preview (of the next point) that helps to bring the audience back on track with the subject.

One potential drawback to taking comments during the course of a presentation is the risk of losing control—of people in the audience or of the time allotted for the program. A presenter can better manage both by voicing phrases like these:

> "In the ten minutes we have before taking a break, what questions or comments do you have?"

> "Based on the material we've considered, what are your thoughts on Point A?" (When the time allotted for comments is up, the speaker would state something like the next remark.) "You have raised some very good points. Now, let's consider Point B."

> "We have time for just one more question before moving on."

When a speaker opens the floor to audience feedback during a presentation, it sometimes happens that a debate occurs between two or three people in the group. It is the speaker's responsibility (as group leader) to exercise command of the situation and assertively bring any debate to an end. A speaker can intervene with a statement like, "I appreciate your obvious enthusiasm for this subject. You have both offered some valid points. Since the next point will shed additional light on the issue, let's consider that now."

Q & A at the End of a Presentation

In more structured settings, with larger audiences, or with a limited time frame, it is customary to defer audience comments and questions until the end of a presentation. A presenter should let the audience know at the outset if there will be a Q & A session at the end. After the introductory opener and preview, the speaker would add, "At the end of the program, I will be happy to answer any questions you may have." If a Q & A session is promised, it is imperative to finish the presentation early enough to allow sufficient time for questions.

Many speakers signal that they will take comments from the audience by asking, "Do you have any questions?" It is a closed question which often elicits no response. It is sometimes voiced with a tone reminiscent of a school teacher. People in the audience think (but do not voice), "Yes, I have a question but I don't want to sound stupid" or "No, I don't want to speak out." The better way to invite audience feedback is to ask, "*What* questions do you have?" This *open* question conveys that the speaker presumes people will have questions, and suggests that the speaker is receptive to hearing them.

After inviting questions from the audience, a presenter should pause at least 30 seconds. Presenters who immediately start talking after asking "What questions do you have?" signal that they are not really interested in hearing from the audience. If no one in the audience responds, the presenter should voice a question to encourage the audience to speak up, saying something like, "One question I'm often asked is . . ." (and then volunteer a question that can be answered in a simple sentence or two).

A Q & A period should never end a presentation. The final question or comment from the audience could be such that it would end the presentation on a sour note. In addition, it is more awkward for a presenter to bring a program to a close when it ends with audience feedback. It is preferable to insert a Q & A period after the last key point but before the speaker's summary and close, sandwiched in toward (but not at) the end of a presentation. In this way, audience attention can be refocused on the speaker and the subject, and the speaker can control the manner in which the presentation ends. It is effective to end with an inspiring, amusing, or compelling anecdote or verbal illustration that reinforces the core concept of the message and brings the presentation to a powerful close.

Key Concept 57

An effective response to verbal feedback involves four steps: listen, discern, affirm, and answer.

Planning and experience enable a speaker to anticipate most of what will occur during a presentation. However, no amount of planning or experience enable a presenter to predict or to prepare for every possible question, comment, or objection. When a speaker opens the floor to feedback from an audience, anything can happen. It is then that a speaker must exercise particularly good communication skills—in terms of both receiving and sending.

The following four steps are essential to an effective response. In the first two, a presenter is in the role of "receiver." In the third and fourth, the presenter resumes the "sender" role.

1. Listen

2. Discern

3. Affirm

4. Answer

These four steps are essential to skillfully field questions or objections. In the terminology of sports, to **field** means to stop or catch a ball and throw it in to prevent the opposing team from scoring a point. The term is aptly applied to presenting. Figuratively, to field a question or objection means to answer it so skillfully that the presenter does not lose an opportunity to score a "winning point" with the audience.

Listen Attentively

Obviously, for a presenter to be effective, speaking skills are important. Listening skills are equally important. By listening attentively, a presenter signals interest in the audience and in what other people have to say. In addition, listening (or failing to listen) affects how a presenter responds to verbal feedback. When they ask a question or make a comment, some people do not communicate clearly. On the surface, what they say may not sound like it makes sense. By listening attentively, a presenter can sift through a confusing communication, clarify the point, and provide a satisfactory response.

Platform behaviors indicate if a presenter is listening attentively. When someone from the audience speaks, a presenter should:

- Make focused, meaningful eye contact with the person who is talking.

- Nod gently in a manner that suggests, "Yes, I hear you."

- Lean forward (slightly) to visually convey interest.

- Match facial expression to the nature of the question or objection. In some cases, a gracious smile is appropriate; in other cases, an expression of genuine concern.

In addition, a skilled listener will:

- Listen for the meaning in the message. To extract the main point of a question or objection, concentrate on key words. Conjunctions (and, or, but) and modifying words (descriptive adjectives and adverbs) are extraneous to the *real* meaning.

- Listen to determine if the person communicates in a concrete or conceptual manner. Typically, concrete thinkers communicate in shorter sentences and use words like "bottom-line." (They prefer a succinct, "bottom-line" response based on facts.) Conceptual thinkers tend to be more expressive and use words like "possibilities." (They prefer a more comprehensive response that conveys ideas.)

- Paraphrase (when appropriate). A **paraphrase** restates in abbreviated form what a person has said. It begins with wording such as that shown in the following examples.

  "Let me be sure I understand. You are asking . . . Is that right?"

  "Am I correct in understanding that you are concerned about . . . ?"

  "So, what you're saying is . . . Yes?"

Paraphrasing serves to clarify a question or objection, and confirms that the presenter correctly understands what a person has said. It is especially useful when a question or objection has been stated in a muddled manner. In addition, a paraphrase "buys time" when a speaker needs a moment to formulate a response.

Discern the Nature and Intent of Verbal Feedback

A presenter who listens attentively is better able to discern the nature and intent of feedback from the audience. A question may sound simple, but an attentive speaker may discern a complex issue within it. Another question may be worded in a complicated manner, but a discerning speaker will understand that the question is an easy one to answer in a straightforward manner.

Discernment is related to perception. A presenter perceives things about people in an audience in the same way an audience perceives things about a presenter: by watching and listening. When a member of the audience speaks up, a discerning presenter will observe visual cues and listen for vocal cues. Facial expression, gestures, and posture can indicate whether a question or an objection is motivated by genuine interest or by the intent to challenge and disprove the speaker. Tone of voice can convey intent. Generally (when considered in combination), vocal and visual cues express the attitude of the person who is speaking.

Affirm the Person

A skillful response consists of two parts: affirmation and answer. An affirmation (as Chapter 5 pointed out) is a relational technique that acknowledges and validates people. Even when a question or objection challenges a speaker, it is essential to maintain an affirmative relationship with the audience—*everyone* in the audience. How a speaker responds to one person is observed by the audience as a whole, and influences how an audience reacts to the speaker. The manner in which a presenter responds to audience feedback demonstrates finesse and professionalism—or lack of it.

An affirmation is expressed before stating an answer. If the presenter knows the people in a group, they should be addressed by name. The statements shown below are examples of affirmations.

"That's an interesting question."

"You make a good point, Jane."

"It's obvious you have given this some thought."

"I'm glad you brought that to our attention, Joe."

"You've raised an important point."

While it is relational to affirm people, it is important to refrain from overdoing it. An affirmation will appear insincere if the wording or the presenter's tone of voice are out of proportion with the point a person raised. Gushing affirmations can encourage attention-seekers in an audience to raise questions and objections repeatedly—just for the sake of it. An appropriate affirmation is a brief statement the presenter can voice honestly. For example, there is a ring of falsehood to an exclamation expressed with undue excitement, such as "What a *wonderful* question! I'm *so* glad you asked that!" It is more appropriate to simply state, "That's a good question."

Just as platform behavior is crucial when a presenter listens, so it is when a presenter starts to voice a response. Beginning with the affirmation and continuing through the answer, a presenter should appear confident and sound conversational. It is important to refrain from an authoritarian "know-it-all" tone of voice, a rigid or "closed" posture, and vocal or visual cues that suggest the presenter is flustered or frustrated. A presenter wants to convey, "I am relaxed, receptive to your comment, and in command of the situation."

Answer the Question, Comment, or Objection

The characteristics of effective communication apply to answering audience feedback. In other words, a presenter's response should be clear, correct, concise, and well-considered.

Clear.   A clear response is "on point." The audience clearly understands the answer because it pertains specifically to the question raised. The response is stated one point at a time, in short sentences, and in language uncluttered by gobbledygook or jargon. In addition, a clear answer clarifies misunderstandings. Circumstances that result in misunderstandings are described in the following examples.

- The presenter neglected to cover a point. A person in the audience is confused and asks a question. Usually, such questions are answered when the presenter states the point that was omitted.

- A question arises because the person was not listening attentively during the presentation. Such questions can be satisfied by summarizing the point the person missed.

- The meaning is not clear because of a difference in the way people think. A message delivered predominately in concrete terms may prompt questions from people who think conceptually, and vice versa. In this case, a point may be clarified by drawing a comparison to something with which the audience would be familiar, by restating the point in another way, or by illustrating the point with a visual aid.

Correct. Answers should be both factually and ethically correct. A factually correct answer is not only accurate; it is complete as well. For example, if someone asks, "How much does the product cost?" a factually correct answer would state, "A hundred dollars, plus applicable taxes and transportation charges." If the presenter said "a hundred dollars," the person may be disgruntled when the amount of the bill is more than they were led to believe.

Ethically correct answers are honest. A presenter who is not honest runs the risk of being caught in a contradiction, or worse, being caught in a lie. For the most part, people appreciate and value an honest answer. They may not agree with the answer; it may not be the answer they wanted to hear, but they will respect the integrity of the presenter. Honesty builds trust, and people are more inclined to deal with those they trust. If given reason to believe the presenter cannot be trusted, an audience is not likely to be persuaded. Dishonesty ultimately leads to a loss of credibility. Without credibility, a presenter might just as well pack up the visual aids, leave the platform, and go home.

Concise. A concise answer is "to the point." Some presenters are pontificators: they respond to every question in great detail and at great length. If asked a question as simple as "Where did you get your overhead projector?" they subject the audience to a 20-minute exposition on the technological development of audiovisual equipment. The principle that applies to verbal style applies equally to answering audience feedback: KISS (Keep It Short and Simple).

Well-considered. Responses to questions and comments should reflect consideration of the setting, and the interests and expectations of the audience. Is the audience gathered for professional, political, social, or personal reasons? Does the setting call for a brief or an in-depth response? Is it more appropriate to offer a serious or a lighthearted answer?

Questions, comments, and objections are addressed in further detail in Key Concepts 58 and 59 that follow. Although they are not delineated with each example, the four steps that comprise an effective response apply in every case. A presenter should always listen, discern, affirm, and then answer.

Key Concept 58

Questions differ as to type and content. A skillful presenter gives an answer appropriate to the nature of the question.

Fielding a question skillfully requires that the presenter correctly identify the nature of the question. Questions are identified in terms of these factors:

Type: simple, composite, or answer unknown

Content: factual or feeling

Types of Questions

Simple. A simple question warrants a simple answer: concise and straightforward. Simple questions are clearly expressed in one or two short sentences. They are commonly concrete in nature and raise one issue that can be answered succinctly and with ease.

Composite. The term **composite** applies to various types of questions. A **composite question** may address one point, the answer to which has several facets. "What is a good way to handle objections?" is an example of such a question. A composite question may raise several aspects of an issue, such as "What are your thoughts on strategic planning, employee motivation, and setting ethical standards as the chief responsibilities of a leader?" (leadership being the issue).

A question is also composite when it is stated in a verbose or confusing manner that makes an otherwise simple question sound as though it were complex. For instance: "I think that humor is a good way to break the ice with an audience, so sometimes I'll use a visual aid of a cartoon at the beginning of a presentation, something that pertains to the subject, of course. It gets people laughing, but because I also want the audience to take me seriously when I present my subject, I change my tone of voice when I start to get into the content. What do you think of that technique?" This question could be stated more simply: "When I begin a presentation, sometimes I use a visual aid of a cartoon as a humorous way to break the ice. What do you think of that technique?"

A composite question can tempt a presenter to respond at length. However, the preferable response to any question is a concise answer stated in the shortest possible time. A presenter must satisfy the question and, at the same time, show regard for the rest of the audience. Unless a presentation is delivered to one person (in a one-on-one situation), others may not have as keen an interest in the question as the person who asked it. Setting and time frame also influence the extent to which a composite question is answered. In formal settings where Q & A sessions are held at the end of a presentation, it is customary to keep answers brief. In more informal and interactive settings, a presenter may elaborate if time allows and if the issue is of interest to the audience as a whole.

Composite questions in particular require attentive listening skills. Often, the real issue of a composite question must be clarified. The following techniques can be useful when responding to composite questions.

■ *Paraphrase.* As previously pointed out, paraphrasing helps to clarify a question.

■ *Ask the person to repeat the question.* It is acceptable to say, "I'm sorry, I'm not sure I understand the question. Could you repeat it for me, please?" Frequently, when restated, a question is worded in shorter and clearer terms.

■ *Ask for time.* When a question probes for in-depth knowledge of facts of which a speaker may not be apprised, it is appropriate to say something like, "Before offering an answer, I want to be sure I have the facts straight. If you will give me a couple of days to check on that, I'll get back to you." When a question seeks an opinion on a significant issue, it is appropriate to respond, "You've raised an important point—so important, in fact, that I'd like to think about it. I'll have an answer for you after the break." The time frame a presenter specifies (after the break, by the end of the program, follow-up within a week) will depend on the situation. To maintain credibility, it is essential to respond with an answer within the specified time frame—in person, by telephone, or in writing.

■ *Confine answers to the most important points.* The answer to a multifaceted question should focus on two or three key points. For the sake of clarity (for both speaker and audience), the answer can be structured like a presentation (with an introduction, body, and conclusion). It may be stated in a manner similar to "First . . . Then . . . Finally. . . ." The following example suggests how this approach would work to answer the composite question, "What are your thoughts about handling questions from the audience?"

> [Affirm] "That's a good question."
>
> [Answer] "First, listen attentively. Next, affirm the person who asked the question. Then, provide an honest answer in a concise manner."

In this example, not everything was said that could be said about answering questions. A presenter could talk at length on the matter. However, the question was not "What are *all* of your thoughts . . . ?," nor was it "Tell us *everything* you know about . . ." The question was "What are your thoughts . . . ?" and the presenter answered the question. If audience members want to know more, they will ask more questions. If they do, the presenter can elaborate if time allows, suggest reference materials that cover the topic in detail, or offer to address the matter further in a follow-up visit, telephone call, or by letter.

Answer Unknown. When a person asks a question to which a speaker does not know the answer, the most appropriate reply is to say, "I don't know." Credibility is damaged by making up an answer that may be incorrect, or by responding in a manner in which the audience detects uncertainty. In some situations, it is appropriate to respond (with a tone of good-natured humor), "That's a good question. I wish I had a good answer on the tip of my tongue, but I don't."

Somewhere, there is an answer for virtually every question. The techniques listed here are useful for finding answers to "I don't know" questions:

- Refer the question back to the person who asked it. Ask, "Based on your experience, what are your thoughts about that?"

- Elicit responses from the audience. Ask, "Does anyone in the group know about that?"

- Offer to research the answer and get back to the person within a specified and reasonable period of time. Write down the question in view of the audience. Doing so conveys the intention to perform as promised.

Content of Questions

Just the Facts. Questions of fact are concrete in nature. They seek information, data, statistics, or specifications. These questions are examples of questions of fact:

"What is the source of the statistics you cited?"

"When can you deliver?"

"How did actual expenditures compare with budgeted amounts?"

"Do you provide after-sales service?"

"What is your voting record on this issue?"

Questions of fact should be fielded with ease. If a presenter is hesitant or evasive when responding to a question of fact, an audience will perceive that the presenter lacks expertise in the subject or lacks honesty.

Feelings. Questions of feeling are conceptual. They seek ideas, alternatives, or the presenter's opinion on a matter. As the following examples indicate, implicit in a question of feeling is the query, "How do you (the presenter) *feel* about this?"

"How important is an open-door policy?"

"Do you agree with Dr. Stefanson's approach?"

"What would you recommend in this situation?"

"How should a manager respond to employee misconduct?"

"You suggested Point X. Why is that?"

When asked questions of feeling, a presenter should refrain from answering "I think . . ." or "I feel . . ." Such wording lacks conviction and authority. Phrases like "Based on my experience . . ." or "During the course of my career, I've observed . . ." sound more substantive. With some questions of feeling, the answer need not be qualified at all. Rather than respond, "I *feel* this proposal will meet your needs," it is more convincing to state, "This proposal will meet your needs."

If a question of feeling asks about someone else's opinion, the presenter should decline answering. If someone poses a question such as, "What does the CEO think of your proposal?" an appropriate answer would be, "I can appreciate your interest in asking. However, as I'm sure you can appreciate, I can't speak for the CEO."

Questions of feeling should be fielded with professional discretion. In a business presentation, it is inadvisable to risk unnecessary controversy by instigating a discussion of a political, ethnic, or religious nature. In a business presentation, it is inappropriate to debate personal values.

Reflection Question

From your reading of Key Concepts 57 and 58, what ideas have you gained that will help you field questions with greater skill and confidence?

Key Concept 59

Comments from an audience differ as to type. A skillful speaker voices a reply appropriate to the type of comment.

When a member of the audience comments on some point of a presentation, the comment will express one of the following:

- Agreement
- Addition
- Objection

As with questions, attentive listening skills help a presenter discern the nature of a comment, which conditions the presenter's reply.

Comments of Agreement

A comment of agreement expresses concurrence with a point made during a presentation. Such comments characteristically reflect a desire to be heard or an interest in having the presenter's proposal adopted. Statements such as "I like what you said about . . ." and "You've presented some good ideas for . . ." are comments of agreement. The appropriate response to a comment of agreement is to say, simply, "Thank you." Agreement from the audience does not require any further commentary from the presenter.

Comments of Addition

A comment of addition also implies agreement, but adds to what the presenter has said. The following statements are examples of comments of addition.

> "I like what you said about reducing costs. In fact, I think we could apply your recommendations to the distribution group as well."

> "You've presented some good ideas for increasing productivity. We could computerize the learning labs, too."

The appropriate reply to a comment of addition is to offer a brief acknowledgment such as, "Thank you. That's a very good point" or "I appreciate your bringing that up."

When responding to comments of agreement or addition, a presenter must take care to avoid two common pitfalls: talking at length and misinterpreting the comment. A Q & A session is considered by people in an audience to be *their* turn to talk. A presenter who responds to a comment with a dissertation can irritate an otherwise receptive audience, or may say something that will neutralize or negate the point of agreement. A presenter who neglects to listen attentively may misinterpret the feedback and respond as though the comment were a difference of opinion or an objection. Doing so can create unnecessary confusion or discord.

Objections

The term **objection** is commonly understood to mean disagreement or disapproval. Comments that sound like objections may, in fact, express a genuine interest in seeking further information or clarification. They may express an opinion that differs from the presenter's as a result of a difference in experience or understanding of the facts. When responding to objections, it is helpful to bear in mind that disagreement on an issue need not (and should not) spark a disagreeable attitude toward the person who voices an objection. Effective presenters consider it more important to remain in a right relationship with the audience than to be proved right on every point.

The key to fielding objections skillfully is to refrain from taking objections personally. Objections must be handled with composure and tact. The objective is to dissipate the issue, not to dispute the other person's point of view. It is imperative to avoid engaging in a verbal battle of wits. A presenter who becomes defensive or argumentative will lose credibility.

There are three appropriate responses to an objection:

- Agree
- Reapproach
- Arbitrate

In every case, the person who voices an objection should be affirmed and not confronted. Negative words (like *don't, no,* and *not*) fuel confrontation. The following examples show a confrontational response in contrast to an affirming response.

CONFRONTS: "I don't agree with you."

AFFIRMS: "That's an interesting point. There is another aspect to consider, though."

CONFRONTS: "No, that's not right."

AFFIRMS: "I can see where that might seem to be the case. However, let's consider this in terms of . . ."

Agree.   On occasion, someone in an audience will raise a point that is correct—even though it expresses disagreement with the presenter. If the objection is not an obstacle to acceptance of the message, the appropriate response is to acknowledge that the person is right. A presenter should never put an entire presentation at risk by insisting on "the right to be right." It is preferable to say, "Thank you for bringing that to our attention. I wasn't aware of those findings," or simply state, "You've made a good point."

Reapproach.   When someone voices an objection but the point is not valid, approaching the issue from another perspective can resolve the objection. People sometimes object, not to what has been said, but to how the point was put. Presenting the matter in different terms may prompt agreement. A reapproach is phrased, "You've brought up an interesting point. However, let's consider this from another angle." The point is then explained in a manner other than how it was first stated. The "other angle" may be presented through the use of a comparison, analogy, rhetorical question, or a scenario that describes a situation to which the objector may be better able to relate.

Arbitrate.   Objections can be dissolved with the use of a "feel-felt-found" response. The presenter states, "I can understand why you would *feel* that way. I worked with someone recently who *felt* the same way, until they *found* that . . ." After "found that," the presenter describes the value that offsets the objection.

This method diffuses the potential for conflict. The "feel" phrase acknowledges the person who voiced the objection. To arbitrate the point of disagreement in an agreeable way, the "felt" phrase introduces (hypothetically, in some cases) an objective third party. The "found that" conclusion suggests the benefit of accepting the point. The example below indicates how the "feel-felt-found" response works.

> In a presentation to plant managers, a sales representative proposed upgrading factory operations with the installation of state-of-the-art automated equipment. At the end of the presentation, one manager remarked, "I like some of your ideas, but the equipment is too costly. We can't afford that kind of investment." The presenter replied, "I can see how you might *feel* that way. I worked with a company last year that *felt* the same way, until they *found* that they gained a considerable return on their investment as a result of safer working conditions, improvements in product quality, reduced turnaround time, and an increase in the value of the business."

Key Concept 60

One measure of a presenter's skill is the ability to deal with disruptions with aplomb.

By planning, preparation, and practice, a presenter accounts for most factors that affect a presentation. The aim is to do, in advance of a presentation, everything possible to eliminate surprises—especially unpleasant ones. Nevertheless, unforeseen situations occur, namely in the forms of disruptive incidents or behavior.

The Appropriate Response to Disruptions

Naturally, how a presenter responds will vary depending on the nature and degree of the disruption. In general, as the person on the platform who commands the attention of the audience, a presenter should demonstrate leadership. Audience members look to the presenter for cues. They wonder, "What is going to happen next?" and expect the presenter to deal with the situation. Skilled presenters do so with aplomb, which is best described as "grace under pressure." With confidence and poise, they remain in control of the presentation event by following the three steps listed below.

- Remain calm
- Take action
- Be flexible

Remain Calm. A presenter who becomes visibly upset or flustered by a disruption may aggravate the situation. Staying calm and composed keeps the mind clear to consider how to handle the disruption, and has a reassuring effect on an audience. When it is appropriate to the situation, humor is useful to relieve the tension that often accompanies a disruption. Humor can make an awkward moment enjoyable for both the audience and the presenter. A disruption can be turned to advantage by finding something amusing in it. People are inclined to respect the presenter who remains sufficiently composed to laugh at a difficult situation.

Take Action. An incident or behavior may be so minor that only the speaker is aware of it, and the presentation can proceed as planned. However, when something threatens to disrupt others, action must be taken to minimize the degree to which the disruption detracts from the presentation. The action is determined by whether the disruption is related to an incident or to behavior.

Be Flexible. Responding to unforeseen situations often requires flexibility. Speakers find they have to adapt to disruptions as varied as last-minute changes in time frame, more or fewer people than expected, a heckler in the audience, or a power failure in the meeting room. Disruptions are handled with greater ease when one is very well prepared. A presenter who is not preoccupied with a script or trying to "wing it" is free to be flexible. In the examples of techniques for dealing with potential disruptions (described here), the value of flexibility is evident.

Disruptive Incidents

Three tactics can be employed for dealing with disruptive incidents: detour, delay, or dismiss.

Detour.   A detour is a way around a disruption that enables a presenter to still reach the objective of a presentation. In the following situation, the presenter took a detour around a potential disruption.

> Joe had an appointment to deliver a presentation at 9:30 A.M. in the conference room of the client's office. Midafternoon the day before, the client telephoned to cancel the presentation because another department needed the use of the meeting room. After confirming that the people scheduled to attend his presentation were still free to do so, Joe arranged for an off-site meeting at a facility near the client's office.

Delay.   Out of respect for the audience, a presentation should always start on time. However, it may not proceed as planned. As the following situation shows, a disruptive incident may cause a delay.

> During Jody's presentation of a computer system, the electric power failed. Since the windows in the room let in enough natural light to continue, Jody asked, "Before we go on, what questions or comments do you have about what you've seen so far?" Jody delayed by inviting questions from the group and initiating a discussion. When the power was restored a few minutes later, Jody made a smooth transition back into the presentation. "I'm glad that happened," she said. "It gives me a chance to show you how easy it is to start up the system." She turned a delay to an advantage.

Dismiss.   Although they rarely occur, some disruptions are best handled by dismissing the audience. Acts of nature such as fire and earthquakes are reasons to dismiss an audience, as are some medical emergencies. In a crisis, it is imperative that the presenter remain calm to provide leadership and direction to the group.

Disruptive Behavior

Few incidents disrupt a presentation as much as a person in the audience who repeatedly interrupts, voices objections, contradicts the presenter, or jokes around. Disruptive behavior signals an intent not to hear but to be heard. The disruptive person speaks out at every opportunity. Persons who behave in such a manner are "detractors." A **detractor** is someone whose behavior detracts from the quality of a presentation, from the attentiveness of other members of the audience, and from what the presenter is trying to accomplish. Detractors have a negative effect on an otherwise professional atmosphere. They diminish the value the majority of people in an audience might receive if they were allowed to hear the presentation without disruption. For the benefit of the audience as a whole, and to keep a presentation moving forward toward its objective, a presenter must deal with disruptive behavior—promptly and assertively.

Common reasons for disruptive behavior are:

- Resistance to change

- Resentment of the presenter

- Repetition of behavior that is successful for the detractor

Resistance to Change.   Frequently, a presentation delivers information and ideas that challenge customary ways of thinking or of doing things. Some people are not receptive to anything new. They feel threatened by new ideas, new information, new systems, new procedures, new policies. They are unwilling to consider attitudes or actions that differ from those they have harbored for a long time. In such cases, disruptive behavior is a form of "self-defense." It is a means of counteracting ideas and information the detractor does not want to accept. A disruptive person may think (albeit subconsciously), "If I ask a question she can't answer, then this information is no good" or "If I raise an objection he can't deal with, then the proposal won't be approved."

Resentment.   During the course of a presentation, an effective speaker fills a leadership role: leading the audience through material and managing the people in the group. An accomplished speaker exhibits enviable attributes: organization and communication skills, energy and enthusiasm, presence and personal power. There are those who may resent what they see and hear. Especially when a presenter is perceived to be an "outsider" (a consultant, salesperson, contract trainer, guest speaker, someone from another department, or an upper-level executive), some people in the audience may feel that the presentation is an intrusion.

Repeating Successful Behavior.   People are inclined to repeat behavior that has worked for them in the past. When they get what they want by acting in a certain manner, they will act that way again to get what they want.

What a disruptive person wants is what every person wants: attention. A child throws a temper tantrum to gain attention. When the parent pays attention, the child has succeeded and so throws temper tantrums again. In a similar manner, a detractor has learned that disruptive behavior succeeds in getting a presenter's attention.

Most presenters are not pleased by the rude interruptions, sarcastic remarks, testy questions, and pointless objections that are trademarks of people intent on disrupting a presentation. (The majority of people in an audience are not pleased either.) It is easier to respond to such behavior when a presenter recognizes that it is not a "personal attack" but an acting out of the need for attention.

Dealing with Disruptive Behavior

With an awareness of the reasons that underlie disruptive behavior, a presenter can more easily deal with it with aplomb by practicing these techniques:

- Be courteous
- Exercise control
- Confront

Be Courteous.   Detractors try to provoke presenters. If a presenter reacts to disruptive behavior with frustration, aggravation, or impatience, the detractor has "won" and will likely continue to disrupt the presentation. Therefore, a presenter's first response to disruptive behavior should be to deal with the person with the same courtesy that a professional would extend to a courteous and reasonable member of the group. Courtesy is expressed by more than words alone. It is conveyed through vocal and visual cues: a pleasant tone of voice, a relaxed posture, a pleasant facial expression. The example that follows describes a common form of disruptive behavior and an appropriate response to it.

> Early in the presentation, a member of the audience interrupts the speaker in midsentence and asks a question that is out of context with the message. Unruffled, the presenter replies courteously, "That's an interesting question." The presenter then offers an answer, prefacing the reply with phrases such as "studies indicate . . . ," "the trends suggest . . . ," or "Experts in the field agree that . . ." Phrases like these convey authority and depersonalize the response.

Exercise Control.   When a courteous response does not suffice to quell disruptive behavior, a presenter must next exert control over the situation. Maintaining control is one of the responsibilities of presenting. To give an audience a meaningful and memorable experience, the presenter needs to manage the setting in which that experience occurs. In a manner of speaking, a presenter is a "traffic cop" who monitors the actions and interactions of people within the group. The following phrases, stated assertively, are useful for expressing control.

> "I'm pleased that you are interested in this subject, but in the interests of time, I'm going to have to ask you to hold any further questions until the end."

> "For the benefit of the rest of the audience, I'd appreciate it if you would refrain from interrupting. I'll be happy to discuss any other points with you during the break."

> "We have time for just one more comment." (The presenter then turns away from the disruptive person and purposely recognizes someone else in the audience.)

Confront.   When a person persists in being disruptive, a presenter must confront the behavior. The experience of the many in the audience takes precedence over one or two detractors. If the situation allows, it is helpful to announce a brief refreshment break or to direct the group to engage in an activity (such as a workbook exercise or discussion with persons seated nearby). A brief break provides an opportunity to deal with a disruptive person on an individual basis. In a steady tone of voice and maintaining focused eye contact, the disruptive behavior is addressed with statements like these:

> "For the benefit of the group, please refrain from [specify the disruptive behavior] until the meeting is over."

> "Frequent interruptions are distracting to the other people here. For that reason, I'm going to have to ask you to please leave."

In view of the peer pressure that exists within any group, the first two tactics—courtesy and control—usually serve to bring disruptive behavior to a halt. However, on the rare occasions when it does not, it is preferable to confront a detractor than to allow one person to destroy a presentation. Phrases like "in the interests of time" and "for the benefit of the group" convey that the presenter's response is not personal, but professional regard for others in the audience.

Unplugging

A potential detractor can be likened to a buzz saw that is plugged into an electrical outlet. Something during the course of a presentation acts like an "on" switch that sets off disruptive behavior. **Unplugging** is aimed at "pulling the plug" on resistance or negative reactions by affirming the "right" of the audience to their point of view. The following statements are examples of unplugging.

> "I appreciate the fact that there are many points of view on this issue. I will be glad to hear yours when we open the floor to comments and questions at the end of the session."

> "I do not expect that everyone will agree with all of the points you will hear. However, others have found value in this program that made it worth their while. I hope you do, too."

Unplugging is not necessary if an audience is wholly receptive to the presenter and to the presentation event. It is most useful when a presenter observes a potential detractor in the audience, when a message is charged with emotion, or when the subject is controversial. An unplugging statement is expressed after the attention-getting opener and preview, or may be voiced as a preface to a key point that addresses a sensitive issue.

Reflection Questions

What disruptions—incidents or behavior—have you observed or encountered in presentations? What ideas have you gained from this section that will help you better deal with disruptions should they occur when you present in the future?

Summary

Verbal feedback from an audience can be fielded more effectively when a presenter has anticipated probable questions and objections, and prepared and rehearsed responses to them. Questions and comments may be solicited before or during a presentation, or during a Q & A session at the end. To effectively field questions and comments, a presenter must follow four steps: listen attentively, discern the nature of the feedback, affirm the person who raised the point, and provide an answer. In addition to responding to questions and comments, a presenter must also be able to deal with disruptive incidents and behavior—calmly and decisively.

Sample Situation

Overcoming Objections in a Sales Presentation

By their very nature, presentations conducted for sales or promotional purposes tend to trigger objections from the audience. An objection may be an expression of natural buyer resistance. It may represent a prospective buyer's attempt to determine the presenter's sincerity or expertise. An objection may be stated with the intent of establishing the prospect's decision-making power. Whatever the motivation, the astute salesperson recognizes that an objection is not a "No."

The experienced sales presenter also recognizes that the first objection often is a "smokescreen," not the *real* objection. A presenter should refrain from answering the first objection voiced and proceed instead through a line of questioning that asks "What else . . . ?" or "In addition to that . . . ?" These questions are used to remove "smokescreens" in order to uncover any true objections that stand in the way of approval of the product, service, or proposal presented. The dialogue outlined below indicates how the method works.

PROSPECT: "It costs too much."

PRESENTER: "What other concerns do you have?"

PROSPECT: "I have to discuss the decision with my partner."

PRESENTER: "In addition to that?"

PROSPECT: "We just don't have the time it will take to implement it."

PRESENTER: "Is there anything else?"

PROSPECT: "No, that's it."

Generally, the last objection raised is the *real* objection (and often the only one).

PRESENTER: [*paraphrase*] "Let me be sure I understand. You are concerned that what I've proposed will take too much of your time. Is that right?

PROSPECT: "Yes."

At this point, the sales presenter would overcome the objection by either the reapproach or arbitrate method (described under Key Concept 59), selecting the response that would be most appropriate to the situation.

Comprehension Check

The answers to the following appear on page 334.

1. "What kind of after-sales service do you provide?" is _____.
   a. a question of fact
   b. an objection
   c. a question of feeling
   d. a composite question
   e. disruptive behavior

2. At the beginning of your one-hour presentation, you announced that you
   would take questions at the end. Ten minutes into the presentation, the
   same person interrupts for the second time and asks another question.
   What would be the preferred way to respond to the person? _____
   a. "Thank you for bringing that up."
   b. "I said I would answer questions when I'm finished!!"
   c. Ignore the interruption and go on with your presentation.
   d. "For the benefit of the group, I'm going to have to ask you to hold any
   further questions until the end of the presentation."
   e. Ask the person to leave.

3. A technique of attentive listening is to _____.
   a. give a concise answer
   b. paraphrase
   c. ask an open question
   d. affirm
   e. formulate a response

4. An objection may be overcome by using _____.
   a. diplomacy
   b. a humorous anecdote
   c. a delay tactic
   d. assertive communication
   e. a feel-felt-found response

Match.   The statements on the left are examples of questions and comments
that may be voiced by a member of the audience or by a presenter. Terms
that identify the types of statements are listed on the right. Match each numbered statement with one of the lettered terms. (A lettered item will be used
only once.)

5. _____ Audience: "You have a good   *a.* Paraphrase
   grasp of the situation."   *b.* Objection
6. _____ Audience: "How do you think   *c.* Comment of agreement
   we should implement your pro-   *d.* Affirmation
   posal?"   *e.* Question of feeling
7. _____ Presenter: "If I understand
   correctly, your chief concern is
   cost. Is that right?"
8. _____ Audience: "I like your ideas,
   but we won't have the time to
   act on them for at least a year."
9. _____ Presenter: "You've raised an
   interesting point."

To Do

For the presentation you are developing for this course, list the probable questions and objections you would anticipate and your answers to them. Use this format:

Questions   Answers

Objections   Response to Overcome Objection

Of the questions and objections you have listed, are there any points that would be better addressed as part of your presentation? If so, you may want to revise your message to incorporate those points in the content.

10
Settings and Surroundings

The effective presenter plans, prepares, and delivers every aspect of a presentation with two considerations in mind: to break down audience resistance and to build an affirmative response. In addition to the message and the manner in which it is presented, thought must be given to the meeting room in which a presentation occurs. The setting and surroundings convey a "message," too. They affect how an audience feels and how a presenter performs.

In many instances, the presenter does not choose the location for a presentation. In some instances, the presenter may have little control over how a room is set up. Nonetheless, it is important to understand the physical factors that influence a presentation and, whenever possible, to make arrangements that create an enjoyable experience for the audience and a positive outcome for the presenter.

Objectives

To understand the impact of the setting on a presentation; to identify the various seating arrangements and factors related to environment and surroundings; and to be able to apply the information when selecting and arranging the setting of a presentation.

Key Concepts

61. Setting is one of the decisive factors that affects the conduct and outcome of a presentation. It is preferable to select a setting that complements the presentation.

279

62. Room arrangements and audience seating are critical components of a presentation setting.

63. A presentation is influenced by environmental factors: lighting, temperature, air quality, and sounds.

64. The atmosphere of the setting in which a presentation occurs is enhanced by certain colors, accessories, and amenities.

Key Terms

To make full use of the key concepts, you will need to understand the following terms:

Setting	Environment
On-site, off-site	Ambiance

Key Concept 61

Setting is one of the decisive factors that affects the conduct and outcome of a presentation. Therefore, it is preferable to select a setting that complements the presentation.

In Chapter 2, Key Concept 14 (on planning a presentation), **setting** is defined as inclusive of the environment and surroundings within which a presentation occurs. Although the term is also used to refer to the nature of a presentation event (as formal, professional, or casual), in the context of this chapter, **setting** applies to the physical facility.

The Significance of the Setting

Setting is a significant consideration for the following reasons.

Psychological.   Physical factors influence the audience frame of mind. People think, feel, and respond much differently in a room that is light, spacious, cool, quiet, and fresh than in one that is dark, crowded, stuffy, noisy, or musty. An unpleasant physical environment is detrimental to the psychological environment. Since persuasion involves engendering good thoughts and feelings in people, the setting should feel like a good place to be.

Perceptual.   A meeting room conveys a "message." Chapter 8 (on the subject of nonverbal style) pointed out that a presenter communicates through vocal and visual cues, from which an audience forms perceptions. In a similar manner, every room contains visible and audible components which likewise shape audience perceptions. When selecting and arranging the setting for a presentation, it behooves a presenter to ask, "What does this room 'say' about me, about the organization I represent, about the import of my message? What do I want the setting to convey?"

Speaker Concentration.   A setting may contain elements that disrupt a speaker's ability to concentrate. In distracting or disruptive situations, it is doubly difficult to conduct a productive presentation and bring about a successful outcome. While presenting, a speaker should not be concerned with having to overcome limitations of the setting, but should be free to give undivided attention to the dynamics of delivering the message.

Complementary Characteristics

A setting should be selected on the basis of what will complement the presentation. A setting is most effective when it is comfortable for the audience, well suited to the intent of the presentation event, and serves the needs of the presenter in relation to the audience.

Comfortable for the Audience.   A primary factor to consider when deciding on the setting for a presentation is how to create the greatest degree of comfort for the audience. Presentations commonly introduce something new: a new product, service, supplier, a new policy, new information, or a new approach. Frequently, people prefer to maintain the status quo, to leave things as they are rather than adopt the unknown. A common cause of "buyer resistance" is reluctance to commit to a decision that will bring about change. Since people initially may feel uncomfortable about making a change, it is crucial to provide a comfortable setting.

In a comfortable setting, people in the audience can:

- See clearly
- Hear clearly
- Sit comfortably
- Focus attentively

They do not have to squint or lean or stretch to view the presenter and visual aids. They do not have to strain to listen, nor are they bothered by extraneous noise. They do not have to shift uneasily in their chairs in a vain attempt to find a position that is comfortable. As a result, the audience can concentrate attention on the message without distractions or discomfort.

Well-suited to the Intent of the Presentation Event. People attend a business presentation with the intent of engaging in one of the activities listed below.

- Learning
- Planning
- Decision making

Of course, presentations are also made on occasions when people gather for social, political, or religious reasons, which occur in settings that range from outdoor parks to platforms at railroad stations. The discussion in this chapter is limited to settings common to business presentations.

A setting that is ideally suited to a learning situation will not appear the same as one arranged for a planning meeting. Likewise, the setting for an external promotional presentation aimed at persuading people to reach a decision would differ from settings appropriate for learning or planning. A business consultant, for example, may make presentations that differ in intent: public seminars that attract a hundred people or so, proposals to prospective clients, and facilitation of small-group planning sessions. The same setting would not work equally well for presentations with different intents.

Serves the Needs of the Presenter. The setting should be equipped with fixtures for audiovisual aids the speaker will require: a sound system, electrical outlets for projection equipment, a projection screen, or visual boards. Most important, the setting should enhance a presenter's platform behaviors—notably, visibility and movement in relation to the audience.

Often, the selection of the setting for a presentation is based on personal preference, convenience, familiarity, frugality, or the fact that the location is a popular spot. Although it is not inappropriate to consider these factors, they should be secondary to the preceding three characteristics. The setting of a presentation should never be the random result of a presenter having overlooked the importance of setting.

Selection of the Setting

Ideally, the setting for a presentation is selected by the person or team who will be presenting. Presumably, the presenter knows better than anyone else the type of setting that will be most conducive to success. In actuality, presenters frequently find they must present in settings that are mandated, either by custom or by someone else.

By custom, many business presentations are given in established meeting rooms—even when the room is not the best possible location for a given presentation. Without giving the matter much thought, people gather in whichever conference room is available. Frequently, conference rooms become multipurpose rooms, used for everything from coffee breaks to meetings of the board of directors. In the public sector, presentations customarily occur in the chambers where city council or board of supervisors meetings are held. In the same setting, a bid proposal amounting to millions of dollars can be followed by citizens speaking out on the subject of the local leash law. It is also customary, and an increasingly popular option, to reserve a hotel facility for a presentation. In this case, care needs to be taken to ensure that the meeting room is indeed designed for business presentations. Too often, hotel meeting facilities (like office conference rooms) serve a multiplicity of uses. The meeting room in which a serious business presentation is held one morning may reek of alcohol and cigarette smoke, because the night before a convention group used the same room for a hospitality hour.

In addition to custom, the setting of a presentation may be selected by the person (such as a client) or the organization for whom the presentation will be given. In such cases, it behooves the presenter to check out the facilities ahead of time. If the location will not complement the presentation, and if the situation permits, the presenter should negotiate for a more suitable site. If the meeting site cannot be changed, the presenter should make whatever adjustments necessary to improve the quality of the setting.

On-site or Off-site

When a presentation is scheduled, a decision must be made about whether to conduct it on-site or off-site. When an internal presentation is done by a member of an organization's staff at the usual work location, the setting is on-site. With external presentations (in which audience and presenter come from different organizations), the distinction between on-site and off-site locations becomes blurred. For the sake of clarity, the term **on-site** applies to presentations done at the normal place of business of either the presenter or the audience: typically, a client's office or an organization's conference room. The term **off-site** refers to a setting reserved specifically for a given presentation: a meeting, training, conference, or convention facility.

On-site locations frequently are limited in terms of what a presenter can do to alter or customize the setting. Rooms used for purposes other than business presentations offer little or no flexibility with regard to floor space, furnishings, seating arrangements, lighting, or audiovisual aids. Furthermore, in familiar surroundings, people are inclined to be preoccupied with other matters going on in their workplace. They may be less alert because the setting is "ordinary." For these reasons, an off-site setting is preferable. High-stakes presentations, in particular, may warrant the additional expense of renting an off-site meeting room.

An off-site location must be selected with care. That a facility advertises meeting rooms in no way guarantees that the site will be agreeable, appropriate, or acceptable. A presenter should "comparison-shop" the options and visit probable locations before making a final decision.

Generally, an off-site presentation entails a greater degree of planning and coordination to ensure that the staff at the off-site facility clearly understand the requirements and comply with directions regarding set-up. In addition to the specific requirements of a given presentation, and the considerations discussed in the key concepts that follow, the factors listed below should be considered when selecting an off-site facility.

- Location: convenient for the audience and easy to find (A map with easy-to-read directions should be provided to those who will be attending the presentation.) In some locations, security is also a factor to consider.
- Adequate parking (preferably free or validated)
- Well-trained, courteous, prompt, and responsive staff
- Adequate restroom facilities near the meeting room
- Ample room for displays (if applicable)
- Dining facilities (if applicable)

Whether a presentation is to be held on-site or off-site, the meeting room should be reserved in advance and confirmed a few days prior to the date of the presentation. On the day of the presentation, it is advisable to arrive at the site early enough to attend to last-minute details or adjustments that may need to be made.

Key Concept 62

Room arrangements and audience seating are critical components of a presentation setting.

Ideally, seating arrangements for a presentation conform to the characteristics of an effective setting (introduced in the preceding Key Concept 61). Seating should:

- Be comfortable for the audience.
- Serve the intent of the presentation event.

■ Suit the needs of the presenter in relation to the audience, specifically in terms of the group dynamics the presenter hopes to generate and audience viewing of the presenter and visual aids.

In actuality, seating arrangements often are conditioned by the size and shape of a room that is customarily used for meetings (especially in cases of on-site presentations). In many instances, seating is arranged according to conventional norms. In no case should seating for a presentation be the haphazard result of neglect on the part of the presenter. Regardless of the circumstances or space limitations, a presenter should always arrange seating in the best manner possible. It is, after all, the presenter who has to "work the room."

Seating Considerations and Room Arrangements

When the presenter has the option to select the site and direct the set-up of the room, primary consideration should be given to audience seating. In addition to reflecting the characteristics of an effective setting, the seating arrangement is determined on the basis of the following factors.

Audience Size.   How many people will be attending the presentation? In this situation, is it common for additional people to show up unexpectedly? (If so, extra seating should be available.)

Audience Composition.   Who will be attending the presentation? Does the status of those who will attend influence how seating will be arranged?

Workspace.   Will attendees need a workspace and, if so, for what: taking notes, working with handouts, spreading out materials for study or review?

Interaction.   Will members of the group be asked to interact with one another and, if so, for what: opening introductions, discussion, activities in break-out groups? Is it preferable to seat members of the audience so that their focus of attention is on the presenter? Or so they can exchange feedback and make eye contact with one another?

Duration.   How long will people be seated? The longer a presentation, the more important it is to provide chairs that are comfortable for long-term seating, but firm enough to encourage people to remain alert.

Tables.   How many tables (total) are needed for seating and for registration, refreshments, workshop materials, or displays? Will a table(s) be needed at the head of the room for the speaker or for placement of audio-visual equipment?

In some situations, presenters work from a head table on which they place an overhead projector, transparencies, and speaker notes. Rooms are commonly set up with the head table placed horizontal to the audience. If space permits, it is preferable to place a head table lengthwise (perpendicular to the audience) to reduce the barrier between presenter and audience. Doing so also allows greater freedom of movement for the presenter. To move across the platform directly in front of the audience, it is easier to simply step away from a table placed vertically than it is to have to walk around from behind a table situated horizontally. When a head table is placed lengthwise, materials can be kept out of view of the audience by setting them behind the projector (if one is used).

Aisles. Between seating, aisles need to be created to provide for a safe and smooth flow of traffic in and out of a room. Access for persons with disabilities must be considered as well.

Visibility. Seating should be arranged in such a manner that the presenter will be clearly visible to everyone in the audience. For a presentation to a large group meeting in an oblong room, it may be necessary to speak from a raised platform or riser. As Chapter 6 pointed out, every seat should also afford a clear view of visual aids.

The visibility factor must be taken into account when selecting a facility for a presentation to a large audience. If people are seated in the back of a narrow and deep room, they may have to raise up out of their chairs and crane their necks to see the presenter. They may miss meaningful expressions and gestures. On the other hand, in a shallow room that is very wide, people seated at the far sides (along either wall) will be viewing visual aids from a severe and distorting angle.

Open Space. If the time frame is such that a presentation includes a break period(s), consideration should be given to the area where people will gather during the break. Like other aspects of room and seating arrangements, the space needed for a break area and how it is arranged will depend upon the size of the audience and the nature of the presentation. To remind people of their reason for being there and to reconvene on a timely basis, it is advisable to have open space for breaks in or near the meeting room. The space should be sufficient for the number of people in the audience to mingle comfortably, with freedom of movement.

Setup Diagram. A setup diagram illustrates the space and seating requirements for a presentation. It indicates the type and placement of furnishings, fixtures, and audiovisual equipment. If a presentation is going to be held off-site, a setup diagram is useful to describe requirements to the facility staff to confirm that they can provide what is needed. If room and seating arrangements are going to be set up by someone other than the presenter, a setup diagram visually clarifies verbal instructions to avoid misunderstandings.

Types of Seating Arrangements

As the diagrams that follow illustrate, audience seating can be arranged in a number of different ways.

Conventional Theater Style (Figure 10-1). With a theater-style arrangement, people in the audience are seated in rows and columns without tables. Theater-style seating is most common with ProActive presentations delivered to large audiences. Seating may also be arranged in this manner for a presentation to a smaller group that must meet in a room with limited space. As Figure 10-1 indicates, if a podium is required, it should be placed to the side and toward the back of the platform (rather than in the center). Doing so opens up the platform for movement by the presenter, reduces the barrier a podium creates between presenter and audience, and discourages a presenter from dependence on the podium.

Theater-style seating is the least comfortable for an audience, especially for presentations that last longer than an hour. Many people feel constrained when seated shoulder-to-shoulder in closely packed rows. If the audience is seated in movable chairs and if space permits, the presenter may want to invite people to move their chairs back, to the sides, or farther toward the front to gain more "elbow room" (provided a center aisle is kept open for exiting the room). To compensate for the possible discomfort of theater-style seating, a dynamic style of delivery is essential.

Conventional Classroom Style (Figure 10-2). A conventional classroom style is so called because it first appeared in instructional settings where the primary intent is learning. People in the audience are seated at tables which are arranged in columns and rows. The classroom style is used for presentations in both ProActive and InterActive modes. Figure 10-2 shows the head table placed lengthwise (the advantages of which were pointed out earlier).

T-formation (Figure 10-3). Similar to seating at a conference table, the T-formation is suitable for presentations to smaller groups. People seated at the table(s) can alternately direct their attention toward the presenter or, for purposes of discussion, they can turn to others seated nearby.

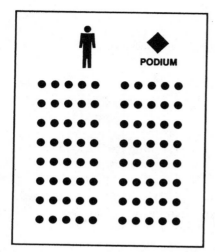

Figure 10-1. Conventional theater-style seating.

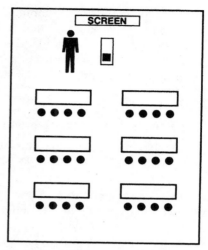

Figure 10-2. Conventional classroom-style seating.

A table(s) is added across the back, perpendicular to the lengthwise table(s), when a "special situation" applies. In an instructional situation, for example, some persons may attend for the express purpose of auditing the presentation. In other instances, such as policy or product announcement meetings, managers already familiar with the message may want to step in for part of the presentation but not remain for all of it. Being seated at the back allows "visitors" to come and go without disrupting members of the group.

Modified T-Formation (Figure 10-4). This seating arrangement is an adaptation of the conventional classroom style. It is useful for InterActive presentations to smaller groups, especially those that involve breaking out into pairs or groups of four for activities. The pair of participants seated at each side of the first table at the front can turn their chairs to join the pair immediately behind them, and so form a group of four. Likewise, the pairs at the third table back can join up with those seated at the last table. Tables placed lengthwise down the center of the arrangement can be used for the placement of materials or audiovisual equipment.

If the dimensions of the meeting room permit, seating capacity is doubled by setting up two modified T-formations (preferably side by side and angled to provide better viewing of the presenter and visual aids). One advantage to the modified T-formation is that it creates a somewhat unexpected setting. Variety (even in seating arrangements) sparks interest.

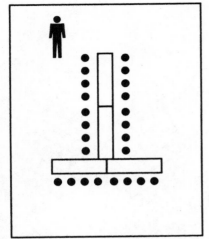

Figure 10-3. T-formation seating.

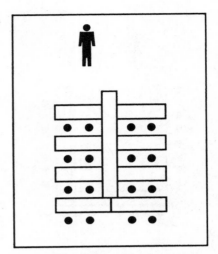

Figure 10-4. Modified T-formation seating.

U-Formation (Figure 10-5). The U-formation is suitable for both promotional and informational presentations in either the ProActive or InterActive modes. It is one arrangement that allows every person in the audience to view not only the presenter, but every other person in the audience as well. Accordingly, the U-formation tends to generate livelier group dynamics. The open area of the "U" at the front of the room gives a presenter access to everyone in the group on a more "up close and personal" basis. Thus, it fosters a more relational presentation style, which commonly results in greater responsiveness from the audience. One potential drawback to the U-formation (as with the "T" and "modified T") is that seating capacity is limited.

V-Formation (Figure 10-6). This arrangement is a modification of conventional classroom seating. To seat the same number of people in a V-formation as would be seated classroom style requires a wider room. However, staggering the tables and setting them at an angle improves audience viewing of the presenter, of visual aids, and of other persons in the group. In addition, the V-formation (like the modified T) is visually more interesting than conventional arrangements.

Reflection Question

For the presentations you give (or plan to give), which seating arrangement(s) would be ideal?

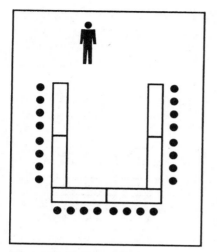

Figure 10-5. U-formation seating.

Figure 10-6. V-formation seating.

Key Concept 63

A presentation is influenced by environmental factors: lighting, temperature, air quality, and sounds.

Environment is literally defined as the conditions that affect the growth or development of living things. In a presentation setting, environmental conditions affect the mood that develops among an audience. In a pleasing environment, people are inclined to be more receptive, listen more attentively, think more clearly, and respond in a more positive manner. Environmental factors also affect a presenter's performance.

When the presenter has the option to choose the setting for a presentation, environmental factors should be carefully considered. The preferred facility features controls that are placed inside the meeting room and are easily accessible to the presenter, so that adjustments can be made if necessary. Other considerations are described next.

Lighting

Lighting affects the mood in a meeting room. Dim lighting or a dark room produce a dreary, somber mood. Lighting that approximates natural daylight (on a sunny day) creates a livelier, happy mood. For that reason, a presentation should not be held in a room without windows. Letting in natural light can improve the audience mood (provided the view outside is not distracting). Incandescent lighting is more pleasing than fluorescent lighting. Bright lighting that glares becomes annoying and should be dimmed.

Temperature

When choosing a facility, it is important to check if meeting rooms are individually climate-controlled. In partitioned meeting spaces, often temperature is controlled from a single thermostat and the presenter may not be able to adjust it.

The temperature should be cool (68 to 70 degrees), but not cold or chilly. An audience will remain more alert in a cooler room. People become uncomfortable in a room that is too cold or too hot. For presentations to larger groups, prior to the presentation the thermostat should be set lower than normal. As people gather, natural body heat raises the temperature and a meeting room can become stuffy. If the presenter starts to feel warm from moving around, before adjusting the climate control, people seated in the audience should be asked if the temperature is comfortable for *them*.

Air Quality

To prevent a room from becoming stuffy, the meeting room should be well-ventilated. When considering prospective sites for a presentation, a presenter should be alert to unpleasant odors. Older facilities, for instance, may smell musty. Meeting rooms in hotels that host convention business sometimes smell of alcohol or cigar smoke, odors that are potentially offensive. Presenters themselves should refrain from wearing heavily scented colognes or perfumes.

Sound

In a presentation setting, the only sound that should be prominent is that of the speaker's voice (or members of the audience when they voice feedback). Unfortunately, extraneous sounds can fill a meeting room and disrupt a presentation. Within the room itself, noise "pollution" may come from a fan on projector equipment that whirrs continuously or from fans in a heating or cooling system. Electronic feedback from a sound system is distracting, as are music or announcements that may be piped into the room over a public address system. At events where meals are served, a speaker should avoid presenting before or during the meal service. Serving personnel, the clinking of glassware, and the clatter of dishes are disruptive.

A presentation may be disrupted by noise that originates from outside a meeting room: airplanes flying overhead, the operation of jackhammers and lawnmowers, noise from a kitchen adjacent to the meeting room, people moving about or conversing in outer hallways, children shrieking at a nearby swimming pool. The likelihood of noise interference can be eliminated or at least minimized by applying these suggestions:

- Before the date of a presentation, check out the facilities. If the site is situated in a noisy or potentially noisy area, consider relocating. Check out audiovisual equipment and replace it if it is noisy. Test the sound system.

- When possible, conduct a presentation in a room situated above ground level.

- Remove any telephones from the meeting room or make arrangements to have all calls held. Arrange for someone to take messages and relay them in the event of an emergency.

- Present in a setting that has good acoustics.

Key Concept 64

The atmosphere of the setting in which a presentation occurs is enhanced by certain colors, accessories, and amenities.

Restaurants often are described in terms of **ambiance**, a term that refers to the surroundings or atmosphere of a place. The place in which a presentation is held has ambiance—good or bad. A speaker's aim is to create an ambiance that generates good feelings and so contributes to the audience experience. Ambiance is created by the colors, accessories, and amenities that surround the area in which a presentation is given.

Colors

The discussion of visual aids in Chapter 6 pointed out that colors create emotional impact and convey meaning. Colors affect the atmosphere of the setting in which a presentation occurs. Ideally, the prominent colors in a meeting room will be pale: off-white, ivory, or a pale hue of dusty rose or aquamarine. These lighter colors brighten the atmosphere and at the same time produce a calming effect.

Brown, black, and battleship or tombstone gray should be avoided. They are dreary, dull the senses, and create an atmosphere that depresses. Dark colors (deep burgundy, red, green, or blue) and rooms with dark wood paneling should be avoided. Dark colors can be oppressive. A presentation should not be conducted in a room with bold or busy patterns on wallpaper or carpeting. Like extraneous noise, such patterns compete for attention and can be distracting.

Accessories

A secondary definition of **ambiance** is the arrangement of accessories to support or intensify the main effect of a piece of art. In a manner of speaking, an effective presentation is a "piece of art" in that it is crafted to convey a message. Accessories, like props and fixtures, are added to the setting of a presentation to enliven the atmosphere and to reinforce the effect of the message. Accessories also serve to heighten the interest of an audience because in most cases they are unexpected.

One speaker covers the front of the podium with a colorful photographic poster related to the subject of his presentation. Another places around the meeting room foil balloons imprinted with the word "Celebrate!" and relates her message to a cause to celebrate. Another situation in which a presenter used accessories effectively is described here:

> Edna, a supervisor for a public sector agency, was asked to present the agency's new performance planning system at the next staff meeting. Staff meetings were regularly held in a conference room with yellowed linoleum flooring, wood-panelled walls, and a gray table and chairs that looked as though they had been purchased from a navy surplus store. Before her presentation, Edna "dressed up" the room. She draped the table with a sky-blue cloth and set two potted live green plants in the middle of the table. On a corner of the lectern, she placed a bud vase with three yellow roses in it. When she began her presentation, Edna announced that she would be asking three questions during the session. With each question, the first person to shout out the correct answer would receive a yellow rose.

With the addition of colorful or symbolic accessories, even a drab meeting room can be brightened to create more pleasing surroundings.

Amenities

It is common to serve amenities like beverages and refreshments. Since many people are more health-conscious today than in previous years, beverage service should include both regular and decaffeinated coffees, herbal teas, and a selection of juices. Where people are seated at tables, it adds a nice touch to place on the tables plastic cups filled with wrapped candies or mints. One businessperson, who makes high-stakes presentations, brings an arrangement of fresh-cut flowers and leaves it in the client's office after the meeting.

Reflection Questions

What effect do you think it has on people to meet in the same room repeatedly? If there is a room where you work where it is customary to gather for meetings and presentations, what changes would you make to improve the surroundings for business presentations?

Summary

The setting of a presentation is significant in terms of the effect it has on an audience and on the presenter. To select and set up a setting and surroundings conducive to success, a presenter must consider room requirements and seating arrangements, environmental factors, and the atmosphere of the meeting room. Factors related to the setting of a presentation are summarized on the planning checklist (Part III: The Setting) that appears at the end of Chapter 2.

Sample Situations

Situation 1: Avoid Surprises

Bob was invited to give a presentation at an annual business conference to be held at a downtown convention center. Every year, the conference was attended by about 3000 people. Speakers were provided space free of charge to display promotional materials. Knowing that such events offered visibility that helped him advance in his career, Bob eagerly accepted the invitation to speak. Since he had been to the convention center on previous occasions, Bob knew the meeting rooms were well designed for business presentations. He saw no reason to check them out ahead of time.

Two weeks before the event, the meeting planner called to ask Bob if he would present a second session during the conference. Bob agreed. The meeting planner explained that since registrations had exceeded expectations, Bob's first presentation at 9:00 A.M. had been rescheduled to be held in an annex adjacent to the convention center. Pleased to be on the conference agenda twice, Bob didn't hesitate to agree to the change.

At 8:15 on the morning of the conference, Bob signed in at the speaker's desk and picked up a map to the annex. Ten minutes later, he arrived at the site for his presentation. He was appalled! He was situated in a damp and drafty, gray cement passageway that led from the convention center to the adjacent sports arena. Fifty hard-backed, aluminum folding chairs were set up facing an old rickety table that marked the area for his presentation. When Bob spoke, his voice reverberated off the walls. When people moved in their chairs, the legs scraped on the hard floor. Bob learned a lasting lesson that day: never do a presentation without first checking the facilities.

Situation 2: Choose a Fresh Location

Becky, a successful salesperson for a high-tech medical products company, regularly presented proposals to her customers. After months of effort to develop a major account, Becky had the opportunity to make a high-stakes presentation to five members of the board of directors. The week before the presentation, Becky met with the administrator to confirm arrangements for the meeting.

The presentation was scheduled to be held in the board room: a narrow and windowless room located in the center of an upper floor. It was furnished with an enormous dark wood table with seating for 30 people. High-backed overstuffed chairs upholstered in dark green fabric were arranged around the table. Aging portraits of previous board members lined the dark wood walls. The setting was somber. It emitted a sense of "ghosts" of old business conducted there over the years.

Becky quickly realized the room was not well-suited to her presentation. She recommended to the administrator that the meeting be held off-site. The administrator agreed. Becky made arrangements at a nearby conference facility where she reserved a light, airy, modern room that was more appropriate to her high-tech presentation. For the board members, it was a fresh location consistent with the fresh approach Becky's presentation proposed.

Situation 3: Create Interest

Ian and Casey were delegated the task of leading a forthcoming sales meeting at which a new desktop computer would be announced. The budget did not allow for moving the meeting off-site, so they considered how to change the atmosphere of the conference room in which meetings were regularly held. They wanted to create surroundings that would generate excitement and reflect the theme of the product-announcement presentation.

They arranged seating in a modified T-formation to make it easy for the salespeople to pair up during product training exercises. They hung computer diskettes from the ceiling and crepe paper streamers around the walls to create a festive atmosphere. At each table, they placed rolls of Life Saver candies, which they referred to when making a point in their presentation: "This product will be a lifesaver for our business!"

Comprehension Check

The answers to the following appear on page 334.

1. A primary factor to consider when deciding on the setting for a presentation is the _____.
   a. setup diagram
   b. presenter's personal preferences
   c. availability of the meeting room
   d. comfort of the audience
   e. client's office location

2. An advantage to conducting a presentation off-site is _____.
   a. convenience for people attending the meeting
   b. people are inclined to be more focused in fresh surroundings
   c. it is more economical
   d. the client has less control
   e. the decor is more conducive to a favorable experience

3. Conventional theater-style seating _____.
   a. is recommended for sales presentations to small groups
   b. heightens audience interest
   c. requires a dynamic style of delivery
   d. is suitable for planning sessions
   e. is conducive to interaction among persons in a group

4. The environmental factor most likely to disrupt a presentation is _____.
   a. lighting
   b. noise
   c. room temperature
   d. air quality
   e. coffee service

5. A presenter might add accessories to the setting of a presentation to _____.
   a. heighten the interest of the audience
   b. call attention away from dark carpeting
   c. mask offensive odors
   d. make people more comfortable
   e. improve learning

To Do

For the presentation you have prepared for this course, sketch a setup diagram that illustrates the ideal setting. Indicate room requirements and seating arrangements. Describe the surroundings. Make note of any accessories or amenities you would add to create a pleasing ambiance.

11

Written Presentations

In a typical workplace, stacked high in in-baskets and on desks are volumes of memos, letters, documents, reports, proposals, brochures, newsletters, publications, and the like. Businesspeople handle hundreds of pieces of paper every week. (Notice the word is *handle,* not *read.*) Much of what comes across the desk of a busy person is not read or attracts little more than a cursory glance. Busy people have more to read than time in which to read it all. A host of documents and proposals compete for attention. Who are these busy people? They are the people who make or who influence decisions on the proposals you write.

In situations that require a screening process, frequently a written presentation is preliminary to an oral one. Written proposals are the basis for selecting the candidates, suppliers, contractors, or service providers who are then asked to make an oral presentation. In other cases, a written proposal follows an oral presentation. It furnishes additional information relating to the spoken message and may determine whether the matter is acted upon as the presenter recommended. In both cases, a written presentation is a contributing factor to the decision an audience makes in response to the writer/presenter. For that reason, even the most effective presenters need to be (or need to use the services of) effective writers.

Objectives

To recognize the concepts and communication skills that apply in common to both oral and written presentations; to describe formats and elements of structure and content that make a document more readable; and to write an effective proposal.

Key Concepts

65. There are three types of written materials related to the subject of business presentations: confirmation letters, handouts, and proposals.

66. Many of the principles and techniques that apply to oral presentations apply equally to written presentations.

67. Format affects the readability of a written proposal.

68. Structure affects the readability of written presentations.

69. A three-stage approach facilitates the writing process. The aim is to compose content that reflects an appropriate style, an effective use of language, and correct use of grammar, punctuation, and spelling.

Key Terms

You will need to understand the terms listed below to fully understand the key concepts:

Written presentation(s)	Structure
Handouts	Mechanics
Proposal	Passive voice, active voice
Readability	Reader-oriented language
Format	

Key Concept 65

There are three types of written materials related to the subject of business presentations: confirmation letters, handouts, and proposals.

The term **written presentation**(s) is used to refer to any one or a combination of the three types of documents commonly associated with oral presentations. These are described here.

Confirmation Letters

Three to five days before the date of a presentation, the person(s) for whom the presentation is being done should receive a confirmation letter.

The letter should be not more than one page in length and not more than two paragraphs. The first paragraph confirms the date, time, and location of the presentation. The second paragraph (if applicable) refers to any enclosures, which may include the following items.

- A synopsis of the message that advises the reader "you will hear about . . ." Synopsis means brief. The synopsis does not divulge the contents of the oral presentation, but highlights the benefits of attending it.
- A biographical sketch(es) of the person(s) who will be presenting.
- For off-site presentations, a map that provides clear directions to the meeting facility.

The letter not only confirms the arrangements for a presentation. It also confirms that the presenter is well prepared and follows through. In those respects, a confirmation letter conveys professionalism.

Handouts

Distributed at the time of the presentation, **handouts** are printed materials provided to the audience for reference. (Other items such as promotional material or product samples may be handed out at a presentation, but are not included in this discussion of written presentations.) A handout may consist of a one-page agenda, an outline of the message, or a workbook. When preparing handouts, it is important to consider two factors in particular: appearance and usability.

Appearance.   The point has been made in previous chapters that an audience forms perceptions on the basis of what they see as well as from what they hear. In a business presentation, the visual appearance of handouts conveys an impression of the presenter and the organization represented. Thus, handouts (like all written materials) should reflect quality. They should be preprinted. Poor quality photocopies made from faded or blotched originals create a poor impression. The information in handouts should be current and accurate. The order of material in a handout should parallel the oral presentation. It is frustrating for an audience to have to skip back and forth between the pages of a handout that does not correspond to what the speaker is saying.

Usability.   A usable handout is written in outline form. It is not a transcript of the text of the message. It provides ample space for the audience to write notes. A presenter wants to encourage note taking because people who take notes mentally interact with the information presented, tend to better remember what they write (as opposed to what they hear only), and leave with something they can review.

Written Proposals

In the context of this chapter, the term **proposal** refers to a document that supports or augments an oral presentation. The term includes (but is not limited to) sales proposals, specifications, resumes, reports, and responses to an RFP (Request for Proposal). In addition to other factors discussed throughout this chapter, two in particular are essential to proposals: brevity and benefit.

Brevity.   As a listener must be "hooked" by the opener to an oral presentation, a reader must be enticed to spend the time to peruse a written proposal. An executive summary, written as a preface to a proposal, prompts the reader to "stay tuned" and read on. It is limited to one page so that the reader can view it at a glance. An executive summary begins with a statement of interest or value to the reader. It then *briefly* highlights the key points of the proposal.

Benefit.   The prospect of benefit entices people. An effective proposal states, up front, something the reader stands to gain. To build acceptance of how the information applies to and will benefit the reader, it incorporates value statements throughout. Costs or fees are presented at the end, after the reader has been acquainted with the advantages of adopting the proposal.

Packaging Handouts and Proposals

A handout is written to be used. A proposal is written to be read. Both should therefore be put together in a manner that makes it easy for a person to handle and review the material. Handouts and proposals longer than three pages should include the following items.

- A cover sheet or cover letter which identifies the originator and contact information: logo, name, address, telephone number, and fax number. To establish an association between the party presenting the material and the party for whom it is intended, the recipient's name and logo should also be prominently featured.

- A table of contents with page numbers, to make it easier for the reader to locate selected information.

■ The date, page number, and originator's name should appear on every page of the document. Page numbers are easier to find when placed in the upper or lower outside corner.

For the convenience of the reader, a multipage handout or proposal should be put together in the form of a booklet that can be fully opened and laid flat: spiral bound, placed in a 3-ring binder, or stapled along the centerfold. The use of pocketed portfolios and certain types of report covers should be avoided. With pocketed portfolios, pages cannot be viewed at a glance unless removed from the pocket, when they are then too easily mixed up or misplaced. With a report cover that holds pages together with a clip or sliding plastic "backbone," sheets curl and cannot be laid flat, making reading and note taking cumbersome. A standard size that can be easily filed for reference is preferable to oversized or odd-sized booklets.

A proposal should also be packaged with eye appeal. An appealing appearance invites a reader to pick up a written presentation, and distinguishes it from the many other documents that appear on the average desk. Eye appeal is enhanced by the use of color: bold colors, striking contrasts, or the recipient's company colors.

Key Concept 66

Many of the principles and techniques that apply to oral presentations apply equally to written materials.

A written message differs from a spoken one in several respects. In a document, the writer (presenter) cannot express or reinforce meaning through vocal or visual cues. The writer does not receive the benefit of immediate audience feedback that may signal a need to clarify, elaborate, or amend a point. In oral presentations, a speaker can observe if the listener's attention is waning and can respond with techniques to reawaken interest. A writer does not have that advantage. In fact, the author of a proposal has no assurance that the reader even "attends" (reads) the written presentation.

On the other hand, there are benefits to presenting a message in written form. It can be expressed with greater exactitude. Without the digressions that occur during spoken presentations, a writer can get "right to the point." While many a presenter has regretted a "slip of the tongue" that could not be recalled, a writer has a second (third or fourth) chance to correct and

clarify the message before presenting a written proposal. A document establishes a record that reinforces the spoken message, and provides a tangible
item that can be reviewed at the reader's convenience. In addition to a
dynamic oral presentation, well-prepared and well-packaged written materials serve as a means to distinguish oneself from competing proposals.

Although there are obvious differences between spoken and written
presentations, both are forms of communication. As such, many of the
concepts and techniques discussed to this point in the course apply as
much to writing as to speaking. Figure 1-1, for example, depicts the communication process from the standpoint of an oral presentation. With a
few changes in terminology, Figure 1-1 also illustrates the process of written communications.

Change "Presenter" to "Writer," "Audience" to "Reader," omit "Vocal
Cues," reduce the impact of "Visual Cues" (some still apply to a limited
degree), and extend the time it takes to receive Feedback. The prominent
factors remain the same: a person expresses a message, a person receives the
message, and perceptions are formed that influence how the audience (listener or reader) responds. In view of the factors the two forms of communication share in common, throughout this chapter you will find references to
previous chapters and key concepts as they pertain to written materials.

Attributes of Effective Written Presentations

To be effective, a written presentation must exhibit the same attributes as
an effective oral presentation. It must be attention-getting, meaningful,
memorable, activating, and balanced. It must satisfy the purpose of making
a presentation, which is to persuade. An effective confirmation letter persuades the reader to show up for the presentation as scheduled. An effective handout persuades people to follow along and take notes as the
speaker presents. An effective proposal persuades people to buy or adopt
the recommendations or information it contains.

An additional quality is required to make a written presentation effective.
It must be readable. **Readability** refers to the ability to read material easily
and quickly. Readability sustains interest. It creates a sense that the writer is
speaking to the reader.

Key Concept 67

Format affects the readability of a written proposal.

The term **format** refers to the arrangement of material on a page. It consists of the type face used, line length, line spacing, margins, indents, and the general layout of text, graphics, and white space in relation to one another. Format gives a document its appearance. Computerized word processing and desktop publishing provide a range of formatting choices, making it possible to produce documents with great eye appeal. However, care should be taken to refrain from overdoing the artistic aspect of formatting. For a written business presentation, readability is the chief consideration.

Formatting Considerations

Format affects readability, as indicated by the following factors.

Line Length. The average line length of a standard typewritten document with one-inch left and right margins is 65 or 78 characters, depending on the type size used. The line length that is easiest to read is 40 characters across—little more than half the length that typically appears on a standard typewritten page. A shorter line is more readable because the eyes do not have to shift so much back and forth across the page.

Type. The standard typewriter type size is 10- or 12-pitch (pitch being the number of characters per inch). It is 12 points high (one-sixth of an inch). A 12-point height remains the standard for the text of a written presentation. In place of 10- or 12-pitch type, a proportional typeface is preferred. It is easier to read because the characters have greater definition than standard type.

Typographical Techniques. Underscoring, bold type, type face changes, and capitalization are ways to distinguish points in a document. Typographical changes should be made sparingly and only where appropriate. While variations add interest, too many will deflect the reader's attention from the message and give a document a cluttered appearance.

Dingbats. In printing terminology, a dingbat is a distinguishing character used to accentuate a point or to set apart items in a list. Commonly used dingbats include bullet points, boxes, asterisks, and arrows.

Headings. A document that is organized by sections is more readable than one that is continuous, nonstop text. Bold-type headings and subheadings identify sections and serve to guide the reader through a written presentation.

Graphics. Chapter 6 emphasized the value of pictorial, colorful, and creative visual aids. The types of graphics that enhance an oral presentation also enhance a written one.

Color. Color adds eye appeal and meaning when it appears on a proposal cover, on letterhead, and on visual aids (see Chapter 6, Key Concept 39). In addition, it is striking to highlight with a yellow marking pen a few key words in the text of a document. The unexpected highlighting calls attention to a point and heightens reader interest. It should, however, be used sparingly and reserved for key words only.

White Space. Leaving open spaces at strategic points in a document is an effective formatting technique. White space provides a rest for the reader's eyes. It relieves the intensity of the reading effort. White space adds a cleaner, less crowded look to a page. Space is also used to frame graphics or to set important points apart from the rest of the text.

These foregoing considerations should be taken into account when deciding on the format of a written presentation. The format alone can determine whether or not a person picks up a proposal and reads it from start to finish. In general, written presentations are prepared according to the following formats.

Common Formats

Full Text. A full-text format is most common with letters and proposals. Pages appear filled with lines of typewritten text that extend the full six and a half or seven inches between the left and right margins and within an inch or so from the top and bottom of the page. A full-text format is tiresome to read and ordinary in appearance. It is *not* recommended for a proposal that is written with the intent of getting action.

Columnar. Newspapers and newsletters are typical examples of printed matter that use a columnar format. Columns are easy to read because of their shorter line length.

Headline. A headline format features bold-type headings and subheadings in varying type sizes to distinguish between sections of a written presentation. Frequently, this format uses various levels of indentation to further clarify changes from one section to another.

Sideline. A sideline format incorporates features of both the columnar and headline formats. Headings and subheadings (distinguished by type size and/or style) are placed in a "column" of white space at the left of the page. Text appears to the right of its corresponding heading. Allow one-inch left and right margins, two inches for the heading column, and a half-inch of space between the heading and the text; the sideline format reduces the text line length to a very readable four-inch width. Set apart in white space, headings and subheadings are clearly visible, making it easy for a reader to locate specific points at a glance.

Combination. Figure 11-1 illustrates a page layout that combines several formatting elements. It shows the use of a bold-face heading at the top of the column of text at the right. At the left, white space is used to frame the graphic, its caption, and a list of items that are accented with bullet points. A combination format is more readable than a full-text format. Appropriate colors added to the graphic would spark the reader's interest and add meaning to the message.

Reflection Question

Based on the information presented in the preceding concept, what formatting techniques would improve the readability of the written presentations you prepare?

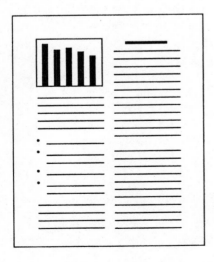

Figure 11-1. A combination format.

Key Concept 68

Structure affects the readability of written presentations.

In Chapter 3, on the subject of structuring an oral presentation, **structure** was defined as the manner in which parts are put together. With respect to the readability of a written presentation, the term refers to the arrangement of textual components and the organization of the material of which a document is composed. Characteristics that contribute to readability are described next.

Sentence Structure

Sentence structure is the arrangement of the various parts of speech (such as nouns and verbs, adjectives and adverbs that modify them, prepositions, and the like). Chapter 5 (Style: Forms of Verbal Expression) pointed out that sentence structure affects the meaning, pace, and rhythm of spoken words. Sentence structure is an even more critical factor with written words because no speaker is adding inflection. The sentence structure must "speak" for itself. The two sentences shown here use the same words and convey the same meaning. The only difference between them is that the parts of speech are rearranged.

> Structure sentences in a manner that creates a rhythm to make a document more readable.

> To make a document more readable, structure sentences in a manner that creates a rhythm.

Shorter sentences are more readable than long compound-complex ones. Shorter words are more readable and more easily understood than multisyllabic terminology. Short words and crisp sentences can be used to add emphasis, or to convey a more declarative or imperative tone. The following example shows the effect of restructuring the two sentences from the preceding example.

> Structure sentences to create a rhythm. It makes a document more readable.

More important than rhythm or tone, sentence structure affects meaning. The two sentences below illustrate this point.

We can proceed immediately with your approval of this proposal.

With your approval of this proposal, we can proceed immediately.

The second sentence is what the writer meant to say. Although the same parts of speech appear in the first sentence as in the second, because they are arranged differently the meaning is different. The implication in the first sentence is somewhat presumptuous: we (the writers) can proceed immediately with *your* (the reader's) approval.

Variations in sentence structure can improve the readability of a written presentation. Mixing up short simple sentences with longer compound ones alters the pace, tone, and rhythm of a document. The same purpose is served by varying the way sentences begin. Several methods for beginning sentences are listed below. The effect of each is shown with variations of the simple sentence, "You save money."

- Dependent clause: "Since you save money . . ."
- Expletive: "It is money you save . . ."
- Interjection: "Yes! You save money."
- Infinitive phrase: "To save money, you . . ."
- Expressive modifier (adverb): "Naturally, you save money."
- Preposition: "With the money you save . . ."
- Rhetorical question: "Will you save money?"
- Verb: "Consider the money you save."

A skilled writer uses parts of speech like a skilled craftsman uses tools— with awareness and purpose. The purpose is to convey the intended meaning accurately, and to sustain the reader's interest and attention.

Paragraphs

As indicators of divisions within the text, paragraphing signals a change in thought. Accordingly, a paragraph should be limited to a single topic or idea. In a single-spaced typewritten document, a paragraph should not exceed half of one page: on average, three to six sentences. While short paragraphs speed reading, variations in paragraph length add eye appeal and sustain interest by altering the tempo with which a document is read.

A key point can be emphasized by isolating it in a one-sentence paragraph (like this one).

Structure and Substance of the Whole

The development of a written presentation corresponds to that of an oral presentation. (With the exception of extemporaneous speaking, an oral presentation *is* a written one before it is spoken.) Chapters 3 and 4 discuss in detail the components of a presentation, how to structure them in a well-organized manner, material to use to substantiate the presenter's (or writer's) case, and sources of data. The information contained in those chapters also applies to written presentations.

The following points in particular merit repeating. It is useful to review them when preparing a written presentation.

■ Key Concept 13 (Chapter 2): Know the nature and needs of the audience. The more a written presentation is tailored to the interests and concerns of the reader, the more effective it will be.

■ Key Concept 21 (Chapter 3): Approach. A written presentation is more effective when it is approached from the perspective of the reader.

■ Key Concept 26 (Chapter 3): Model Outline. The model outline worksheet at the end of Chapter 3 is useful for structuring a written presentation. An effective written proposal will include the same components: an opener, preview, key points in the body, a review, and close.

The Principle of "First and Last"

Prominence is given material by placing it first or last. The first words and last words of a sentence, more so than material in the middle, capture the reader's attention. (Notice, for example, the first sentence of this paragraph. The first word "prominence" and the last words "first or last" are key, and their placement suggests an association between them.) In a paragraph, the first sentence should introduce the idea of the paragraph and the last sentence conclude it. In keeping with the principle of first and last, the first paragraph and the last paragraph of an effective written presentation would feature the highlights of the message.

Frequently, a writer will begin a proposal with an inconsequential introduction and close with equally meaningless content. For example (the proposal opens), "We appreciate the opportunity to submit this proposal . . ." and (the proposal concludes) "We look forward to your response." Such hackneyed phrases have little impact on the reader and may suggest that the proposal lacks substance.

The busy reader wants to get to the point—now! A common practice among business and professional people is to scan written presentations to determine if there *is* a point of interest to them. When scanning, a person previews a document as follows:

- Glances at the first paragraph (the opener).

- Flips through the pages of the proposal, pausing at obvious key words (a reason to use bold-type headlines and highlighting).

- Glances at the last paragraph (the close).

Provided the opener and close create interest, the person will examine the contents of the document more closely. There (in the middle) they should find the key points, explanations, evidence, and detail that substantiate the statements presented first and last.

Since people scan, it is more effective to begin and end written presentations using one of the approaches listed below.

- Identify the problem . . . Recommend the solution.

- Refer to a current condition . . . Anticipate a future improvement.

- Cite findings . . . State how the findings apply.

- Point out the cost . . . Reiterate the savings.

Key Concept 69

A three-stage approach facilitates the writing process. The aim is to compose content with an appropriate style, an effective use of language, and correct use of grammar, punctuation, and spelling.

The task of preparing a written presentation is made more difficult when the writer attempts to compose a finished product on the first try. From early childhood, teachers emphasized the **mechanics** of writing: grammar, punctuation, spelling, and penmanship. Rules were learned, but not the process of giving written expression to one's thoughts. As a result, many businesspeople find their writing efforts constrained by habits formed during years in schoolrooms.

The Writing Process

Writing is easier and often more expressive when it is done in three stages: rough draft, write, and refine. These three stages parallel the process of preparing an oral presentation, as depicted in Figure 3-1.

Rough Draft. Comparable to the stage of structuring a presentation, the purpose of rough drafting is to capture initial ideas on paper—without concern for conforming to rules. In some cases, this stage will start with the formulation of ideas (see Key Concept 25, Chapter 3). The writer's ideas and information are then organized using the Model Outline that appears at the end of Chapter 3. From this framework, the message is drafted in *rough,* recognizing that it will be further developed and corrected as the writing process continues.

Write.   This stage corresponds to the second and third stages depicted in Figure 3-1: substance and style. The purpose is to "fill in the blanks" that remain on the rough draft. The text that explains or describes the substantiating material is written, with some attention given to the matter of style. While the mechanics of writing (grammar, syntax, and such) begin to take shape at this stage, the writer is not preoccupied with absolute correctness. Any needed revisions or corrections will be made during the next stage.

For handouts and proposals that include the support of visual aids, graphics would be prepared and inserted at this stage.

Refine.   The written presentation is reviewed and revised. The writing is refined to achieve the best expression of meaning and a "flow" of text that proceeds logically from one point to the next. Each time a document is revised it should be proofread to ensure that the grammar, punctuation, and spelling are correct.

Especially in cases of high-stakes proposals, it is beneficial to have someone other than the writer review the material. Generally, an "outside party" is more objective than the writer. If acquainted with the circumstances for which the proposal is being written, the reviewer can try to look at the proposal as the intended reader might.

Style, language, and the mechanics of writing warrant careful consideration. These aspects were addressed in Chapter 5 (Style: Forms of Verbal Expression). Additional points that pertain to written presentations in particular are discussed in the sections that follow.

Style

In Chapter 5, style is defined as the manner in which a message is conveyed. A certain type of style results primarily from word choices and the length and structure of sentences.

One aspect of style is the "voice" with which a document is written: active or passive. The term refers to how parts of speech are arranged in a sentence, which affects the resulting tone. In the **active voice**, the person or thing performing an action appears before the receiver of the action. With the **passive voice**, the receiver of the action appears first. As the comparison below indicates, active voice creates a tone that is more conversational than passive voice. Passive voice sometimes sounds awkward.

Active Voice: "A skilled presenter addresses the interests of the audience." (The action verb *addresses* is prominent.)

Passive Voice: "The interests of the audience are addressed by a skilled presenter." (The passive noun *interests* is prominent.)

A writing style is commonly referred to as formal, technical, or conversational. A formal writing style is characterized by longer compound or complex sentences, usually written in the passive voice. The writer chooses words that are predominantly academic or bureaucratic in nature. A formal style conveys a sense of propriety or caution. A technical style, similar to a formal style, makes greater use of specialized technical or professional terminology. A conversational style expresses a message in short sentences, active voice, and familiar words. It makes occasional use of contractions, like people do when they talk. Of the three styles, a conversational style is the most "friendly" and readable.

The style of a given written presentation is determined on the basis of the following factors.

- Who is the intended reader?
- What is the relationship between the writer and the reader?
- What is the nature of the document as to type, purpose, and message?

For example, a legal contract prepared by an attorney for a new client mandates a writing style that is (or should be) different from a letter written to a long-time client who is also a friend.

Language

As Chapter 5 pointed out, language is the chief component of style. Language refers to word choices, terminology, phrasing, and figures of speech. For the sake of optimum readability, it is essential that the language of a written presentation reflect the four fundamentals identified in Key Concept 34. The language must be clear, correct, concise, and well-considered.

An effective, readable written presentation refrains from ambiguities and does *not* use gobbledygook, jargon, overworked adjectives, cliches, euphemisms, hackneyed phrases, redundancy, or language that expresses bias. All abbreviations and acronyms are clearly defined for the benefit of the reader. These forms of expression are discussed in Chapter 5.

A type of language *to* use is reader-oriented. **Reader-oriented language** places the reader first in a sentence. Giving prominence to the recipient of a proposal conveys the writer's interest in the reader. It is "you" language as opposed to "I" language, as the following comparisons show.

> Writer-oriented: "I have enclosed . . ."
> Reader-oriented: "You will find . . ." or "Here's the . . . you asked for."
>
> Writer-oriented: "We can provide the benefits of . . ."
> Reader-oriented: "You will gain the benefits of . . ."
>
> Writer-oriented: "Our personnel are well-qualified to serve your needs."
> Reader-oriented: "Your needs will be served by our well-qualified personnel."

For people who give or who write business presentations, language is a potentially powerful tool. An expansive vocabulary and proficiency with all aspects of language equip a person with verbal versatility. The versatile speaker/writer alters the style of a message to suit the circumstances, and so communicates more effectively. Language is the raw material of which persuasion is made.

Grammar, Punctuation, and Spelling

A speaker is concerned with using correct grammar primarily because of what an audience perceives from poor grammar: that the presenter is poorly educated or careless with language. Writers must be concerned with grammar for the same reason. Incorrect grammar is even more noticeable in a written presentation than it is during a spoken one. In a written proposal, there are no vocal or visual cues to deflect the reader's attention or to mask grammatical errors. A mistake that may be missed by a listener is clearly evident to a reader: there it is in print on the page.

Incorrect grammar can change the meaning of a message. In the following example, the intended meaning is altered as a result of a common grammatical error—misplacing a modifying phrase. (The modifying phrase appears in italics.)

> Meaning to impress upon the reader the need for new classrooms, the writer states, "Classrooms will be built with funds from bond sales, *which are desperately needed.*"

The statement implies that bond sales are desperately needed. Written correctly, the modifying phrase would be placed adjacent to the noun it is intended to describe. The statement should read, "Classrooms, which are desperately needed . . ." or "Desperately needed classrooms . . ."

Although a speaker is not at all concerned with spelling or punctuation, the author of a written presentation must be. Spelling errors are obvious to many readers. Some errors in punctuation may not be as noticeable, depending on the gravity of the error and the reader's understanding of the rules of punctuation (which vary). Nonetheless, correct use is important because punctuation can affect meaning, as the following example shows.

"The materials warehoused in Kansas can be delivered within a week."

"The materials, warehoused in Kansas, can be delivered within a week." or "Warehoused in Kansas, the materials can be delivered within a week."

The first statement is subject to misinterpretation. The reader may wonder, "Are materials warehoused somewhere else? If so, can they be delivered sooner?" The second statement, punctuated correctly, conveys the meaning the writer intends.

In addition, punctuation helps to guide a reader through the text. It adds to a written presentation what vocal cues add to a spoken one: pauses, emphasis, and subtle shifts in pace and tone.

When in Doubt, Find Out

Correct grammar, punctuation, and spelling are governed by numerous rules and exceptions to the rules. Conventions change as the use of language changes over time. When a question arises regarding correct usage, the answer can be found in an up-to-date reference book. Anyone who prepares written presentations should have on hand a style guide, a grammar handbook, and a comprehensive dictionary.

Reflection Question

What do you stand to gain by taking the time to prepare effective written presentations?

Summary

Written presentations include the confirmation letter, handout, and proposal that accompany an oral presentation. Since both oral and written presentations are forms of communication, the concepts that govern an effective and persuasive spoken message apply equally to a written message.

In addition, in a written presentation, readability is essential. Readability is influenced by format, structure, style, language, and the mechanics of written work. It is easier to prepare a written presentation by doing the writing in three stages.

Sample Situation

The Effect of Effective Written Presentations

Short-listing is a common practice with many organizations that contract with providers of products or services (notably, architectural and engineering firms, urban planners, advertising agencies, consultants, equipment vendors, and suppliers). The organization issues a Request for Proposal (RFP). Of the companies that respond by submitting a written proposal, a few are selected and named on a "short list." The firms that are short-listed are invited to make an oral presentation, typically to a selection committee or board. It is a competitive screening process that demands more than the ability to provide the requested product or service. It requires excellent writing and speaking skills to make convincing written and oral presentations.

As a case in point: during their first three years in business, Alpha Associates built a reputation in the local community for providing professional services of the highest quality. To expand the geographical market they served, the firm began to respond to RFPs from organizations throughout a three-state region. When they measured the results of their efforts after six months, Alpha Associates discovered they had been short-listed just 20 percent of the time. In other words, they had lost 8 out of 10 opportunities for new business. They concluded that, in situations when they did not have the advantage of local contacts and word-of-mouth advertising, the written proposal was more of a deciding factor.

To improve the impact and effectiveness of their proposals, Alpha Associates engaged a writer and graphic artist to produce samples of text and page layouts. Intended to serve as "models" for future written proposals, the samples suggested three major changes from previous proposals.

- The full-text format was eliminated. A one-page executive summary in sideline format appeared as the cover sheet to proposals. A combination format was used for the body of the text.
- Color illustrations were inserted.
- Content was written in a more conversational style that made greater use of the active voice and reader-oriented language. Value statements were added to each key point and in the concluding paragraph.

After putting the new proposal format and style into effect, instances in which the firm was short-listed more than doubled.

Comprehension Check

The answers to the following appear on page 334.

1. A confirmation letter _____.
   a. is needed only for off-site presentations
   b. should be written in a formal style
   c. conveys the presenter's professionalism
   d. provides a complete description of the oral presentation
   e. is packaged in a report cover

2. Effective handouts for use in an oral presentation _____.
   a. provide a transcript of the message
   b. feature ample space for notes
   c. use standard type size
   d. appear in a columnar format
   e. are stapled along the centerfold

3. One of the attributes of an effective written presentation, readability _____.
   a. is not as important as packaging
   b. is synonymous with usability
   c. requires an executive summary
   d. refers to the ease with which a document can be read
   e. is a channel of communication

4. Of the following formats, the most readable and interesting format for a written proposal is _____.
   a. headline
   b. combination
   c. full text
   d. full text with bullet points
   e. columnar

5. Preparing a written presentation is made easier if the writer _____.
   a. adheres to the rules of grammar
   b. uses a headline format
   c. follows a process of writing in three stages
   d. applies the principle of "first and last"
   e. keeps it brief

To Do

Suppose that the oral presentation you have prepared for this course will be accompanied by a written proposal. As a preface to the proposal, write a one-page executive summary.

For a guide to the components and structure of a presentation (oral or written), refer to the model outline at the end of Chapter 3.

12

Preparing Yourself to Present

For everyone who presents, there is a first time: a first time speaking from a platform, a first time standing behind a podium, a first time addressing a group. After that first presentation (and sometimes subsequent presentations, as well), often the presenter feels, "I could have done better." This concluding chapter discusses what professional presenters do to do better. It offers numerous suggestions to help you prepare yourself to present, and to progressively improve your business presentation skills.

Objectives

To describe techniques for gaining ease and confidence when speaking before a group; to name resources for further developing professional skills; and to prepare a development plan for becoming an accomplished presenter.

Key Concepts

70. To become a skilled and self-assured presenter entails personal preparation, professional development, and practice.

71. For many people, personal preparation requires overcoming the anxiety of speaking before a group. Beyond that, it is a matter of developing the personal attributes of humor and confidence.

72. Professional development involves skill-building activities and associations.

73. To reach a comfort level presenting requires practice, guided by feedback and a development plan.

Key Terms

To make use of the key concepts, you will need to understand the following terms:

Apply	Inhibitor
Group anxiety	Mentor
Relaxation response	Comfort level
Charisma	

Key Concept 70

To become a skilled and self-assured presenter entails personal preparation, professional development, and practice.

Chapter 3 pointed out that a presentation ends with a close, which encourages the audience to take action in response to the message. As the message of this course draws to a close, you are encouraged to apply the information you have gained. To **apply** is to put into effect, to act on. A person does not become a presenter solely by reading about presentations. It is by personal preparation, professional development, and repeated practice *presenting* that a person becomes a confident and convincing presenter.

Personal Preparation

Dynamic presenters give something of themselves to an audience. They exhibit personal qualities that appeal to people: candor, conviction, enthusiasm, and humor, to name a few. A skilled speaker appears perfectly at ease whether talking to five people or five hundred. Such ease—with oneself and in front of others—does not come naturally for many people. It is the outcome of personal preparation.

Professional Development

At the outset of this course, presenting was introduced as a means to achieving one's goals. Achieving a goal is not an event. It is a process. It entails purposeful actions carried out over time, among them engaging in professional development activities. Through such activities, a person builds job-related skills, gains insight and experience, and forms associations with other success-oriented professionals.

Practice

Ultimately, the ability to present effectively is developed by practice. In every field of endeavor, practice produces proficiency. Without practice, a piano player does not become a great pianist. Without practice, a football player does not become a great quarterback. Without practice, a speaker does not become a great presenter. Practice is the application of what has been gained from personal preparation and professional development.

Key Concept 71

For many people, personal preparation requires overcoming the anxiety of speaking before a group. Beyond that, it is a matter of developing the personal attributes of humor and confidence.

According to some estimates, as many as nine out of ten people dread speaking in public. They experience "butterflies" in the stomach, a racing heartbeat, shortness of breath, a trembling voice, or sweaty palms. Some people avoid presenting altogether and thereby limit their career opportunities. Others will present when asked, but appear nervous or restrained when they do so. As a result, their effectiveness is limited.

For many people, a first step in preparing to present is to overcome **group anxiety**: the condition of feeling apprehensive about appearing before an audience. Group anxiety can be overcome by identifying its cause, and then alleviating the sense of apprehension.

Causes of Group Anxiety

Three common causes of group anxiety are described next.

Perfectionism.   Perfection is the condition of being flawless. It is excellence of the highest order. Realistically, perfection cannot be attained in a business presentation because presenting is affected by too many variables over which the presenter has no control.

One variable is the audience. To attempt the "perfect" presentation, one would have to presume that everyone in the audience will have the same standard of excellence—which will never be the case. What one person finds excellent, another will consider lacking. (A familiar adage points out that you cannot please all of the people all of the time.) An audience is a composite of different temperaments and varying perspectives on a subject. It is impossible for a presenter, any presenter, to appeal "perfectly" to everyone.

Group dynamics, settings, and times vary. The message a speaker delivers one day will not have the same effect when it is presented in a different locale at a different time of day to a different group. The most accomplished presenters have faced what stand-up comics refer to as a "tough crowd": an audience that seemingly cannot be satisfied—no matter what the speaker does. On other occasions, an audience will applaud a presentation—no matter what the speaker does. A further consideration is that information is constantly changing. Content that appears flawless today may not be so tomorrow, when new research findings or results of the latest survey are announced.

In presenting, perfectionism is counterproductive.

Recollection. Group anxiety can be triggered by a memory of a previous unpleasant experience. For some people, the recollection dates back to grammar school when classmates laughed during "Show and Tell" (for reasons which probably had nothing to do with the presenter). Others recall a more recent incident: the first business presentation they gave. They felt nervous that first time and the endeavor was not their most successful. As a result, presenting becomes associated with nervousness and fear of failure.

Like any undertaking, giving a presentation requires skills that must be learned and developed over time. The ability to walk and move one's arms does not make a person a skier, a tennis champ, a pro golfer, or a football star. The ability to talk does not make a person a presenter. On the first occasion (even the second or third) giving a presentation, a person may feel awkward and the outcome may fall short of a sterling success. However, past events need not govern the future. With training and practice, the person who is a novice today can be a masterful presenter tomorrow.

In presenting, recalling former foibles is counterproductive.

Criticism. Undue concern about the possibility of being criticized contributes to group anxiety. Anxiety is a result of fretting: "Maybe someone won't like what I say. Maybe someone won't like my hair. Maybe someone won't like my visual aids." Maybe someone will!

In presenting, preoccupation with possible criticism is counterproductive.

Overcoming Group Anxiety

The causes of group anxiety are rooted in self-consciousness. They are largely self-imposed or learned behaviors. As the discussion in Chapter 5 on platform behaviors pointed out, learned behaviors that are counterproductive can be replaced—by learning new behaviors. By applying the techniques described in this section, a person can alleviate apprehensions associated with presenting.

Focus on the Audience. In a presentation setting, a speaker establishes a primary focal point of attention. A speaker can choose to focus either on the nature of his or her experience, or on the quality of the experience the audience receives. Focusing attention on the audience relieves preoccupation with one's self. Furthermore, consideration of the audience prompts a presenter to prepare. Being very well prepared builds a presenter's confidence.

Produce a Relaxation Response. Frequently, group anxiety is the result of conditioning. The first time a person presents, uncertainty may trigger a nervous reaction: a trembling voice, for example. The next time the person presents, worrying that the voice will tremble causes it to tremble. Repeated incidents condition in the speaker the same reaction every time. Nervous reactions that are conditioned responses can be overcome by reconditioning through relaxation exercises.

The method described below conditions a **relaxation response**. The term refers to the response (relaxation) that is produced when a given stimulus is applied.

> Select a recording that helps you relax: soothing mood or inspirational music, or a relaxation-training tape. Select a fragrance that is pleasing to you. Scent a handkerchief with the fragrance. Sit or recline in a position in which you are comfortable. Listen to the recording. Close your eyes and breathe slowly and deeply. When you are relaxed, hold the handkerchief to your nose and inhale the fragrance.

Using this technique, you are associating the scent of the fragrance with the condition of being relaxed. If you tend to feel anxious before speaking to a group, carry the scented handkerchief with you and, before presenting, take a whiff of the fragrance. It acts as a sensory stimulus that recalls a relaxation response. You may need to repeat the exercise several times. Repetition conditions and reinforces the relaxation response.

Imagine a Positive Experience. Some speakers have active imaginations. They imagine the worst that could happen during a presentation— and create anxiety. Instead, envision the best that can happen. Doing so will help to alleviate anxiety. Use your imagination to create mentally the experience that you want to occur in actuality. Figuratively speaking, "see" and "feel" and "hear" yourself giving a wonderfully effective presentation. Positive imagining (synonymous with visualization) is most effective when it is paired with relaxation techniques.

Forge Past the Fear. The speaker who consistently applies the concepts and skills of presenting effectively will eventually experience success. The pleasure of succeeding, repeated from one presentation to another, will condition a new response to the prospect of presenting. The speaker will begin to look forward to it—without fear.

In the interim, if feelings of anxiety do arise, face up to them and forge past the fear. Think of "F-E-A-R" in terms of an acronym that signifies the following points.

- F: *Focus on the task at hand.*   Refrain from projecting into the future disappointments that have occurred in the past. Refrain from mentally fabricating worst-case scenarios. Focus on the audience. Focus on the positive experience shaped in your imagination.

- E: *Energy.*   The physical reactions to anxiety (a quickened heartbeat, for example) are evidence of heightened levels of adrenalin. Adrenalin increases bodily energy. Think of putting that extra energy to work for you, rather than allowing it to work against you. Apply the energy to action.

- A: *Act.*   Take some action that will enhance your presentation. If you feel apprehensive during the days before a presentation, set yourself to a task that will help you be better prepared. Do not allow apprehensions to build. Instead, direct your attention to productive or relaxing activities.

- R: *Reward yourself.*   After every presentation, identify some aspect that was done well. Recognize that it represents something you learned and applied with success. Treat yourself to something you enjoy as a way of celebrating the success—even one that is seemingly insignificant. Recognize and applaud your accomplishments, because "success breeds success."

Developing Humor

For all speakers—those who get nervous before presenting as well as those who do not—a good-natured sense of humor is an asset. (See Chapter 5, Key Concept 36 on Humor.) Long after people have forgotten what was said during a presentation, they will remember how the presenter made them feel. People prefer to feel good, and a sense of humor generates good feelings.

Humor is not the ability to tell a joke. It is the ability to see in situations (and in oneself) something amusing, comic, or lighthearted. Humor derives from a pleasant disposition, as opposed to an angry or sullen one. It is related to perspective. A sense of humor is lacking in the person who views every situation as potentially tragic or who enlarges issues out of proportion. The person with a sense of humor keeps things in proper perspective. (A presentation, for example, is not a matter of life or death.)

For some people, humor is not an inborn trait. It must be developed by awareness and association. The quality of humor is fostered by applying these suggestions:

- Read comic strips.
- Read humorous books.
- Watch selected situation-comedy programs on television: those that feature good-natured humor (not sarcasm or belittling humor).
- Associate with optimistic people who have a good sense of humor.
- Avoid the company of people who are often angry, somber, or pessimistic.
- Listen to presenters who express humor.
- Be willing to laugh at yourself, and invite others to laugh with you.

Building Confidence That Conveys Charisma

The most persuasive presenters exhibit charisma. **Charisma** is the quality of personal magnetism. It is the power to appeal to and attract others. The word is derived from the Greek *charis,* meaning *favor,* which implies that a person with charisma is favored with special abilities. Since everyone possesses abilities of some sort, everyone has the potential to present with charisma. So what distinguishes a powerful presenter from others? Confidence.

Confidence comes from being very well prepared. It develops as successes are repeated. Confidence results from learning to freely express one's personal attributes and demonstrate one's professional abilities without reserve. A person can build confidence by applying the following suggestions.

Identify and Affirm Your Strengths.   Write on a tablet a list of your strengths: personal and professional. For each, write a statement that is self-affirming. Self-affirming statements begin with one of these phrases:

> I am . . . (state a quality)
>
> I have . . . (name an attribute or accomplishment)
>
> I do . . . (describe a skill)
>
> I can . . . (state an ability)

Periodically, read aloud your list of affirmations as a reminder of the reasons you have to be confident. Periodically, add to the list. For example, when you have finished this course, you would add, "I have successfully completed *The McGraw-Hill 36-Hour Course: Business Presentations.*"

Clarify Motivators.   Motivators are incentives that move a person to want to achieve and excel. They can be thought of as "the fuel that keeps your motor running." In what way are motivators related to confidence? Motivated people tend to produce positive results, repeatedly.

People who experience a pattern of success are characteristically more confident than those who are uncertain about themselves.

Motivators differ from one individual to another. One person may be motivated by the prospect of financial reward, another by personal recognition. Write on a tablet a list of what motivates you: to learn, to try, to work, to achieve. Beside each, make note of a source(s) of the motivation. For example, finishing a task may give you a motivating sense of accomplishment. Spending time with an encouraging friend or inspiring colleague may be motivating. Make a point of doing more of what motivates you.

Identify Inhibitors. An **inhibitor** is a thought or emotion that is irrational, pessimistic, negative, self-deprecating, or self-defeating. Inhibitors hinder the process of confidence building. They interfere with personal and professional development aims. An inhibitor restrains a person from trying, seeking, or doing something different or more.

Common to people who experience group anxiety is an inhibitor that sounds something like this: "I made a fool of myself when I gave that speech in high school. I am not going to do that again!" The person who harbors such thoughts may refrain from ever making a presentation or even attempting to learn how to present. Not only does the inhibitor limit the person's development. It may interfere with opportunities and career advancement.

The inhibiting thought just noted is irrational because it equates what happened in high school with what will happen now. (Ten, fifteen, or twenty years may have gone by, during which time the person has grown up and gained experience.) It is irrational to assume that something that happened once (years before) will be repeated in kind. The self-deprecating aspect of the thought is the assumption "I made a fool of myself." In fact, the person may have given a good speech, but felt awkward about it at the time. (Most adolescents feel awkward, no matter how well they do something.) Moreover, looking or sounding foolish on one occasion does not make a person a fool.

If motivators are "the fuel that keeps your motor running," inhibitors are "pollutants, clogs, or breaks in the gas line." In order to sustain motivation, inhibitors must be identified, recognized for what they are, and dispelled.

Write on a tablet a list of irrational or self-defeating thoughts or emotions that inhibit you from learning, trying, working, and achieving. To call attention to inhibitors you want to concentrate on overcoming, place an asterisk by those that undermine your confidence. Then, rewrite each inhibitor on the list, stating the case in positive and self-affirming terms. An example is shown below.

Inhibitor: "I made a fool of myself when I gave that speech in high school. I am not going to do that again!"

Restated: "It took courage to give that speech in high school. It was pretty good for a teenager. I'm going to learn how to speak before a group—with skill and confidence. As an adult now, skillful presenting will help my career."

Do Your Best.   Earlier, the point was made that confidence builds as a person repeatedly produces good results. Good results are the outcome of doing one's best. To prepare yourself to present—at your best—apply the following suggestions.

- To do your best, you must feel your best. To feel your best, spend time with people who believe in you, who support your aspirations, and who encourage you in your efforts to achieve them. To feel your best, look your best. (See Chapter 8, Situation 1, Presenting 2-Up.)

- To do your best as a presenter, apply the information and insights you have gained from this course. If presenting is a relatively new undertaking for you, you will find it easier to begin with a topic with which you are well acquainted. You will be more motivated to invest the time to prepare if the topic is one in which you have a vested interest. You will find the experience more gratifying if you present a topic(s) that is personally meaningful to you.

- To do your best, take advantage of the many resources that are readily available for continued professional development.

Reflection Questions

What personal attributes have you observed in presenters that you felt were becoming? What traits did you find bothersome?

Key Concept 72

Professional development involves skill-building activities and associations.

An amusing maxim observes, "If it walks like a duck and squawks like a duck, it's probably a duck." Applied to business presentations, the saying would be amended to read, "If it walks like a presenter and talks like a presenter, it's probably a presenter." How does a presenter walk? Like a person with a purpose, with the self-assurance gained from developing skilled platform behavior. How does a presenter talk? Like a skilled communicator. How does a person further develop the skills related to business presentations? By involvement in professional development activities and associations.

Think Like a Presenter

Professionals who regularly make business presentations are regularly on the lookout for resources, role models, and opportunities.

Collect Resource Materials.   Generally, professional presenters speak on one topic or on a range of related topics. They are constantly on the lookout for new information and ideas to update or enhance an existing presentation or to speed and simplify the task of preparing a new one. Anyone who presents should develop the habit of being alert to useful material that appears in publications or on television. Interesting or appropriate items are filed for reference, as described here.

Set up two types of reference files: hanging file folders or 3-ring binders for storing pages, and a 3″ × 5″ index card box for notations. Label the files with subject titles so that material can be quickly and easily located.

If, while reading a book, material catches your attention as something that you might use in a presentation, make note on a 3 × 5 card of the book title, author, publisher, edition, and page number on which the item is found. File the index card behind the appropriate label in the card-file box. If you come across material in a publication to which you subscribe, tear the item out of the publication and file it in the applicable hanging folder or binder section. If you hear material on a televised news, interview, or documentary program, contact the television station to learn if you can order a transcript of the program.

Having references readily available enables a person to prepare a presentation on short notice. In addition, the habit of spotting quotes, anecdotes, survey data, and the like helps to develop a presenter's "mind set."

Observe Role Models.   Most people attend seminars or business conferences to learn about a subject. Presenters should occasionally attend for the purpose of observing and hearing professional speakers. Most people watch television for entertainment. Presenters should occasionally view selected programs to watch and listen to professional newscasters and broadcast journalists. By emulating "role models" who present for a living, a person can learn many communication and presentation skills.

Seek Opportunities to Present.   The activity that best prepares a person to present is *presenting*. With any endeavor—riding a bicycle, running a business, or giving business presentations—it is doing the thing that develops skill and confidence. A presenter (or potential presenter) can gain experience by volunteering to speak to groups.

At work, volunteer to make presentations at meetings or training sessions. Volunteer to teach an adult class at church or for a community organization. Contact service clubs and offer to appear as a luncheon speaker. Welcome roles that require addressing an audience, such as serving as president of a club or association.

Become Involved in Skill-building Activities and Associations

Accomplished professionals in all fields make a practice of refining and expanding their skills: formally, through learning programs, and informally, through association with other professionals.

Training. An effective business presentation encompasses a range of skills and abilities, which are developed by taking courses in the following areas.

- Communication skills
- Business writing
- Creative thinking
- Negotiation skills
- Selling skills
- Theater arts

Training in business writing is useful for those who prepare written presentations. Courses in negotiation and selling skills are especially appropriate for presenters who must field questions and objections in interactive or promotional presentations. Stage presence, expressive platform behaviors, and confidence are developed by training in theater arts or by participation in a theater group.

Training and professional development can be acquired through numerous avenues, including the following.

- Continuing education courses
- Corporate training programs
- Courses offered at colleges and universities
- Individual coaching
- Public seminars
- Videotape, audiocassette, and multimedia programs

Associations. Participation in an association provides peer support, an exchange of information and ideas, and opportunities to present. Of the many business and professional associations in operation, several which specifically address the needs and interests of presenters are listed here.

- American Society for Training & Development
- International Platform Association
- National Speakers' Association
- Speech Communications Association
- Toastmasters International

Develop a Personal Association with a Mentor.   In addition to membership in a group association, it behooves a person to associate, on an individual basis, with a mentor. A **mentor** is a wise and trusted adviser. For an aspiring presenter, the ideal mentor is an accomplished speaker who is a knowledgeable, creative, and confident professional. A mentor is more than a role model. A mentor discerns potential in the up-and-coming presenter, and so takes the time to provide coaching and counsel.

Reflection Questions

What professional development activities are you currently engaged in? In what respects do they (or could they) help you prepare yourself to present? What opportunities to present do they (or could they) offer you?

Key Concept 73

To reach a comfort level presenting requires practice, guided by feedback and a development plan.

Successfully completing an effective business presentation is an exhilarating, and often profitable, experience. Planning, preparing, and delivering one requires skill. Usually, a person who has presented rarely or not at all must develop a **comfort level**. The term describes the point at which a person feels at ease applying recently learned skills.

Trying out new skills can produce discomfiture. For persons for whom presenting is a new endeavor, it is common to feel awkward or uncertain when first applying the concepts and techniques described in this course. However, by practice a person becomes accustomed to being a "presenter." By repeated practice, a person gains proficiency and a comfort level making business presentations.

Previous concepts have recommended practicing business presentations by:

- Rehearsing with colleagues
- Videotaping presentations
- Volunteering to present

Greater benefit will be gained when practice presentations are critiqued and evaluations reviewed.

Evaluations

By pointing out aspects of a presentation that need improvement, evaluations help a presenter develop proficiency. They also serve to reinforce a presenter's strengths. A cumulative record of evaluations collected over time indicates progress achieved.

Two forms are useful for evaluating practice presentations: the *evaluation of platform behavior* (included at the end of Chapter 8), and the *presentation evaluation* that appears on the last page of this chapter. Colleagues or a mentor who view your presentations can use the form(s) to make note of their observations. If you videotape your presentations, use the forms for self-evaluation. With each presentation, select one aspect you will concentrate on improving before your next presentation.

In addition, the *feedback form* included in Chapter 2 (Key Concept 17) is recommended in situations when it is appropriate to solicit evaluative information from members of an audience.

A Development Plan

A development plan is a "blueprint" for action. It details what a person will do to become a more skilled and confident presenter. Each action is numbered in order of priority and specifies a target date for completion. An example of a development plan is shown here.

#1—Join a speakers' group. Target date: 6/1.

#2—Prepare a presentation on customer service. Ask manager for opportunity to present at staff meeting. Target date: 7/15.

#3—Enroll in a theater arts class. Target date: 9/5.

A development plan represents a commitment: to master the skills and attributes that are hallmarks of professional presenters.

Summary

Skillful presenting is the result of personal preparation, professional development, and repeated practice. Personal preparation may involve overcoming group anxiety so as to be at ease when addressing an audience. It entails developing humor and confidence. Professional development begins with thinking like a presenter, and then engaging in learning activities and professional associations that further one's skills and experience. The best preparation for presenting is practice and evaluation. Mastery is achieved by applying, repeatedly, the concepts and techniques of effective business presentations.

Comprehension Check

The answers to the following appear on page 334.

1. Group anxiety is _____.
   a. the fear of going out in public
   b. synonymous with claustrophobia
   c. apprehensiveness about speaking before an audience
   d. rare among businesspeople
   e. the fear of being criticized by one's peers

2. In a presenter, a sense of humor is an asset because _____.
   a. humor makes people in an audience feel good
   b. an effective presentation is loaded with jokes
   c. it helps a speaker field objections
   d. it is a motivator for speakers
   e. it is obvious in role models

3. A person who "thinks like a presenter" _____.
   a. is ready to speak extemporaneously on any subject
   b. never experiences group anxiety
   c. is always self-assured
   d. notices and saves resource materials that might be usable for a presentation
   e. teaches communication skills

4. A person who wants to improve platform behaviors would benefit from a course in _____.
   a. creative thinking
   b. business writing
   c. theater arts
   d. fashion modelling
   e. humor

5. To become an effective presenter, a person who is new to presenting must _____.
   a. join a professional association for speakers
   b. collect and file reference material for speeches
   c. befriend a mentor
   d. develop a comfort level by practicing presentation skills
   e. exhibit charisma

Presentation Evaluation   Name _____

Date _____   Topic _____

	Strengths	To improve

Informational
Opener
Preview
Body: key points
   Support/evidence
   Transitions
Review
Close

Relational
Related to audience needs
Recognized audience
Involved audience
Applied message (value)

Platform Behaviors
Verbal: style and language
Vocal: pitch, rate, volume,
   and tone of voice
Visual: expressions, gestures,
   movement, and attire

Visual Aids
Pictorial? Colorful? Creative?

Overall: Based on what they see and hear, what will the audience perceive?

_____

How effective is the presentation? Will it persuade people to accept and
act on the message? _____

_____

To Do

Prepare a development plan that describes activities that will most help you prepare yourself to present. Include opportunities for practice and evaluation of your presentations. Set it up using columns with the following headings:

#	Activity	Target Date

Answer Key to Comprehension Checks

Comprehension checks are found at the ends of the chapters.

Chapter 1

1. c   4. a
2. b   5. b, c, f, h, i
3. b

Chapter 2

1. b   4. a
2. e   5. b
3. c

Chapter 3

1. b   3. b
2. d   4. c

5. Prepare in this order: Body,
   Preview, Review, Opener, Close
   Present in this order: Opener,
   Preview, Body, Review, Close

Chapter 4

1. b   3. a
2. e   4. d

5. Audience, Subject, Objectives,
   Setting, Time Frame

Chapter 5

1. b   4. c
2. e   5. d
3. b

Chapter 6

1. d   4. b
2. b   5. d
3. a

Chapter 7

1. d   5. a
2. b   6. b
3. b   7. d
4. e   8. c

Chapter 8

1. b   4. a
2. d   5. e
3. b

Chapter 9

1. a	6. e
2. d	7. a
3. b	8. b
4. e	9. d
5. c	

Chapter 10

1. d	4. b
2. b	5. a
3. c	

Chapter 11

1. c	4. b
2. b	5. c
3. d	

Chapter 12

1. c	4. c
2. a	5. d
3. d	

Index

About the Author

Lani Arredondo is the principal of Resource Associates and a veteran of more than 20 years' experience presenting in corporate, classroom, and guest-speaker settings. A popular international speaker, she has trained and coached managers and staff of government agencies, educational institutions, and numerous companies including AT&T, Argonaut Insurance, Eastman Kodak, IBM, and Pacific Bell. She is the author of *How to Present Like a Pro,* also published by McGraw-Hill.

Final Examination

The McGraw-Hill
36-Hour Course:
Business Presentations

If you have completed your study of *The McGraw-Hill 36-Hour Course: Business Presentations,* you should be prepared to take this final examination. It is a comprehensive examination, consisting of 50 questions.

Instructions

1. You may treat this as an "open-book" exam and consult this textbook while taking it. Doing so will help to reinforce your learning and to correct any misconceptions. If you prefer to establish a superior understanding of the subject matter, you may choose to take the examination without reference to the textbook.

2. An answer sheet appears at the end of the exam. Answer each of the test questions on this answer sheet. For each question, write the letter of your choice on the answer blank that corresponds to the number of the question you are answering.

3. Questions are multiple-choice or matching. Always select the option that represents the *best* answer.

4. Each correct answer is worth 2 points on a scale of 100 percent. For a passing grade of 70 percent, you must correctly answer 35 questions. A passing grade entitles you to receive a handsome *certificate of achievement* suitable for framing. The certificate attests to your proven knowledge of business presentations.

5. Print your name and address in the spaces provided at the top of the answer sheet, remove the completed answer sheet from the book, and send it to:

Jim Bessent
Certification Examiner
36-Hour Course: Business Presentations
Professional Books Group
McGraw-Hill, Inc.
11 West 19th Street
New York, NY 10011

---

1. A presenter communicates to an audience through _____.
   a. the creative and distillation processes
   b. sensory perceptions
   c. verbal, vocal, and visual cues
   d. feedback

2. A presenter should be ever mindful of the key principle that _____.
   a. the verbal message has greater impact than visual cues
   b. perception is more powerful than fact
   c. visibility ensures a person's success
   d. the purpose of presenting is to inform the audience

3. A presentation is *effective* when it _____.
   a. generates feedback
   b. produces the outcome the presenter intended
   c. capitalizes on the creative process
   d. makes people feel comfortable

4. It is crucial to distill information for presentation because of _____.
   a. information overload
   b. limited time frames
   c. the need to alleviate boredom
   d. audience attitudes

5. A common barrier to presenting effectively is _____.
   a. a disinterested audience
   b. insufficient time
   c. inadequate planning and preparation
   d. neglecting to identify the type of presentation

6. The first stage in the process of presenting, planning _____.
   a. guarantees a successful outcome
   b. gives a presenter complete control of a presentation event
   c. reduces the possibility of oversights or last-minute crises that can have an adverse affect on a presentation
   d. can be eliminated if the presenter has spoken on the same subject before

7. Of the numerous considerations planning entails, it is *most* important that a presenter _____.
   a. prepare an action plan
   b. choose the setting
   c. understand the audience
   d. study the subject

8. To gain insights and information about an audience, it is most useful for a presenter to _____.
   a. develop a demographic profile
   b. solicit feedback from the audience
   c. seek input from respected colleagues
   d. research results from previous presentations to similar groups

9. An action plan _____.
   a. identifies the type of presentation as internal or external
   b. is prepared mutually by the contact person and the planning team
   c. details dates, times, and tasks to be completed to ready a presentation
   d. evaluates feedback from a presentation and recommends the appropriate follow-up action to take

Match. Aspects of structuring a presentation are shown here. Each numbered phrase on the left describes a chief characteristic of a lettered item that appears on the right. Match each numbered phrase to the lettered item it describes. (A lettered item will be used once only.)

10. _____ Reflects the perspective of the audience   a. Preview
11. _____ Follows the Rule-of-3   b. Approach
12. _____ Captures the attention of the audience   c. Opener
13. _____ Calls the audience to action   d. Body
14. _____ Serves to satisfy for an audience   e. Close
the need to know what to expect

15. It can help to make a message more memorable by labelling key points using a mnemonic device, such as _____.
   a. definition or quotation
   b. metaphor or simile
   c. alliteration or acronym
   d. transition or question

16. When selecting material to substantiate one's point of view, it is most important that the material is _____.
   a. statistically accurate
   b. humorous
   c. believable
   d. emotive

17. A presenter builds balance into the content of a presentation by using a mix of materials, both _____.
    a. concrete and conceptual
    b. traditional and contemporary
    c. personal and self-disclosing
    d. informative and interesting

18. _____ can speed and simplify research on a subject.
    a. Administrative assistants
    b. Library catalogs
    c. Computerized database services
    d. Extensive reading

19. Ultimately, material for the content of a presentation is selected on the basis of the "litmus test," which determines if it is _____.
    a. current and correct
    b. suited to the audience, subject, setting, and time frame
    c. addresses the audience in an inspiring manner
    d. sufficiently varied and balanced

20. The verbal style of a presentation refers to _____.
    a. language and phrasing
    b. word choices and platform behaviors
    c. verbal illustrations as opposed to statistical data
    d. tone of voice

21. An effective verbal style is characterized by language that is _____.
    a. humorous
    b. clear, correct, concise, and well-considered
    c. attention-getting and activating
    d. tailored to the reading grade level of the audience

22. "This is representative of an egregious infraction of the rights of entre-preneurialists" is an example of _____.
    a. jargon
    b. incorrect syntax
    c. evocative expression
    d. gobbledygook

23. Figures of speech that use imagery _____.
    a. are effective because they communicate in visual terms as well as verbal
    b. are ineffective because they are confusing
    c. are effective because they always add emphasis to significant points
    d. are ineffective because they rarely convey a point clearly

24. Effective visual aids add support to a presentation because _____.
    a. people in an audience find them interesting to look at
    b. they help to alleviate group anxiety
    c. an audience expects to see visual aids
    d. they clarify or reinforce verbal statements

25. The most effective visual aids are pictorial, meaning they make use of _____.
    a. numeric tables
    b. graphics and illustrations
    c. a variety of type styles
    d. photocopies on transparencies or slides

26. In a business presentation, it is preferable to use _____.
    a. contrasting black-on-white visual aids, because it is easier for an audience to view them
    b. visual aids accompanied by an audio recording, because people respond to music
    c. colorized visual aids, because color adds meaning and emotional impact
    d. visual aids that show an outline of the message, because they help a presenter stay on track

27. In a ProActive presentation to a large group, the type of media that would likely be least effective would be _____.
    a. overhead transparencies
    b. photographic slides
    c. flip charts
    d. props

28. Computer-driven multimedia presentations _____.
    a. are preferable to any other type of audio or visual aid
    b. will eliminate the need for making presentations in person, once the technology is perfected
    c. cannot be used for large groups
    d. should not be considered a substitute for a well-prepared and skillfully delivered "live" presentation

29. The term "information-bound" describes a presenter who _____.
    a. is articulate communicating information
    b. is dependent upon the use of a podium and notes
    c. has carefully researched the subject of a presentation
    d. is chiefly concerned with gathering substantive evidence

Match.   The factors that appear on the right add to the relational content of a presentation. Match each numbered phrase on the left to the lettered item it describes. (A lettered item will be used once only.)

30. _____ builds trust   *a.* Rhetorical questions

31. _____ recognizes an audience   *b.* Value statements

32. _____ encourage audience participation   *c.* Self-disclosure

33. _____ apply the message to the audience   *d.* Appropriate termi-
                                                    nology

34. Platform behavior refers to _____.
    a. the way a speaker walks around a meeting room
    b. the degree to which an audience interacts with a presenter
    c. the sum total of vocal and visual cues a presenter conveys
    d. the presenter's comfort level when speaking to large groups that are seated theater-style

35. It is most effective for a presenter to exhibit a style that is _____.
    a. passive
    b. expressive
    c. aggressive
    d. suited to the setting

36. The "voice image" a presenter projects to an audience _____.
    a. is most impressive when it is emphatic
    b. is synonymous with vocal vitality
    c. is comprised of pitch, rate, volume, and tone of voice
    d. is an inborn trait that cannot be modified

37. People in an audience commonly form perceptions based on what they see. Of the following visual cues, from the standpoint of the audience a presenter's professional credibility is most affected by _____.
    a. attire and demeanor
    b. eye contact
    c. the appearance of handouts
    d. movement around a podium

38. In a well-paced presentation _____.
    a. short sound bites relieve boredom
    b. vocal and visual cues are varied
    c. material is well organized
    d. each key point takes the same amount of time to present

39. Four steps comprise an effective response to audience questions and comments. They are _____.
    a. listen, paraphrase, nod, and answer the question
    b. discern, paraphrase, affirm, and respond

    c. listen, discern, affirm, and respond

    d. affirm, paraphrase, respond, and invite the next question or comment

40. When a person in the audience voices a question with a sarcastic tone of voice, it would be appropriate to begin to answer by saying, _____.

    a. "It's obvious you don't agree with me, but . . ."

    b. "I don't know the answer, but I'll be glad to find out."

    c. "For the benefit of the group, I would appreciate it if you didn't use that tone of voice."

    d. "You've raised an interesting point."

41. When a person in an audience is disruptive, it is essential that the presenter _____.

    a. remove him or her from the group as soon as possible

    b. apologize for the detractor's behavior

    c. remain calm

    d. ignore the disruptive behavior, even if it is repeated

42. It is advisable to use the technique of "unplugging" early in a presentation when _____.

    a. a presenter anticipates audience resistance to the message

    b. one person in the group is a detractor

    c. a medical emergency arises

    d. a presenter invites questions at the beginning of a presentation

43. It is important that the setting for a presentation is _____.

    a. brightly lighted

    b. entirely free of noise

    c. comfortable for the audience

    d. familiar to the presenter

44. The chief reason to consider the surroundings in which a presentation will occur is that surroundings affect _____.

    a. a speaker's concentration

    b. the frame of mind of the audience

    c. the clarity of visual aids

    d. the arrangement of seating

45. For a ProActive presentation to a group that will be using handouts, the least favorable seating arrangement is _____.

    a. classroom style

    b. theater style

    c. U-formation

    d. V-formation

46. It is preferable to present in a meeting room with _____.

    a. gray walls that do not distract from the message

    b. dark wood paneling that suggests a prestigious environment

c. bright wallpaper that enlivens the atmosphere

d. pale hues that are simultaneously light and calming

47. The readability of a written proposal is improved by _____.
    a. reducing the line length from a standard 60- or 70-character width to a narrower width of 40 or so characters
    b. alternating boldface and italic type throughout
    c. removing headlines that can distract the reader
    d. using the recipient's company colors on the cover

48. The primary reason it is important to use correct grammar, spelling, and punctuation is _____.
    a. readers respect conformance to the mechanics of writing
    b. correct usage may distinguish a presenter from competitors
    c. the affect on how a presenter/writer is perceived
    d. they establish the reading grade level of a document

49. Group anxiety can be overcome by _____.
    a. intensive therapy
    b. practicing relaxation and positive-imagining techniques
    c. emulating humorous speakers
    d. networking with a mentor

50. The best way to sharpen one's presentation skills is to _____.
    a. take advantage of every opportunity to present
    c. become a member of a professional association
    b. take courses in selling and negotiation skills
    d. view videotapes of role model presenters

Name _____

Address _____

City _____ State _____ Zip _____

Final Examination
Answer Sheet
The McGraw-Hill 36-Hour
Course: Business Presentations

See instructions on page 1 of the Final Examination.

1. _____	11. _____	21. _____	31. _____	41. _____
2. _____	12. _____	22. _____	32. _____	42. _____
3. _____	13. _____	23. _____	33. _____	43. _____
4. _____	14. _____	24. _____	34. _____	44. _____
5. _____	15. _____	25. _____	35. _____	45. _____
6. _____	16. _____	26. _____	36. _____	46. _____
7. _____	17. _____	27. _____	37. _____	47. _____
8. _____	18. _____	28. _____	38. _____	48. _____
9. _____	19. _____	29. _____	39. _____	49. _____
10. _____	20. _____	30. _____	40. _____	50. _____